Table of Contents

Chapter 5: Employee Expenses 227

Chapter 6: Miscellaneous Policies 269

Charts, Forms, and Outlines

Preface

Sound human resource policy is a necessity in the growth of any business or company.

You may recognize this necessity when you realize that an increasing amount of your company's time is being devoted to human resource issues. This is time that could be used for production, marketing, and planning for growth. Effective, consistent, and fair human resource decisions often become more time consuming because of a lack of written standardized policies and procedures.

When issues of employee rights and company policies come before federal and state courts, the decisions generally regard company policies, written or verbal, as part of an employment contract between the employee and the company. Without clearly written policies, the company is at a disadvantage.

A Company Policy and Personnel Workbook is designed to assist a business create clearly-written policies. This book presents a comprehensive and adaptable set of policies that balance employee and employer rights and expectations. Adapting these to your business can make the challenge of putting your company policy manual together a much easier process and take the drudgery out of developing policies from scratch.

If your company is revising its existing manual, *A Company Policy and Personnel Workbook* also provides a discussion of current laws and regulations and serves as an orientation package for the staff that is preparing for the assigned revision responsibility. The discussions of current laws and regulations and other important related issues are featured in the book's *Comment* sections, located before each policy. See *How to Use this Book.*

This practical, easy-to-use workbook will save you valuable time and expense in researching, developing, drafting, and revising your company policy manual. These policies will establish clear procedures that will increase your company's efficiency and communication.

We, the authors, would like to thank the many contributors who generously gave their time to make suggestions for the development of this workbook — in particular, the employees at PSI Research in Grants Pass, Oregon.

Introduction

This book was written to help you and your management team make efficient use of your time in developing a cohesive and up-to-date policy manual.

The person or committee who has the responsibility of writing the manual will find this book makes the whole process of selecting, understanding, and tailoring personnel policies much easier than researching and constructing them from scratch.

Before you begin this process, consider some of the benefits your company can gain from a policy manual:

- A set of written guidelines for human resource decisions
- A means of communication with employees;
- A framework for consistency and fairness;
- A way to promote the company philosophy;
- A tool to save management time; and
- A means to protect the legal interests of the company.

Consider each of these benefits in more detail.

1. *A set of written guidelines for human resource decisions.*

    The process your company management team undergoes when comparing the policy alternatives, understanding their importance, and evaluating your company's current practices will help you to develop your company's guidelines and procedures.

2. *A means of communication with employees*

The policy manual serves first as a way to communicate with employees. It demonstrates awareness of and interest in employees' individual security needs. It helps to organize and announce management's plans for growth, and it communicates the company's investment in its employees.

3. *A framework for consistency and fairness*

The policy manual defines management's standards for making decisions on various personnel and organizational issues. The clearly defined procedures and standards express the company's intent to make consistent and evenhanded decisions.

4. *A way to promote the company philosophy*

The policies will reflect the company's philosophy of business and employee relations as they demonstrate:

- Your creativity in solving policy issues;
- The competitive position of the company in providing a variety of employee benefits; and
- The respect and appreciation for human resource management.

5. *A tool to save management time*

Carefully drafted and standardized policies and procedures save the company countless hours of management time. The consistent use and interpretation of such policies, in an evenhanded and fair manner, reduces management's concern about legal issues becoming legal problems.

6. *A means to protect the legal interests of a company*

A company's policies and procedures define the rights and obligations of the employee and of the company. The policy manual is an expression of the rules governing the employment relationship. In the 1990s, probably more than ever, a company must protect its rights within that relationship by adopting policies that are fair to both sides, clearly stated, and legally permissible.

Caution

If your company's employees are represented by a labor union, any collective bargaining agreement (CBA) between you and the union will, in effect, serve as a policy manual with respect to the employees covered by the CBA.

In this case, you may utilize a policy manual which covers non-union employees. A CBA may also limit your ability to modify your policy manual at will, requiring instead negotiation of matters covered by the CBA.

The discussion of the above six points will help clarify the responsibility that you accept in developing your policy manual. The authors' own experiences and research provides the basis for information throughout this workbook. The next three sections will outline a process to help you easily develop your policy manual.

Develop and Maintain Your Policy Manual

Upper management must be directly involved in the development of the manual and its presentation to employees.

When management is involved in selecting and wording the policies and in establishing procedures to implement policies, it "buys in" on the success of the total process. Management involvement assures greater understanding of the policy manual by those required to interpret and administer it, provides insight into employee concerns, and promotes greater employee-employee communication.

Select a committee from operational employees and from mid to upper-management. The size of the committee will vary depending on the size of the company and management's willingness to broaden the process. Broader representation will bring different viewpoints and perspectives to the discussions and help to develop a better set of policies. The involvement of upper management ensures that the company philosophies of business, production, and employee satisfaction, among others, will be found in the manual.

Here are some suggestions the committee can follow when developing the policy manual.

- Select a person on the committee to coordinate development of the manual;
- Study this workbook to become familiar with its contents and the *Comment* sections;
- Meet with upper management to outline what is to be accomplished by the manual;
- Determine which present company policies will be included in the manual and whether or not they need to be revised;
- Have supervisors/managers respond to a checklist of tentative policies and an outline of instructions for implementing policies; and
- Set deadlines and arrange for progress reports.

Another important responsibility of the committee is a training session to introduce the policy and personnel manual to all employees. If this is your first manual, consider an employee orientation meeting during which:

- The company president comments on the importance of the manual and its purposes;
- One or more of the committee members who worked to develop the manual presents a brief discussion of its organization, each of its policies, and the reasons for including them in the manual; and
- Time for questions and comments from the employees.

If your company has made only revisions to current established policies, or is adding only a few new policies, a more informal meeting would be appropriate. An important part of the process, before introducing the manual to your employees, is to have the company attorney review its contents.

The manual's publication does not complete the project. As the company grows and the workforce becomes larger and more diverse, new issues will have to be faced and new policies developed to cover them. Similarly, changes in laws, regulations, employee benefits, and other areas will make revisions necessary. You may choose to maintain the committee to make revisions or for new policy development. Or you may appoint one person, possibly a committee member or department head, for this purpose. The responsible party should have access to the committee's notes, research, drafts of discarded policies, and meeting minutes for reference.

Create a master file and index it by policy number to store the materials, including management memos regarding policy issues. Maintain a record of revisions when changes to a policy are made. These records can save valuable time when drafting revisions or looking for policy alternatives.

When the policy manual is published, consider numbering each copy and having a master log which identifies the person or department that received each manual. Numbering the manuals assists in their distribution and revision as well as maintaining control of them. Have your employees sign a statement indicating their receipt of the policy manual. You may not want the manual distributed outside of the company or kept by employees who leave the company.

You may want the committee or a committee member to be the sole source of policy and procedure interpretation. Whoever has this responsibility must also have access to the developmental records and be aware of the changes in upper management's desires and philosophies. To ensure evenhanded and fair treatment of employees, document an important interpretation of a policy, including the facts giving rise to the issue. These interpretations are valuable as precedents for future use.

As new employees join your company, part of the employee orientation process includes presenting them with a copy of the manual. Once they have had an opportunity to read the manual, schedule a time to discuss and answer any questions.

Suggested Formats for Your Policy Manual

There are several formats available to you when organizing your policy manual. This section discusses loose-leaf, numeric, and alphabetical organizational formats. It also assists you in determining your manual's size, binding, and printing options. To help decide on a format, answer these questions:

- What image does your company want to portray to employees through the policy and procedures manual?
- How much money is budgeted for the manual?
- What method of upkeep of the manual will the company initiate? For example, will employee manuals be returned to one location for updating, or will updated policies be distributed and employees expected to maintain their own manuals?
- Does the assigned work location of employees have an effect on the type of manual that should be selected? For example, are they working at a desk or are they assigned to trucks out in the field?
- Do you anticipate major revisions in the manual in the next couple of years?

Here are some general points to consider regarding the content of policies:

- Keep in mind who the policies are written for. Who is the audience?
- Organize each policy in a logical operational sequence.
- Stay on the subject.
- Keep sentences and paragraphs short.
- Avoid rigid formality.
- Check for understanding. Be flexible but avoid vague, unclear, or indirect statements.

If you choose the loose-leaf binder format for your manual, we suggest that your company name or logo be prominent on each page. The section name and policy title on each page help to organize and reference the manual. The use of "Page ___ of ___ pages" makes it easy for everyone to determine if he or she has the complete policy in their manual. The use of "effective date" and "revision date" assists in researching the history and changes to each policy. The inclusion of "Approved by" legitimizes the policy and ensures that policy language has been reviewed by the responsible person. A sample policy format that incorporates these aids is on page 16.

Your company will probably already have an established terminology for key words that should be used throughout the manual, such as references to gender, organization, department, division, and positions. You may easily alter the policies in this book to continue this terminology or, in some cases, you may wish to make changes to clarify your in-house communication.

The authors have chosen to use "his" or "her" when referring to employees. There are some additional choices you can consider using.

- Instead of "his" or "her", you could use the word, "the." For example, you could say, "Return to the shift" rather than "Return to his or her shift."
- Write a disclaimer statement in the introduction of the manual that states the use of either a masculine or feminine gender which will refer to both "his" and "her."
- Simply use the word "person" or "employee."

Throughout this workbook, the personnel department and personnel manager are referred to in a number of the policies. The role and responsibilities taken by your company's personnel or accounting department will determine your need to tailor each policy. See *How to Use this Book*.

As you select the appropriate department or individual title reference, consider the role and responsibilities of the respective department or person as well as the image management wishes to communicate to employees. In some cases, especially in small companies, one person is responsible for all personnel duties and operations.

What you do in implementing the policy can be as important as what is said in the manual. Be sure that personnel administrators and supervisors/managers have the skills to understand the manual's contents and to deal with company employees in a responsive and caring manner. You may want to refer to a member of upper management for certain approvals or decisions, depending on the position of this person within the organization.

Numeric and alphabetic formats are commonly used to organize personnel and policy manuals. If you select the numeric format, incorporate a flexible numbering system. With this system, your company can add more statements without having to renumber the system each time. For example, *600.1–Our Company, 600.2–Employment, 600.3–Compensation*; or *100–Our Company, 200–Employment, 300–Compensation*. The policies under these headings would then be assigned in tens, ones, or additional decimals. For example, regarding *600.1–Our Company*, you would number any subsections and their respective policies in the following manner: *Company History–600.1.1* or *110, Company Objectives–600.1.2* or *120*. This allows other policies relating to *Company History* to be assigned *600.1.1.1* or *111, 112*.

In selecting an alphabetical format, the same considerations should be followed. Usually a combination of alphabetic and numeric is chosen, e.g., *A-1-b*.

Some companies have a less detailed, informational employee handbook that dwells less on company procedures than a policy and procedures manual would. In this case, the policy manual is usually distributed to management or supervisory personnel only. All employees are given the employee handbook. For convenience and clarity, it is also wise to select the same organizational format if you plan to issue an employee handbook.

You can reduce the cost of reprinting a bound booklet by adopting the loose-leaf format. However, circumstances may not make this format practical in all cases, such as when the policies must be used "in the field" where a large notebook would be cumbersome. If this is the case, place only one policy on any individual page or pages.

We also recommend that 10% of the pages be left blank. If any policy needs to be revised, or if policies are added, the revision or additional policies can be printed on separate gummed sheets and glued over old policies or onto the blank pages. This practice can save printing or duplication cost until the revisions or additions become extensive enough to warrant printing a new bound version.

How to Use this Book

This workbook is organized into six chapters. Each chapter features its own introduction and selection of alternate policies.

Chapter topics range from hiring practices to employee benefits and expenses. Each policy within the chapters has its own *Comment* section. *Comment* gives the staff and policy committee an overview of considerations that should be discussed before developing that particular policy. If there are important federal laws relating to a policy, they are discussed within this section.

Throughout this book, the authors use *Note* and italicize subsequent warnings or reminders for you to research for any peculiarities or variations in your state's laws or to take action on other important related issues. Be sure your typist deletes any *Notes* when typing policy drafts or final copies. Consult your company attorney or legal counsel before your policy manual is printed and distributed throughout the company because of the many variations in state laws. Ask your attorney to keep you updated regarding changes in employment-related laws and court decisions which may impact your policy.

The policies in this workbook are integrated to be used as a complete policy manual with a minimum amount of tailoring. However, some companies may choose to expand upon some policies when special circumstances warrant. If you would like to make changes to a policy, its *Comment* section will help you tailor the wording.

Other companies may choose to use only a few policies from each chapter and add them to already-established policies. Whichever choice you make, *A Company Policy and Personnel Workbook* will be a valuable resource that will save countless hours of research and drafting time.

For easier and more effective use of this workbook, the authors suggest you freely use pencils and various-colored highlight pens to make this a working document.

As you read the chapters, make use of the margins to jot down your ideas or to make notes of the issues you want to clarify or discuss with management. Use colored highlight pens to identify specifics you want covered in policies (e.g., yellow); federal or state laws you want to discuss with your company attorney for further clarification (e.g., red); and alternatives that you want to explore with other committee members (e.g., green). This workbook is planned to be your organizer as well as a working document.

You may have noticed the four-digit numbers in the *Table of Contents* and in the following chapters after each policy title. The purpose of these four-digit numbers is to:

- Provide an easy-to-follow, chronological numbering system for this workbook's policy sections and their respective alternate policies; and
- Correspond with the companion software program, *Company Policy*, which is available for this workbook.

The first digit of the section number indicates which chapter the policy is located in. The subsequent three numbers indicate its sequential listing within that particular chapter. For example, in the text, the authors may refer you to *Section 2010* on *Equal Opportunity*. By using the section number, you would know the section is located in Chapter 2 and would be listed sequentially by the last three numbers. The four-digit number is also used as a prefix in the number which identifies and lists any alternate policies contained within a policy section. Any alternate policies listed in *Section 2010*, would have the following identification numbers: *2010.1*, *2010.2*, and *2010.3*, etc.

Company Policy Software is a valuable tool if you have an IBM compatible computer and would like to create and develop your policy manual on screen. ASCII text files are available for the Macintosh computer. For ordering information on this software, see the order form at the end of this workbook.

Many of the policies have alternate statements for your comparison and selection. The authors give no preference or priority to the Alternate Policy 1 versus the Alternate Policy 2.

Write your policies as they will be implemented within your company, considering the policies as means to an end, not ends in themselves.

Select the policies to be included in your manual by asking these questions:

- Are we required by federal or state law or contract to have this policy?
- What is the reason for having this policy?
- Does our organization with its size, business, and work force justify having this policy?
- Does enforcing this policy accomplish our company goals?
- Is the policy consistent with the company's management or business philosophy?
- What have we done in the past to solve issues related to this policy?
- Does this policy strike a proper balance between management flexibility and fairness to employees?
- Is the cost, such as the time and expense, of administering this policy reasonable in relationship to the benefits to be obtained?

As you select policies to be included in your manual, refer back to these questions to make certain that your policy will strike a balance between fairness to your employees and flexibility and cost effectiveness for your business.

Select the policies that you want to include in your manual and place the other policies in the back of this workbook for future reference or consideration. Select only those policies you need and to which you are willing to devote adequate time, expense, and resources.

Read the *Comment* section, highlighting the points that you believe your committee should discuss together or with upper management before developing your company's policy statement.

Read Alternate Policy 1 to see if it covers your company's main objectives and management's philosophies. Then read Alternate Policy 2 and ask yourself:

- How does each policy relate to the points highlighted in the *Comment* section?
- Is this the solution to our problem?
- Is this a procedure we can implement?

For your convenience, the alternate policies have been spaced for making changes or adding statements unique to your company. You may pick and choose parts of each of the two alternate policies and combine them into one. Avoid contradictions within one policy and ensure that other related policies, such as *Recruitment* and *Selection Process*, *Employee Classifications*, and *Position Descriptions* are consistent with that policy.

Throughout the policies in this workbook, there are several job titles and subjects that are capitalized and put in parentheses. For example, the job title of the individual your employees should contact for additional information, approval, or assistance may be indicated by (VICE PRESIDENT), (PERSONNEL MANAGER), or (PRESIDENT). Modify these titles to fit your particular company's in-house communications and organization. Although an individual's name may seem to be a wise choice, the policy may become outdated with company promotions and employee mobility.

You also will see department names and other related topics presented in the same manner, e.g., (ACCOUNTING DEPARTMENT), (PERSONNEL DEPARTMENT), (DATE), (ADD TIME), and (ADD NUMBER). Insert the appropriate information for your business, and whenever (COMPANY) is used, you should replaced it with your company's name. When your manual is complete, carefully proofread it to make certain that it is internally consistent and that the appropriate departments or individuals are named or referred to throughout the manual.

If neither of the alternate policies reflects management's or employees' desires, use the *Comment* section and the alternate policies as a guide to develop your own policy. Keep in mind that the policies should comply with federal and state laws and regulations.

At a minimum, you may wish to include policy statements on the following subjects in your initial manual:

1. *Equal Opportunity*
2. *Employee Classifications*
3. *Workday, Payday, and Pay Advances*
4. *Overtime Compensation*
5. *Meal Period and Rest Period*
6. *Payroll Deductions*
7. *Vacation*
8. *Holidays*
9. *Sick–Personal Leave*
10. *Performance Evaluation*
11. *Performance Improvement*
12. *Termination*
13. *Internet*
14. *Termination E-mail*

You can combine some of the topics into one policy. For example, items numbered three, four, and five could be addressed under one policy until management chooses to prepare a more comprehensive statement on those topics.

The management team must closely monitor the types of human resource questions and concerns that confront the company. This will help to determine when additional policies are added and when existing policies need to be revised or deleted. Avoid writing a policy for every problem. It is important to weigh the burden of not having the policy against adding an unlimited number of policies. Allow a potential policy to simmer for 30 days before adding it to your manual. Also, consider a periodic group orientation to explain your policy manual to new employees and to answer any questions concerning it.

Some companies find it is an advantage to begin with a management policy manual that gives supervisors/managers guidance on the company's philosophy in managing its human resources. The manual is usually presented in outline form and provides guidelines for handling employee issues. It is then clarified by discussion of interpretations at management meetings.

When companies choose to begin with the management policy manual, its companion communication to the employee is an employee handbook. The contents of the employee handbook are presented in informal language. It should include the basic information concerning the organization and its policies.

The employee handbook would include a brief statement about:

- Management and the company
- General wage and salary information
- Hours of work and attendance
- Standards of conduct
- Brief descriptions of benefits and services.

Though it may be easier to write, the employee handbook remains a statement of the relationship between the employee and the employer. It is important to have the handbook reviewed by your company attorney.

The policy manual is ready to be typed and reproduced when you have selected the policies, made changes, and tailored each policy. Select the format for the manual by reviewing the section, *Suggested Formats for Your Manual.* Don't forget to ask the company attorney to review your manual for completeness and compliance with state and federal laws before you distribute it to employees.

If this is your company's first policy manual, you may want to start with a limited number of policies and add others as they become appropriate. Every three to six months, the individual or committee responsible for the manual should review its contents to determine if there should be any revisions or additions.

A policy can also be deleted as the company outgrows the need for it. Keeping the manual current is also important. It communicates the importance of its contents to the employees and it assists managers in their supervisory role. Such changes also signify to the employees that the company keeps up with the times and the competition. Remember, undefined policies and inconsistencies in policies consume a great amount of management time and become a hidden cost to the company. They also create unnecessary confusion and miscommunication among employees.

Before You Begin

Before you begin, some final thoughts merit consideration:

- What an employer does in practice is as important as what is written in the policy manual. The actions and words of management must be consistent with the manual.
- Don't include policies you don't understand and therefore cannot consistently or properly administer.
- Select persons charged with the responsibility of administering the policy manual with great care and skill. If managers and supervisors are not capable of uniformly and consistently applying the policies or if they lack good interpersonal skills, the policy manual will not work.
- Recognize the non-static nature of business and the business environment, and be flexible and able to adapt to changes. Case law, statutes, and regulations change. Your policy manual must be able to change as well.
- Your manual should overstate the employer's rights to modify or terminate policies set forth in the manual at any time and from time to time. The manual must indicate clearly that it is not to be considered a contract of employment.
- Treat employees within the same classification equally.
- Use good common sense.
- Do what makes sense for your business. What works for one business may not work for another. A sample policy manual cover page follows for your convenience.

Sample Policy Manual Cover Page

(COMPANY NAME) Policy Manual

The policies and procedures in this manual are not intended to be contractual commitments by (COMPANY), and they shall not be construed as such by employees.

The policies and procedures are intended to be guides to management and are merely descriptive of suggested procedures to be followed. (COMPANY) reserves the right to revoke, change or supplement guidelines at any time without notice.

No policy is intended as a guarantee of continuity of benefits or rights. No permanent employment or employment for any term is intended or can be implied from any statements in this manual.

(COMPANY NAME)

(ADDRESS)

(DATE)

Equal Opportunity

Sample Policy _____ #2010.1

(COMPANY)

Policy and Procedures Manual

Equal Opportunity is (COMPANY) policy. It is (COMPANY) policy to select the best qualified person for each position in the organization. No employee of (COMPANY) will discriminate against an applicant for employment or fellow employee because of race, creed, color, religion, sex, national origin, ancestry, age, disability status or any other statutorily prohibited basis.

This policy applies to all employment practices and personnel actions. (COMPANY) has adopted an affirmative action policy which essentially means that the company will aggressively seek out, hire, develop and promote qualified members of protected groups (defined as racial minorities, women, physically or mentally disabled, disabled veterans, veterans of the Vietnam era and persons between the ages of 40 to 70).

Any person having inquiries concerning (COMPANY'S) compliance with the above is directed to contact the (VICE PRESIDENT), who has been designated as Compliance Coordinator. The office is located at (ADDRESS AND PHONE NUMBER).

Revised: 3/1/99   Approved by: _____
                                                      President

Page 1 of __ pages

Chapter 1

Our Company

Introduction

The first section of your policy and personnel manual should describe your company. This will include a brief overview of your company and a welcome to the new employee.

Including this section in your manual offers other advantages. The employees will learn the history of the company, who the founders are or were, and how the company grew to its present status. As an employee reads this section, he or she will become familiar with the company's objectives for growth and become a valuable participant in meeting those objectives.

The policy manual is primarily designed to reveal how management will treat its employees and vice versa. You should also emphasize that it is designed to ensure that all employees know the company's organizational rules in order to succeed both individually and as a company. This first section will give the employee a sense of what the company is all about and what he or she is a part of.

The amount and detail of information provided in the company section will be determined, in part, by the number of employees and the age of the company. If the company is small and young, less information may be necessary. New employees joining the staff will probably interact with everyone and will quickly gain a perspective of the company. At some point in the company's growth, you will want to start developing the historical information for later use. Regardless of how young your company is, an awareness of its history and its projected future is valuable to all employees.

For a company with 15 or more employees, the work setting becomes more impersonal. You save money by offering assistance to help the new employee adjust.

You should have maximum flexibility in drafting the company policies. You or your management already have adopted a way of communicating with your employees. Do not impose a structure which would be contrary to your company's current philosophy and style. Every company is unique and the company section, more than others, is where that individuality really appears.

Therefore, this chapter offers you advice and suggestions on how to organize your policy manual's introduction rather than construct a policy or use language that might be uncomfortable for you.

This initial section of your policy manual may take more thought. Therefore, you may want to save it for last or work on it concurrently with other chapters.

Welcome Letter from the President 1010

Comment

The president's letter welcomes new employees to the company. It is the first opportunity to set the tone of the manual and introduce the company philosophy.

The letter may be just a short welcome or it may include three or four sentences that summarize the history of the company, the number of company employees, the locations of other company offices, and the unique features about your company's product, service, and management. The letter may thank the employee for selecting the company as his or her place to work and stress the importance of becoming a productive part of the organization.

Above all, the letter is a personal statement from the chief executive who is ultimately responsible for the company's fortunes and the policy manual.

Company History 1020

Comment

A brief company history helps the employee be aware of the change and growth experienced by the company since its inception. Information about the founders of the company and a brief statement of their original objectives helps a new employee gain an historical perspective and appreciate what the company has accomplished.

Other possible topics to consider in writing this section are:

- The company's achievements and its products or services;
- Any major changes or additions to the company's products or services which allowed the company to remain competitive in the marketplace or to gain a greater market share; and
- A brief statement concerning the profit curve or major financial accomplishments of the company. Be aware that this statement may become outdated at the end of every important fiscal period.

Consider also mentioning and crediting any investor or venture capital firm that supports your company, especially a parent company, which has a vested interest in your firm's existence. You want your employees to be just as proud of the company as you are. Show them your pride.

Company Objectives 1030

Comment

Exercise caution when you detail the company objectives in the policy and personnel manual. It is difficulty to control the confidentiality of this information. Yet, it is important that the employee be made aware of the company's goals and objectives in a general sense.

Some topics to include are:

- The role profit plays in directing or changing the focus of your business;
- The importance of the customer and the value of customer satisfaction;
- The potential areas for growth in relation to foreseen customer needs;
- The employees' role in the success of the business;
- The company's role of service and support to the surrounding community; and
- The company's encouragement of employees' activity in community organizations.

Organization Chart 1040

Comment

The organization chart identifies and formalizes the reporting and working relationships of all the positions identified within it. The inclusion of an organization chart in the policy manual helps new employees to quickly become familiar with the structure of the company and the relationship held by each of the departments or individuals to one another.

If your company is growing rapidly, you may provide an organization chart identifying only the management staff in order to avoid frequent updating. Another possibility would be to identify the positions on the chart by title only. This will avoid the need to reprint the manual as staff changes occur. A third way to introduce the key people in your organization would be to include a list of their names, titles, telephone extensions, and the names of their assistants or secretaries with their telephone extensions.

There are two examples of a simple organization chart on the following page. In Example 1, each Vice President shares equal responsibility in management along with the leadership of the Chief Executive Officer (CEO).

Example 2 is the traditional form of an organizational chart. The CEO assumes the key management responsibility and is joined by the three Vice Presidents in comprising the management team. The positioning of the three Vice Presidents at the same level of management responsibility communicates to employees equal importance of each department.

Downsizing of staff within many companies during the past decade has meant the flattening of organizational charts. Many managers were relieved of their responsibilities allowing for closer interaction between employees and managers.

Organization Chart

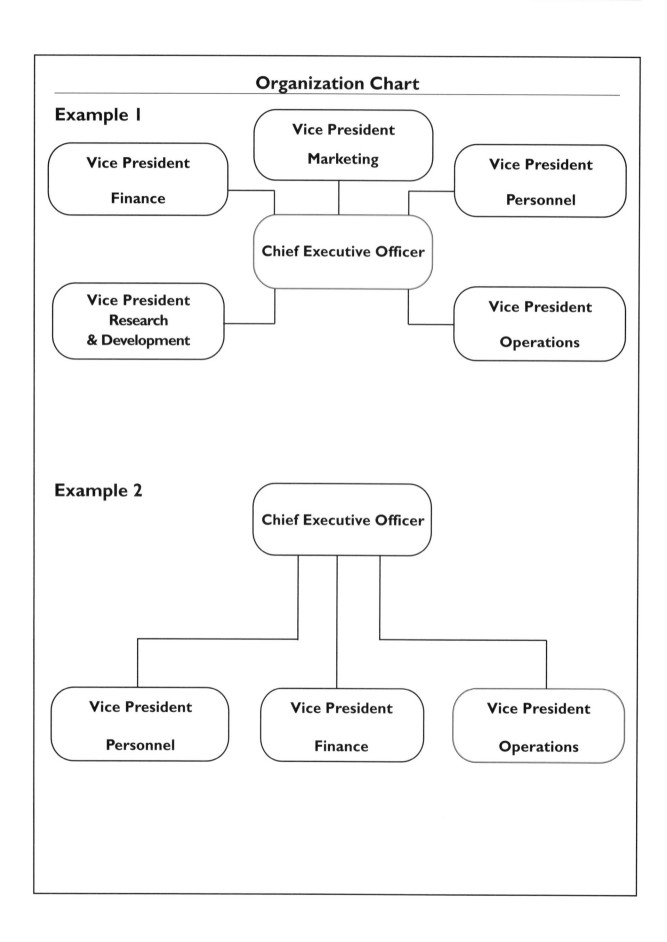

Example 1

Vice President Marketing

Vice President Finance

Vice President Personnel

Chief Executive Officer

Vice President Research & Development

Vice President Operations

Example 2

Chief Executive Officer

Vice President Personnel

Vice President Finance

Vice President Operations

Statement of Growth, Profit, and Business Plan 1050

Comment

If you accept the premise that an informed employee is a more productive employee, you will want to provide your employees with brief and broadly stated information concerning the company's growth plans. Consideration should be given to the confidentiality of this information. Even a sanitized version of confidential growth or marketing plans may give valuable information to a competitor.

You might consider including statistical or profit projections, or explaining the company's plans for expansion or introduction of new products. You could also provide information about the company's competitive role in the marketplace. Such information may require updating too frequently to be of any value unless your projections and plans are for several years in advance.

A few brief statements concerning the company's plans for the next two to five years depicts the leadership role of management in planning and preparing for the future. Planning may give employees a more secure feeling about the strength of the company.

Statement of Commitment to Employees   1060

Comment

Nothing frustrates or demoralizes an employee more than not knowing where his or her job fits into the total operation or being uncertain of the value of the work accomplished. Even more demoralizing is not having anyone show appreciation for what the employee is doing.

Possibly the first commitment you should consider making is to keep the employee informed about his or her job responsibilities and any changes which will impact those responsibilities. When new employees come to work, a staff member should be assigned to introduce them to fellow workers, the company layout, and the facilities.

Whenever possible, a supervisor should also review their responsibilities. Printed material, such as the policy manual, should be given to all new employees on the first day of work. After introductions and a brief orientation, the supervisor can set a time to meet again in a few days and respond to their questions. We suggest that you plan a periodic group orientation meeting for new employees if the size of your company warrants it.

Employees are much happier and better workers when they respect the management of their company and believe their supervisors are competent, fair, and alert to employees' contributions. This statement of commitment can facilitate these beliefs. Some examples of general statements about the company's commitment to its employees include the following:

- The company's recruitment and selection of highly capable and innovative employees;
- Management's commitment to provide a work environment and leadership which unites employees and generates enthusiasm for the company and its products and services;
- A commitment to maintain the highest standards of business ethics;
- An understanding of the importance of the employees' role in the company's success; and
- A commitment to provide training and opportunities for advancement.

Depending on your management style, another commitment worth considering is an open door policy. Under this policy, the president or owner commits to being available to any employee at any convenient time to discuss any job-related problems the employee may have. No manager likes to have an employee go over his or her head. However, the effect that this commitment has on the responsiveness of supervisory personnel or middle management may be worthwhile to everyone. Obviously, you must also commit to being fair and objective. If you manage this commitment well, the word will get out that you are responsive to every employee's problems.

A grievance procedure is a different, more formal approach to being fair and objective. An open door policy emphasizes availability. A grievance procedure emphasizes due process. For more information about a grievance procedure, see *Grievance Procedure — Section 6060*.

A job's income or potential for income is often given as the reason for why people work. However, the reason people stay at one company for a long time often has to do with the non-monetary work environment. Your commitment to your employees is a statement of how you value them as people and how you intend to treat them.

Your attitude toward management-employee relations will set the tone and style of employee-employer communications. These communications, and how you perform your commitments, have a significant impact on the work environment. This subsection, or the welcoming letter, is the place to state your business and employee relations philosophy.

You may not be able to state it as a commitment, but if you have a set of principles or rules for running your business, let your employees know what they are. Your wish to share the principles or philosophy with others reflects a leadership quality that will enhance respect for management and improve the work environment.

Continuity of Policies — Right to Change or Discontinue   1070

Comment

To allow for maximum flexibility, you should include a concise statement in the introduction or first section of your policy manual. This statement should clearly reserve the company's right to change or discontinue policies at any time without notice.

Ensure that all employees understand that a policy, once in force, is not irrevocable and can be modified or deleted at any time. For example, a change in the law might require you to immediately modify or discontinue a policy. A business downturn may require a quick revision of certain policies. The size of your organization and the location of your employees might make it difficult to instantly announce such changes. Therefore, you need to protect the company's rights to make such changes effective without notice.

Give prompt and reasonable notice of any such changes to avoid the problems caused by someone's reliance on a discontinued or modified policy. However, your employees have been forewarned that such changes may occur without notice and will be effective regardless.

Here is a statement you could use or modify to state your right to change or discontinue a policy:

- To preserve the ability to meet company needs under changing conditions, (COMPANY) may modify, augment, delete or revoke any and all policies, procedures, practices, and statements contained in this manual at any time without notice.

  Such changes shall be effective immediately upon approval by management unless otherwise stated.

If the laws of your state recognize a company handbook or policy manual as a contractual commitment to employees, some stronger, more direct language may avoid such a result in future cases. For example:

- The policies and procedures in this manual are not intended to be contractual commitments by (COMPANY) and they shall not be construed as such by employees. They are intended to be guides to management and merely descriptive of suggested procedures to be followed.

  (COMPANY) reserves the right to revoke, change, or supplement guidelines at any time without notice. No policy is intended as a guarantee of continuity of benefits or rights. No permanent employment or employment for any term is intended or can be implied by statements in this book.

Caution

The right to modify a policy does not allow an employer to revoke employee rights or benefits which may have already accrued.

For example, if an employee has earned a certain amount of vacation time or sick leave based on years of service under your existing policy, a subsequent policy revision can't reduce or eliminate benefits already accrued. The new policy can only apply on a going forward basis.

Acknowledging Receipt of Policy Manual   1080

Comment

It is in the company's and employees' best interests to have a sign-off sheet to acknowledge receipt of the policy manual.

It serves as documentation for the company in case the employee denies having received a copy of the manual or being aware of a particular company policy. For all new employees, this form would be signed, dated, and given to the administrative/personnel office before receipt of his or her first paycheck. In the second sample provided, the employee acknowledges that any future changes in policy will supercede what is written in the manual.

Receipt of Policy Manual

Sample 1

I have received a copy of the (COMPANY) *Policy Manual,* specifying policies, practices, and regulations, which I agree to observe and follow during my employment with the company. I understand that it is my responsibility to be familiar with its contents and to ask questions on any matters I don't understand.

_____
Employee's Signature   Date

Receipt of Policy Manual

Sample 2

I have received my copy of the *Policy Manual* which outlines the policies, practices, and benefit guidelines of the company, and I have read and I understand the information contained in the manual.

Since the information in this manual is necessarily subject to change as situations warrant, it is understood that changes in the manual may supercede, revise, or eliminate one or more of the policies in this manual. These changes will be communicated to me by my supervisor or through official notices. I accept responsibility for keeping informed of these changes.

I further acknowledge my understanding that my employment with (COMPANY) may be terminated at any time with or without cause.

Note: The preceding sentence should be included only in states where termination at will is permitted and where the employer desires this status.

_____
Employee's Signature   Date

Chapter 2

Hiring Practices

Introduction

The next section of your policy manual should help your employee understand the process used by the company to recruit, hire, classify, and counsel its employees.

The philosophy of the company and the important role played by each employee in the success of the company should continue to unfold in this section. Many of the policies in this chapter are regulated by federal statutes, such as Title VII of The Civil Rights Act of 1964. These policies require frequent updating in order to stay in line with the times, the law, and the competition.

All states have laws and regulations that affect the employee recruitment and selection process. Often these laws and regulations are derived from the applicable federal laws. In some cases, states have additional requirements or broader coverage. Consult an expert to learn about these differences and reflect them in your policies.

Although this section covers policies relevant to the hiring practice, federal and state laws that impact the hiring process generally cover all aspects of employment. This includes promotion, compensation, and termination.

Present legislation relating to the Americans with Disabilities Act (ADA) and discrimination lawsuits have increased the "dos and don'ts" relating to job interviews. Questions such as: "Are you married?", "Do you intend to have children?", or "Do you have a baby sitter or spouse who shares childcare responsibility?"are taboo and should be avoided. Focus your questions on whether a person can do the job as defined.

Equal Opportunity 2010

Comment

A number of federal and state laws prohibit discrimination in employment and require companies to adopt affirmative action programs. Title VII of the Civil Rights Act of 1964[1] as amended in 1991, requires employers with 15 or more employees, who work each workday during any 20 weeks of the current or preceding year, to adhere to the prohibitions against employment discrimination based on race, sex, color, religion, or national origin. Under many state laws, civil rights laws apply with as few as a single employee. This is true in Alabama, California, Hawaii, Iowa, Maine, Minnesota, Montana, New Jersey, Oregon, South Dakota, Vermont, and Wisconsin.

While Title VII does not apply to businesses with fewer than 15 employees, there are other federal anti-discrimination laws which do apply. The Civil Rights Act of 1872[2] prohibits discrimination based upon race and national origin without regard to number of employees. The Equal Pay Act of 1963[3] prohibits wage differentials based on sex for equal work under similar working conditions and applies to employers of two or more employees. Seniority, merit, or incentive systems are specifically excepted.

The Equal Pay Act of 1963 is an amendment to the Fair Labor Standards Act of 1938[4] and covers all employees subject to the FLSA. This includes employers with two or more employees if engaged in commerce or in producing goods for commerce. The Age Discrimination in Employment Act of 1967[5] now prohibits discrimination against employees or applicants who are 40 years old and older. This act is applicable to all employers with 20 or more employees within a 20-week period — similar to the rules under Title VII.

The Americans with Disabilities Act of 1990 bars employment discrimination against people with physical or mental disabilities. It also requires employers to provide reasonable accommodation to the disabled including making existing facilities accessible, providing special equipment and training, and arranging part-time or modified work schedules. This excludes accommodations which impose an undue hardship on business operations.

The law applies to employers of 15 or more people. Many states have laws similar to the ADA that apply to companies with fewer employees. See more discussion of this law's impact on employers in *Sections 2050 — Medical Evaluations and Interviews* and *2060 — Substance Abuse.*

There are other federal and state anti-discrimination laws that apply to employers who have federal or state government contracts or subcontracts above a certain dollar value — usually relatively low. The major provisions of these laws will be described in any federal or state government procurement document published to solicit bids, proposals, or quotations.

The anti-discrimination laws relate to hiring. They also define the employer's obligations regarding compensation, promotion, type of work that may be assigned, and working conditions.

Comparable Worth — Equal Pay

Another issue which impacts the decision to hire and administer salary is the concept of comparable worth or equal pay. No employer may pay wages to any employee at a rate less than the employer pays employees of the opposite sex for comparable work requiring comparable skills. Both federal and state statutes obligate employers to provide for comparable worth. Failure to do so can result in claims of wage or sex discrimination.

To avoid these traps, vigilantly monitor your job classifications — especially ones which seem to be primarily occupied by males or females — and pay scales. This area is also considered in *Chapter 3, Compensation.*

When developing the company's equal opportunity statement, it may be important to seek legal counsel or consult with federal, state, or local officials to ensure compliance with all statutes and ordinances.

In his 1999 State of the Union address, President Bill Clinton announced that the government would undertake more strict enforcement of the Equal Pay Act. Employers be forewarned.

Equal Opportunity

Alternate Policy 1   2010.1

Equal Opportunity is (COMPANY) policy. It is our policy to select the best qualified person for each position in the organization.

No employee of the company will discriminate against an applicant for employment or a fellow employee because of race, creed, color, religion, sex, national origin, ancestry, age, or other physical or mental disability. No employee of the company will discriminate against any applicant or fellow employee because of the person's veteran status.

This policy applies to all employment practices and personnel actions including advertising, recruitment, testing, screening, hiring, selection for training, upgrading, transfer, demotion, layoff, termination, rates of pay, and other forms of compensation or overtime.

(COMPANY) has adopted an affirmative action policy which essentially means that the company will aggressively seek out, hire, develop, and promote qualified members of protected groups — defined as racial minorities, women, physically or mentally disabled, disabled veterans, veterans of the Vietnam era, and persons ages of 40 and over.

Note: Affirmative action portion of this policy may only be required for employers who contract with federal, state, or local governments.

Equal Opportunity

Alternate Policy 2   2010.2

It is the intent and resolve of (COMPANY) to comply with the requirements and spirit of the law in the implementation of all facets of equal opportunity and affirmative action. In the recruitment, selection, training, utilization, promotion, termination, or any other personnel action, there will be no discrimination on the basis of race, creed, color, religious belief, sex, age, national origin, ancestry, physical or mental disability, or veteran status. (COMPANY) fully complies with all government requirements for setting up and carrying through affirmative action policies related to the protected classes mentioned above.

It is the responsibility of all managers to see that the company policy of equal opportunity is communicated throughout the organization.

1. A written notice of this policy will be sent to all managers, supervisors, and other employees engaged in employment and training.

2. A copy of our equal opportunity policy will be made available to each new employee or applicant on the first day he or she reports to work or upon request.

3. The company's policy on equal opportunity will be posted in prominent locations.

Recruitment 2020

Comment

The recruitment policy statement sets forth the communication process your company will follow when filling position requisitions within the organization. It should define the methods of recruitment outside of the organization as well as spell out the in-house requisition posting procedures.

The statement should encourage all qualified, present employees to compete for job openings. This provides employees with an opportunity for upward or lateral mobility, increases morale, and saves recruitment costs. Reference should be made to the policy, *Announcement of New Positions — Section 6010,* or it can be combined with this policy under this title.

A reference statement within the policy should reinforce your company's commitment to equal opportunity and, where appropriate, affirmative action. Carefully draft this policy to avoid the potential for discriminatory recruitment practices (e.g., "word of mouth" or "college" recruitment should not be stated as "preferred" methods). This policy should be evaluated in conjunction with the policy on *Employee Selection Process* which follows. You may wish to combine the essentials of each policy into one recruitment policy.

Is an affirmative action policy required? If you engage in government contract work, the answer is almost certainly "Yes." If you are a private employer without government contract work, the answer is generally "No."

Do not misrepresent working conditions, existence of work, the length of time work will last, compensation for such work, or the status of any strike or labor dispute affecting such work. A sample Position Requisition form follows the alternate policy statements on recruitment.

Once your company authorizes the approval for recruitment of a new position, the next step is to collect applications from potential candidates. A sample employment application follows the recruitment policies. Remember various state and federal laws prohibit you from asking questions about age, race, marital status, disability status, injuries and illness.

The questions on the application are to focus on whether a person can do the job. The Sample Employment Policies and Release Form is an introduction to applicants about your company. Review this text very carefully. Be sure each statement applies to your company. The format and wording serve as a model for you to structure a similar company statement.

Recruitment

Alternate Policy 1   2020.1

(COMPANY) leadership position in the business community demands that recruitment be conducted in an aggressive manner to attract top caliber individuals to all levels of the organization. Positions may be filled by transfer or promotion of existing employees or new employees who are recruited or apply directly to the company. Recruitment may be conducted through advertising, employment agencies, schools, employee referrals, or technical and trade referrals. The (PERSONNEL DIRECTOR) is the only person who is authorized to approve recruitment funds. Supervisors/managers should discuss the most appropriate method of recruitment for filling departmental positions with the (PERSONNEL DIRECTOR). All recruitment shall be conducted in an ethical, professional, and non-discriminatory manner.

A list of current openings will be posted on all company bulletin boards. Refer to the policy *Announcement of New Positions — Section 6010.*

Recruitment

Alternate Policy 2   2020.2

(COMPANY) provides equal employment opportunity to all applicants on the basis of demonstrated ability, experience, and training.

As positions become available within the company, prior to outside recruitment, the (PERSONNEL DIRECTOR) and hiring manager shall determine the availability of qualified candidates within the company. Recruitment may be conducted through schools, employment agencies, and company advertising.

Contact the (PERSONNEL DIRECTOR) to discuss the most appropriate method of recruitment. The company bulletin board will display all current openings.

This policy excludes those employed through temporary agencies or "job shops."

Employment Opportunity / Position Requisition

Title of Position:_____

Department:_____ Classification: Exempt _____ Non-Exempt _____

Hiring Supervisor:_____

Reports to:_____

Position Description: _____

_____

_____

Major Job-Related Duties and Functions: _____

_____

_____

Minimum Qualifications: (Knowledge, Skills, and Education):_____

_____

_____

Additional Desired Qualifications:_____

Employment Status: Regular Full-time _____   Regular Part-time _____ Temporary_____

Salary Range: _____

Potential Career Opportunities in the Position:_____

_____

Additional Comments: _____

For additional information, applicants should contact:

_____

Name   Telephone   Date

Employment Application Form

Sample Form

Personal Information

Full Name_____ Social Security #_____ Telephone #_____

Address_____ City and State_____ Zip_____

Employment Desired

Position/s applying for: 1._____ 2._____

Date you can begin _____ Salary Desired _____

Are you currently employed? ■ Yes   ■ No

If yes, may we contact employer? ■ Yes   ■ No

Employment Sought: ■ Full time   ■ Part time

Can you, at the time of employment, submit verification of your legal right to work in the United States? ■ Yes   ■ No

Education

High School_____ Location _____ Graduate? ■ Yes ■ No

College _____ Location _____ Graduate? ■ Yes ■ No Major_____

College _____ Location _____ Graduate? ■ Yes ■ No Major_____

Trade/Business/Graduate School _____ Location _____

Graduate? ■ Yes ■ No   Major_____

List Special Studies or Hobbies: _____

Please Answer

Why are you interested in becoming an employee with (COMPANY)?_____

_____

_____

Employment Application Form

Sample Form (continued)

What are your career goals? _____
_____

Where did you get the information about the position? _____

Employment History — list most recent first

Company Name _____ Supervisor's Name _____ Last Position _____

Address _____ Telephone No._____ Job Responsibilities _____

City,State, Zip _____ Dates of Employment _____ Reason for Leaving _____

Company Name _____ Supervisor's Name _____ Last Position _____

Address _____ Telephone No._____ Job Responsibilities _____

City,State, Zip _____ Dates of Employment _____ Reason for Leaving _____

Company Name _____ Supervisor's Name _____ Last Position _____

Address _____ Telephone No._____ Job Responsibilities _____

City,State, Zip _____ Dates of Employment _____ Reason for Leaving _____

Company Name _____ Supervisor's Name _____ Last Position _____

Address _____ Telephone No._____ Job Responsibilities _____

City,State, Zip _____ Dates of Employment _____ Reason for Leaving _____

References — list 3 individuals (not related to you) who are familiar with your work-related skills

Name	Name of Company	Company Address	Telephone No.	Years Acquainted

Employment Policies and Release Form

Sample Form

There are a number of (COMPANY) policies that an applicant needs to know about and agree to before being employed. There also are a number of activities that (COMPANY) may want to instigate as part of the review and investigation of the appropriate background information on an applicant. The purpose of this document is to present these policies and investigative activities to the applicant to ensure that they are understood and agreed to at the time the application is submitted.

We, therefore, ask that you please read, complete, and sign this form before you complete the Application for Employment.

Policies

Among the policies that have been adopted at (COMPANY) are the following which we believe are important for an applicant to know in advance of employment. These are listed below. Your signature on this Release Form indicates that you have read, understand, and would agree to operate under these policies if employed at (COMPANY).

1. This firm is an equal employment opportunity employer and does not discriminate because of age, sex, race, color, national origin, disability, or religious preference.
2. (COMPANY) is a drug and alcohol free-workplace. To ensure worker safety and integrity of the workplace, (COMPANY) prohibits the illegal manufacture, possession, distribution or use of controlled substances or alcohol in the workplace by its employees or those who engage or seek to engage in business with (COMPANY). Offers of employment, therefore, may be conditioned on a physical examination, including a drug and alcohol screening.

Note: Pre-employment drug testing is permitted under the ADA. Pre-employment alcohol screening is not. If you intend to screen for both drugs and alcohol, a test following a conditional offer of employment is your most cost-effective choice.

3. Smoking is not permitted inside the building at (COMPANY). For the safety and health of its employees, (COMPANY) is committed to a smoke-free building.
4. Your signature on this Release Form indicates that you understand and agree that if employed, that employment is for no definite period, and may, regardless of the date of payment of your wages and salary, be terminated at any time without previous notice
5. An offer of employment must originate from the (PERSONNEL DIRECTOR) of (COMPANY).

Employment Policies and Release Form

Sample Form (continued)

Background Review Activities

The following investigative activities may be conducted by (COMPANY) as part of the background review of prospective employees. Your signature on this Release Form indicates you understand these activities and you authorize them to be performed with the conditions specified as listed below.

1. Certain positions at this company may not be held by persons convicted of specific crimes. If you are applying for such a position and have been convicted of a felony, please note this below. If more space is needed, please provide the additional information on a separate sheet of paper. In addition, you authorize (COMPANY) to undertake a criminal records check with state police officials._____

_____

2. You authorize (COMPANY) to obtain a Motor Vehicle Record report. Our insurance company may also obtain a report through its sources. If the position you are applying for involves driving a motor vehicle, it is imperative that a good driving record exists.
3. You also authorize and request any and all of your former employers to furnish any and all information regarding your job performance. You agree to hold your former employers and their agents harmless from all liability which could relate in any way to the disclosure of private information or an assessment or opinion of your suitability for employment.
4. You understand that an offer of employment must originate from the (PERSONNEL DIRECTOR) of (COMPANY).

In closing, we ask that you read (and complete where needed) the remaining three (3) statements and that your signature on this Release From indicates you understand each.

1. I have read and understand the job description for the position of _____ as approved on the date of _____.
2. I understand that misrepresentation or omission of facts herein is cause for termination, if employed.
3. I have read and understand the attached application and have answered all portions of the application truthfully and correctly with no omissions.

_____   _____
                Signature   Date

Employee Selection Process   2030

Comment

The *Employee Selection Process* policy statement establishes the authority and responsibility of designated management staff in the selection function.

The design of this policy should minimize your company's efforts and maximize its resources in selecting the best candidate available for an open position. The policy should provide assurance of your company's intention to recruit, hire, place, promote, and transfer for all positions without regard to race, religion, color, national origin, sex, age, or physical disability. Excepted are positions which require physical fitness as a valid occupational qualification.

In developing this policy, consider recent innovations. Some companies provide cash awards or other incentives to employees who seek and refer applicants who are then hired. For example, a non-exempt position filled in this way may carry a $100 bonus. An exempt, professional, or executive position may carry a $300 bonus. Other incentives include a day or two off with pay or use of the company condominium for a weekend. The recruitment cost savings is obvious. However, a word of caution is appropriate. Such an incentive system may result in word of mouth recruiting becoming a preferred or sole method of recruiting. This may lead to a charge of discriminatory hiring practices being leveled at the company if there is a lack of minority and female candidates. This can occur even though management's intent is benign.

The Immigration Reform and Control Act of 1986, also known as the Simpson—Rodino Act, makes a notable impact on most employers' recruitment and selection policies and procedures. This law prohibits employers with four or more employees, from practicing employment discrimination based on national origin or citizenship.

A major burden on employers is the:
1. Prohibition against knowingly hiring or continuing to hire illegal aliens;
2. The verification measures required; and
3. The maintenance of records showing the immigration status and certifications required by the law and implementing regulations.

Basically, the immigration status of all new hires must be verified by the examination of documents or records showing both employment and identity. A U.S. passport or a green card satisfies both the employment authorization and identity requirements. Otherwise, both an employment authorization record, such as a Social Security card and U.S. birth certificate, and an identity document, such as a U.S. driver's license or identity card, must be examined. The documents must appear to be genuine to a reasonable person.

Under penalty of perjury, the employer must attest in writing that the employer saw the documentation. Also, the employee attests, in writing and under penalty of perjury, that he or she is authorized to work in the United States. These attestations are made on *Form I–9, Employment Eligibility Verification,* which must be kept by the employer for three years after recruitment or for at least one year after the employee's termination, whichever occurs last. A list of the authorized documents or records and *Form I–9* may be obtained from the Immigration and Naturalization Department. A sample of *Form I–9* for both employer and employee certifications follows the alternate policies.

The law does not require you to maintain photocopies of the documents that you have examined. However, this practice is permitted by the law and is evidence of a good faith attempt to comply, which is a defense to a charge of employing an illegal alien. Hiring, recruiting, continuing to employ, or referring for hire an alien who is not authorized to work in the United States is punishable by civil fines. These range from a $250 minimum fine up to a $10,000 maximum fine for a third offense for each alien. A pattern or practice of violations is a criminal matter. Sentences for this can be up to six months in jail or a $3,000 fine, or both, for each alien. The Act also extends to independent contractors and employment policies.

A critical component of any employee selection process is what questions you can ask job applicants. Recently, the United States Equal Employment Opportunity Commission (EEOC) published an enforcement guide related to pre-employment disability-related inquiries. Further discussion of the EEOC's guidance is included in *Medical Evaluations and Interviews — Section 2050.*

Sample letters also follow the alternate policy statements. The rejection letter expresses your company's appreciation to the applicant for their time and interest in participating in the selection process. Just the few minutes it takes to initiate and send the letter places a positive closure on the application and selection process. The offer of employment letter confirms the verbal agreement made when asking the applicant to join your staff.

A sample *Interview Summary Sheet* follows the alternate policy statements. Forms for employee privacy rights waivers are in *Employee Privacy — Section 6100.* Use these when checking references, background, and before providing similar information concerning company employees to others.

Employee Selection Process

Alternate Policy 1   2030.1

Selection of candidates for all positions will follow (COMPANY) Equal Opportunity and (Affirmative Action) policies. The supervisor/manager is responsible for preparing the position requisition. Only the (PERSONNEL DEPARTMENT) is authorized to place ads, respond to inquiries from employment agencies, and post requisitions on the company bulletin boards.

Job-related duties and qualifications, as listed on the position requisition, will provide the basis for initial screening of applications. All applications and resumés received for the position will be forwarded to the personnel department. Initial screening for the minimum qualifications will be conducted by the personnel department. The supervisor/manager will further screen the applications to select those individuals to be interviewed for the position.

The personnel department and hiring manager will jointly conduct the interviews. Only job-related questions or ones which assess the candidate's experience, skill, and training will be asked. Definite salary commitments will be avoided during the initial interview.

Some positions will require skills for which a known level of competence must exist — for example, typing, mathematics, and keypunch. Under these circumstances, the personnel department may request applicants to demonstrate these skills by completing an exercise involving a job-related work sample. It must be evident that such an exercise measures knowledge or skills required for the particular job. The results of an exercise must prove to be a valid prediction of job performance. All interviewed applicants must be given the same exercise.

Employee Selection Process

Alternate Policy 1 (continued)   2030.1

The personnel department will be responsible for verification of employment information provided by the applicant, if the information is needed in making a candidate selection.

The only information to be verified from prior employers will be the following:

1. Dates of employment
2. Positions held
3. Salary at time of termination

The applicant should be advised that this information will be verified. Additional information should not be requested from prior employers, unless the applicant agrees in writing, because it may violate the applicant's privacy.

Note: See the Comment to Employee Privacy, Section 6100. This verification of information should be documented and will become part of the data used in the selection process.

Every newly-hired employee must verify his or her eligibility for employment within three business days of accepting employment. The personnel department will not notify other candidates that the position has been filled until the new employee has complied with the law.

The employee will fill out and execute the top of *Form I–9.* The personnel department will complete *Form I–9* after examining the employee's documentation of identity and employment eligibility. Each document examined will be photocopied and the copy maintained in the employee's personnel file folder.

Note: See sample of Form I-9 on pages 48-49.

Employee Selection Process

Alternate Policy 2   2030.2

(COMPANY) provides equal opportunity to all applicants on the basis of demonstrated ability, experience, training, and potential. Qualified persons are selected without prejudice or discrimination as stated in the company's Equal Opportunity (and Affirmative Action) policies.

The employment requisitions, initiated by the (SUPERVISOR/MANAGER), will define the job-related tasks and qualifications necessary to assume the position. The defined tasks and stated qualifications will be the basis for screening applications. The (PERSONNEL DEPARTMENT) will conduct structured initial interviews limited to job-related questions to assess the candidates' experience, demonstrated ability, and training. The telephone may be used for these initial interviews.

Pre-employment tests demonstrated to be job-relevant and valid according to accepted professional practices may be used. Such tests are to be administered only by trained personnel in the prescribed professional manner. All interviewed applicants will be asked to take the test.

After initial interviews and testing, the hiring supervisor or department manager will conduct interviews with the candidates he or she selects with the concurrence of the personnel department.

Before extending an employment offer and upon the applicant's prior agreement that inquiries may be made, at least two applicant references must be checked. Inquiries are to be made in a professional manner requesting only factually verifiable and job-related information. The reference data is used only as supplemental information for the hiring decision.

Following employment, the information will be retained for one year before being destroyed.

Note: Check your state law for records retention requirements.

Employee Selection Process

Alternate Policy 2 (continued)   2030.2

After candidate interviews, verification of employment history, and reference inquiries, the hiring manager is responsible for the employment offer. Before a verbal offer is made, the personnel department must be consulted and must give approval. The hiring manager may make the offer personally or may delegate this responsibility to the personnel department.

After the verbal offer has been made and the candidate has agreed to the essential terms of the offer (typically position, employee classification, salary or rate, and starting date), a written offer will be prepared by the personnel department and submitted to the candidate in person or by mail. The written offer will confirm the verbal offer and will include the essential terms of the verbal offer as agreed to by the candidate. The candidate will be required to sign and date an acceptance of the written offer which will state as follows:

"The undersigned accepts the above employment offer and agrees that it contains the terms of employment with (COMPANY) and that there are no other terms express or implied. It is understood that employment is subject to verification of identity and employment eligibility and may be terminated by the (COMPANY) at any time for any reason."

The verbal or written offer must never express or imply that employment is "permanent," "long-term," of a specific duration, or words of similar meaning. An exception may be made where a temporary position of known duration is to be filled. Employment may be made contingent upon certain job-related factors, such as obtaining a specific state or federal license or security clearance when appropriate or desirable.

Once the candidate has accepted the employment offer, she or he will be required to provide documentation of identity and employment eligibility in accordance with federal law. The *Form I–9*, a copy of which is included at the end of this policy, shall be used for this purpose.

Interview Summary Sheet

Applicant's Name _____ Date _____

Position _____ Interviewer _____

Qualifications (taken from job announcement):   Applicant's Background:

_____   _____

_____   _____

Job Functions: Applicant's Experience:

Skills: _____   _____

_____   _____

Education: _____   _____

_____   _____

Knowledge: _____   _____

_____   _____

References of Previous Supervisors or Managers: _____

_____

Preferred Qualifications: _____

_____

Growth in Career: _____

_____

Accomplishments: _____

Applicant's Strengths: _____

Applicant's Limitations: _____

Interviewer Comments: _____

_____

Employment Eligibility Verification — Form I-9

Notice: Authority for collecting the information on this form is in Title 8, United States Code, Section 1324A, which requires employers to verify employment eligibility of individuals on a form approved by the Attorney General. This form will be used to verify the individual's eligibility for employment in the United States. Failure to present this form for inspection to officers of the Immigration and Naturalization Service or Department of Labor within the time period specified by regulation, or improper completion or retention of this form may be a violation of the above law and may result in a civil money penalty.

Section 1 — Instructions to Employee/Preparer for completing this form

Instructions for the employee

All employees, upon being hired, must complete Section 1 of this form. Any person hired after November 6, 1986, must complete this form. (For the purpose of completion of this form the term "hired" applies to those employed, recruited, or referred for a fee.)

All employees must print or type their complete name, address, date of birth and Social Security number. The block which correctly indicates the employee's immigration status must be checked. If the second block is checked, the employee's Alien Registration Number must be provided.

All employees whose present names differ from birth names, because of marriage or other reasons must print or type their birth names in the appropriate space of Section. Also, employees whose names change after employment verification should report these changes to their employer. All employees must sign and date the form.

Instructions for the preparer of the form, if not the employee

If a person assists the employee with completing this form, the preparer must certify the form by signing it and printing or typing his or her complete name and address

Section 2 — Instructions to Employer for completing this form

(For the purpose of completion of this form, the term "employer" applies to employers and those who recruit or refer for a fee.)

Employers must complete this section by examining evidence of identity and employment eligibility and
- Checking the appropriate box in List A or boxes in lists B and C;
- Recording the document identification number and expiration date (if any);
- Recording the type of form if not specifically identified in the list;
- Signing the certification section.

Note: *Employers are responsible for verifying employment eligibility of employees whose employment eligibility documents carry an expiration date*

Copies of documentation presented by an individual for the purpose of establishing identity and employment eligibility may be copied and retained for the purpose of complying with the requirements of this form and no other purpose. Any copies of documentation made for this purpose should be maintained with this form.

Name changes of employees which occur after preparation of this form should be recorded on the form by lining through the old name, printing the new name and the reason (such as marriage) and dating and initialing the changes. Employers should not attempt to delete or erase the old name in any fashion.

Retention of Records

The completed form must be retained by the employer for:
- Three years after the date of hiring; or
- One year after the date the employment is terminated, whichever is later.

Employment Eligibility Verification — Form I-9 (continued)

I. Employee Information and Verification (To be completed and signed by employee)

Name (Print or type) Last	First	Middle	Birth Name

Address: Street Name and Number	City	State	ZIP Code

Date of Birth (Month, Day, Year)	Social Security Number

I attest, under penalty of perjury, that I am (check a box):

- 1. A citizen or national of the United States.
- 2. An alien lawfully admitted for permanent residence (Alien Number A_____.)
- 3. An alien authorized by the Immigration and Naturalization Service to work in the United States (Alien Number A_____ or Admission Number _____). Expiration of employment authorization, if any _____.

I attest, under penalty of perjury, the documents that I have presented as evidence of identity and employment eligibility are genuine and relate to me. I am aware that federal law provides for imprisonment and/or fine for any false statements or use of false documents in connection with this certificate.

_____   _____
Signature   Date (Month, Day, Year)

Preparer Translator Certification (To be completed if prepared by person other than the employee)

I attest, under penalty of perjury, that the above was prepared by me at the request of the named individual and is based on all information of which I have any knowledge.

Signature	Name (Print or Type)		
Address (Street Name and Number)	City	State	ZIP Code

2. Employer Review and Verification (To be completed and signed by employer)

Instructions: Examine one document from List A and check the appropriate box OR examine one document from List B and one from List C and check the appropriate boxes. Provide the Document ID Number and Expiration Date for the document checked.

List A *Documents that Establish Identity & Employment Eligibility*	List B *Documents that Establish Identity*	List C *Documents that Establish Employment Eligibility*
■ 1. United States Passport ■ 2. Certificate of United States Citizenship ■ 3. Certificate of Naturalization ■ 4. Unexpired foreign passport with attached Employment Authorization ■ 5. Alien Registration Card with photograph	■ 1. A state-issued driver's license or a state-issued ID card with a photograph, or information, including name, sex, date of birth, height, weight and color of eyes (Specify State)_____ ■ 2. U.S. Military Card ■ 3. Other (Specify document and issuing authority	■ 1. Original Social Security Number Card (other than a card stating it is not valid for employment). ■ 2. A birth certificate issued by state, county or municipal authority bearing a seal or other certification. ■ 3. Unexpired INS Employment Authorization Specify form_____
Document Identification #_____	Document Identification #_____	Document Identification #_____
Expiration Date (if any) _____	Expiration Date (if any) _____	Expiration Date (if any) _____

Certification: I attest, under penalty of perjury, that I have examined the documents presented by the above individual, that they appear to be genuine and to relate to the individual named, and that the individual, to the best of my knowledge, is eligible to work in the United States.

Signature	Name (Print or Type)	Title
Employer Name	Address	Date

Sample Rejection Letter after Interview

(APPLICANT'S NAME)

(APPLICANT'S ADDRESS)

Dear (APPLICANT),

Thank you for your recent application and interview regarding the position with (COMPANY). We certainly appreciate your interest in our firm.

I want to inform you that we have offered the position to another applicant whom we think best meets our needs for the position. It was a difficult decision because a number of applicants, including yourself, were strong candidates. We would like to keep your application on file for a period of 120 days in the event another position for which you are qualified becomes vacant. If that occurs, we will give your application strong consideration. If your address changes within that period of time, we encourage you to inform us of your new address.

Again, we thank you for your interest in (COMPANY) and for attending the interview. We wish you continued success in your career endeavors.

Sincerely,

(NAME)

Personnel Director

(COMPANY)

Note: Do not send this type of letter to candidates who were plainly not qualified for the position. It will invite complaints of discrimination. Consider using the sample letter found on the next page.

Sample Rejection Letter after Interview

(APPLICANT'S NAME)

(APPLICANT'S ADDRESS)

Dear (APPLICANT),

Thank you for your recent application for a position with (COMPANY). We certainly appreciate your interest in our firm.

☐ We regret to inform you that at this time we do not have a vacancy in a position for which you applied.

☐ We regret to inform you that we have offered the position to another applicant whom we think best meets our needs for the position.

Again, we thank you for your interest in (COMPANY) and the time and effort you spent in submitting an application. We wish you continued success in your career endeavors.

Sincerely,

(NAME)

Personnel Director

(COMPANY)

Sexual Harassment   2040

Comment

Sexual harassment is a form of prohibited employment discrimination under Title VII of the Civil Rights Act. Sexual harassment is defined as unwelcome sexual advances, requests for sexual favors, and other verbal or physical conduct of a sexual nature whenever:

a. Submission to this conduct is made either explicitly or implicitly a term or condition of an individual's employment
b. Submission to or rejection of such conduct by an individual is used as the basis for employment decisions effecting such individuals; or
c. Such conduct has the purpose or effect of unreasonably interfering with an individual's work performance or creating an intimidating, hostile or offensive working environment.

There are two forms of sexual harassment. The first is known as quid pro quo harassment. Here, employment decisions are conditioned upon the granting of sexual favors or being required to tolerate other forms of sexual abuse. Employment decisions cover the full range of employment activities including decisions to hire, fire, promote, grant a raise, or make a job assignment.

Under quid pro quo harassment, an employer is strictly liable for the conduct of supervisory employees who make employment decisions. This is true even if conduct occurs during non-working hours or off premises.

The second category is known as hostile environment sexual harassment. This is a much more difficult area. Under hostile environment harassment, the following elements must exist:

a. The employee is subjected to sexual advances, requests for sexual favors and other verbal or physical conduct of a sexual nature (including sexual jokes, nude photographs, highly personal questions, notes or telephone calls);
b. The conduct is unwelcome; and
c. The conduct is sufficiently severe or pervasive to alter the conditions of employment and create an abusive working environment. Under this type of harassment, an employer is not strictly liable for the acts of supervisory employees. The employer is liable only if the employer knew or should have known that this conduct was occurring.

Prior to 1998, many employers believed that employer liability in quid pro quo cases existed only where some tangible employment action was taken (i.e., fired, demoted, not promoted). This is no longer the case. As a result, employers must take the preventive steps described below.

Sexual harassment claims can be expensive. Successful claimants may be eligible for back pay, compensatory and punitive damages, reinstatement, attorney fees and injunctive relief. Harassment claims are also often brought with claims for wrongful discharge or emotional distress.

In addition to the potential monetary loss, there are other practical damages which may result, including:

- Loss of productivity;
- Diversion of company resources to investigate and resolve the claim;
- Loss of trust and confidence of employee;
- Diminished morale; and
- Time and expense of conducting an investigation.

To avoid or minimize sexual harassment claims, an employer should take the following steps:

- Develop a strong policy regarding sexual harassment that is easy to understand and encourages reporting;
- Provide for a viable problem solving mechanism through which employees can report harassment and from which a prompt and thorough investigation will be made;
- Provide adequate training to all employees so that potentially harassing behavior can be identified and reported at the earliest possible opportunity;
- Conduct a prompt and thorough investigation; and
- Take appropriate corrective measures.

Complete the investigation and take appropriate corrective measures, These two steps are important even in situations where the harasser has stopped the conduct and where no employment action was taken.

There is no clear advice about how you should treat office flirtations or romances. No one can say with certainty where the line between well-meaning social relationships and harassment will be drawn. There seems to be a subjective standard in such a decision.

The cautious employer may consider a policy which prohibits dating between employees and managers or supervisors. However, discipline or termination for violating such a policy may lead to the employee's claim that his or her privacy was violated or that such action was wrongful because dating does not affect the employer's legitimate business interests.

A well-defined company policy is the first step toward the elimination of sexual harassment. Develop appropriate controls to avoid any form of sexual harassment. Develop methods to sensitize employees to rid the work environment of forms of conduct that could be interpreted as sexual in nature. Some employers have a policy against posters, signs, or other displays which might be considered sexually offensive.

An adequate policy is only the first step. Management should ensure that any allegation of sexual harassment will be investigated without embarrassment or negative reaction to the employee reporting the allegation. Being responsive to allegations of employee misconduct and taking appropriate disciplinary action when required are essential management responsibilities in this area. Plainly, in this area, the actions of management in handling sexual harassment complaints are as significant as anything written in the policy manual.

The Internet has added another sexual harassment complexity to the workplace. Guidelines should be defined as to what can be downloaded and how to handle material received from the outside that may be considered sexually explicit.

It is also important to note that sexual harassment laws apply to the actions of customers and suppliers and other non-employees. If you are aware of circumstances which may indicate harassment of employees by customers, suppliers, or others doing business with the employer, your policy may apply and you will be required to investigate and take appropriate action and eliminate harassment.

Recent court decisions in a few small states have permitted employees to file claims against their employers even though the employer did not have enough employees to be covered by federal or state statutes. In those jurisdictions, the courts allowed the employees to proceed on the theory of wrongful discharge in violation of public policy.

Sexual Harassment

Alternate Policy I   2040.1

(COMPANY) will not allow any form of sexual harassment or any such conduct that has the purpose or effect of interfering with an individual's work performance or creating an intimidating, hostile, or offensive work environment.

Such conduct, when experienced or observed, should be reported immediately to the supervisor/manager or personnel department. The (PERSONNEL DEPARTMENT) will conduct an investigation and will be required to report the findings to the (VICE PRESIDENT'S) office or his or her appointed representative. The privacy of the employee filing the report and the employee under investigation shall be respected at all times consistent with the obligation to conduct a fair and thorough investigation.

Any intentional sexual harassment is considered to be a major violation of company policy and will be dealt with accordingly by corrective counseling and/or suspension or termination, depending upon the severity of the violation.

It is the intent of (COMPANY) to provide a work environment free from verbal, physical, and visual forms (e.g., signs, posters, or documents) of sexual harassment and an environment free of harassment, intimidation or coercion in any form. All employees are expected to be sensitive to the individual rights of their co-workers.

Displaying sexually explicit images or text on company property is a violation of (COMPANY) policy. Employees are not allowed to download, archive, edit, or manipulate sexually explicit material from the Internet while using company resources. Any sexually explicit material sent by a fellow employee or received from outside sources should be given to your (MANAGER).

Sexual Harassment

Alternate Policy 2   2040.2

(COMPANY) will not allow any form of sexual harassment within the work environment.

Sexual harassment interferes with work performance; creates an intimidating, hostile, or offensive work environment; influences or tends to affect the career, salary, working conditions, responsibilities, duties, or other aspects of career development of an employee or prospective employee; or creates an explicit or implicit term or condition of an individual's employment. It will not be tolerated.

Sexual harassment, as defined in this policy, includes, but is not limited to, sexual advances, verbal or physical conduct of a sexual nature, visual forms of a sexual or offensive nature (e.g., signs and posters, material downloaded from the Internet, sexually explicit e-mail communications), or requests for sexual favors.

Medical Evaluations and Interviews   2050

Comment

The language that defines a company's medical policy has taken a number of dramatic changes in the past few years. In the past, many companies required all new employees to have a company-paid physical, performed by a physician chosen by the company. Today, more and more companies are omitting the required physical. Other companies require a medical evaluation only if a job has special physical demands or there is some question as to the individual's ability to perform the job-related tasks.

As a general rule, a job applicant cannot be required to submit to a medical or physical exam before hiring. Hiring can be conditioned on subsequent passage of the medical or physical exam. Tests designed to measure strength or ability to perform a job-related task may be administered during the pre-employment phase if required for the performance of the job and if all other employees in that job classification are required to take the same test.

Legal considerations arise with regard to medical evaluations of employees. Some are relatively minor. Others are not minor because the employer may be exposed to the risk of liability and may also have to assume a greater duty to an employee in certain circumstances.

Under certain circumstances, state law may require periodic physicals of employees (e.g. where the employee is exposed to certain hazardous substances). Also, the Occupational Safety and Health Administration, the Environmental Protection Agency, and certain state agencies may require employers to record and report certain employee health complaints or symptoms. To learn if you have such requirements, you can directly contact the agencies themselves or your individual state labor or health agency.

From the standpoint of Title VII and state anti-discrimination laws, medical evaluation standards for employment must be job-related or directly related to a determination of whether the applicant would endanger his or her health or safety or the health and safety of others.

You should also be careful of minimum height or weight requirements. Such requirements must be clearly job-related or else you may face a charge of discrimination against certain national origins or because of gender or disability. Similarly, you cannot exclude women from jobs which are strenuous, dirty, or dangerous.

The decision whether to require medical evaluations should start with the understanding that, generally, the employer has no legal duty to ascertain whether an employee, or prospective employee, is physically fit for the job. However, once this duty is assumed, the employer is liable if the duty is performed negligently or performed negligently by someone else.

One corporation was found to be liable to an employee for failure to evaluate a blood test report through clerical error, the results of which would have led to an earlier diagnosis of bone cancer.[1] Another employer was held liable to an employee for the malpractice of the doctor hired by the company to do the pre-employment physical.[2] The use of a written disclaimer signed by an employee may help insulate an employer from liability in these situations. A sample form of disclaimer follows the alternate policies to this section.

Other legal issues face the employer as well. When medical information is released to the employer (the employee must sign a release for this purpose), the employer is generally legally obligated to keep that information confidential. However, if the report shows some health-jeopardizing condition or illness, the employer is under a duty to disclose this to the employee as soon as reasonably possible, if the doctor has not already done so.

If the medical evaluation reveals an abnormal condition or frailty, this information will be passed on to the employer. After receiving this, if the employer assigns work to the employee which aggravates this condition or is beyond the employee's physical capabilities, the employer will generally be held liable for injuries to the employee.

If the medical evaluation was not negligently performed, a report showing that the employee was in good health can provide some protection to the employer. However, some protection is not full protection. That report may also be evidence in favor of the employee who charges that he or she incurred a disease, illness, or injury purely as a result of the work environment such as in the recent asbestos cases, stress, or injury resulting from lifting heavy objects.

Medical information is often protected by state law to ensure an individual's privacy. Check your state's laws in this area. Whether or not there is a requirement, make sure that the company's records are secure and the employees are aware of the prohibitions. To avoid inadvertent disclosure, keep employee medical records separate from personnel files.

Some companies are required to maintain medical information about employees by law or regulation. For instance, chemical companies must maintain records of employee health complaints under rules of the Environmental Protection Agency. Often states have laws requiring statistical reports and records about occupational injuries and illnesses. Check your state labor office for details.

Based on research and the warnings above, you are not recommended to adopt a policy concerning medical evaluations unless the job or state law requires it. Two policy statements are provided for your consideration should you need to adopt one. Note that there is a distinction made between the policies with respect to interviews and evaluations.

If the medical interview relies solely on verbal or written information provided by the employee, a medical opinion may still be necessary. The employer may face the same legal considerations discussed above.

Special attention may need to be paid to the federal Americans with Disabilities Act of 1990. Generally, the Act prohibits discrimination against persons who are disabled, as defined in the law, as long as they are otherwise qualified for the job.

Under the ADA, an employer may not ask about the existence, nature, or severity of a disability and may not conduct medical examinations until after it makes a conditional job offer to the applicant. Once made, an employer can require medical examinations and make disability-related inquiries if it does so for all entering employees in the job category. To exclude an individual following an exam or inquiry, the employer must show that the exclusion was based on job-related criteria consistent with business necessity and the essential function of the job can't be performed with reasonable accommodation. Questions continue to arise that attempt to extend the definition of disabled workers. Two cases sought coverage for diabetes and vision impairment. Both have lost.

In May 1994, the Equal Employment Opportunity Commission (EEOC) published an enforcement guidance setting forth the EEOC's position on pre-employment disability-related inquiries and medical examinations.

In the fall of 1995, the EEOC published its final rules regarding what can be asked in a job interview. Under the final rule, an employer can ask what accommodation an applicant would require only where the applicant's disability is obvious or where the applicant voluntarily discloses the disability. Caution is required, however, because the employer can't ask about the disability under these circumstances, only the accommodation.

EEOC's final rule includes examples of disability-related and non-disability related inquiries and provides guidance on what constitutes a medical exam. These are set forth on the next page. A copy of the EEOC's rule is available by calling the EEOC at 1-800-669-3362.

Permissible Disability-Related Inquiries

- *Can you perform the functions of this job — essential and/or marginal, (with or without reasonable accommodation?)*

Note: The bracketed portion of this question may only be asked during the pre-employment phase if : 1. the employer reasonably believes the applicant needs reasonable accommodation due to an obvious disability; 2. the applicant has voluntarily disclosed a hidden disability; 3. the applicant voluntarily discloses the need for reasonable accommodations.

- *Please describe/demonstrate how you would perform these functions (essential and/or marginal).*
- *Do you have a cold? Have you ever tried Tylenol for fever? How did you break your leg?*
- *Can you meet the attendance requirements of this job? How many days were you absent last year?*
- *Do you drink alcohol? Have you ever been arrested for drinking under the influence (DUI)?*
- *Do you illegally use drugs? Have you used illegal drugs in the last two years?*
- *Do you have the required licenses to perform this job?*
- *How much do you weigh? How tall are you? Do you regularly eat three meals per day?*

Note: If these questions are to be used, they should be asked of all employees.

Impermissible Disability-Related Inquiries

- *Do you have AIDS?*
- *Do you have asthma?*
- *Do you have a disability which would interfere with your ability to perform the job?*
- *How many days were you sick last year? ("Absent" in place of "sick" is acceptable.)*
- *Have you ever filed for workers' compensation?*
- *Have you ever been injured on the job?*
- *How much alcohol do you drink each week?*
- *Have you ever been treated for alcohol problems?*
- *Have you ever been treated for mental health problems?*
- *What prescription drugs are you currently taking?*

Note: The impermissible inquiries may become permissible after a conditional job offer is made if they are asked of all employees who receive conditional job offers and are reasonable follow-up questions to information provided by the employee.

What is a Medical Examination?

How do you determine if a particular examination is a medical examination?

The following factors are considered by the EEOC in determining whether a particular test is medical in nature:

- Whether the test is administered by a health care professional or trainee;

- Whether the results of the test are interpreted by a health care professional or trainee;

- Whether the test is designed to reveal an impairment or the state of an individual's physical or psychological health;

- Whether the test is given for the purpose of revealing an impairment or the state of an individual's physical or psychological health;

- Whether the test is invasive (e.g., requires drawing of blood, urine, breath, etc.);

- Whether the test measures physiological/psychological responses (as opposed to the performance of a task);

- Whether the test is normally done in a medical setting; and

- Whether medical equipment/devises are used for the test.

While the factors listed above will generally be used to analyze any challenged test, the EEOC considers the following tests to not be medical tests under most circumstances:

- Physical agility/physical fitness tests which do not include medical monitoring;

- Certain psychological tests, such as tests which simply concern an individual's skills or tastes; and

- Tests for illegal use of drugs.

Because it is not always easy to tell what constitutes a medical test or what might include a disability inquiry, a safe course of action may be to make a conditional offer of employment prior to testing, conditioned on successful completion of testing. By moving inquiries to the post-offer context, many problems can be avoided.

Note: Whenever a medical examination is used, careful attention must be given to protecting the confidentiality of the examination results. In addition, medical examinations should be given to all employees seeking the same or similar positions.

Medical Evaluations and Interviews

Alternate Policy 1   2050.1

Once an employee has been hired, medical interviews may be conducted by a health professional chosen by the company to determine the employee's ability to fulfill job-related requirements. Physicals may be authorized for employees, if a job has special physical demands or when an employee's ability to meet the physical demands is reasonably in question.

Only the personnel manager may authorize such interviews or physicals. All costs for required medical interviews or physicals will be borne by (COMPANY). The employee must sign a written release of this information to the company. A copy of any written report received from the health professional respecting the interview will be provided to the employee and employer.

All information received will be deemed confidential. An employee's continued employment with (COMPANY) is conditioned upon successful completion of the medical interview.

Medical Evaluations and Interviews

Alternate Policy 2   2050.2

Once an employee has been hired, medical evaluations may be required to ensure that a prospective employee is capable of performing his or her essential job-related tasks. Such an evaluation will be conducted whenever a job has special physical demands or if a reasonable question exists concerning whether the employee would endanger his or her health or safety or the health or safety of others in performing assigned tasks.

The medical evaluation will be at company expense and performed by a physician chosen by the company. The employee will be required to sign a written release of this information to the company. (COMPANY) will treat as confidential the information contained in a report of medical evaluation. The company will provide the employee with a copy of any written report it receives from the health professional respecting the evaluation.

An employee's continued employment with (COMPANY) is conditioned upon successful completion of the medical evaluation.

Disclaimer of Liability

Alternate Policy 3   2050.3

Note: If used, Alternate Policy 3 should be used in conjunction with Alternate Policy 1 or 2.

(COMPANY) and employee have mutually agreed that a medical interview, evaluation, or examination is required to determine employee's ability to perform his or her essential job-related tasks in a manner which will not create an unreasonable risk of harm to employee or others. Employee acknowledges that the company will rely on the report prepared by the examining physician in determining employee's ability to perform.

Employee releases and agrees to hold harmless (COMPANY), its officers, directors, shareholders, employees, successors, and assigns from any and all liability, of any kind or nature whatsoever, which might arise out of or result from any statement or omission made or contained in said medical report.

The company is not required to undertake any independent investigation of the truthfulness or accuracy of statements made or contained in said medical report.

_____

Employee's Signature   Date

Substance Abuse   2060

Comment

If your management is not sure that this subject should be addressed by your policy manual or administrative guidelines, consider what the cost impact of substance abuse is today on American business. It is estimated that one in ten people suffer from the disease known as alcoholism. Children of alcoholics are four times more likely to have alcohol problems than children of non-alcoholics, and 33% of adult Americans say alcohol causes family problems. Drug abuse is just as likely to have the same impact on our families as alcoholism.

Nationally, drug abuse costs more than $30 billion each year in medical claims, wasted materials, industrial accidents, decreased productivity, and time lost from work. Add to that the cost of more than $116 billion nationally for alcohol abuse in the areas of lost production, health and medical payouts, vehicle accidents, violent crime, social responses, and fire losses.

Robert Taggart, a vice president of Southern Pacific Transportation Company of San Francisco, spoke at a conference sponsored by the University of California's Center for Human Resources Programs. He said his company's testing program was necessary because an employee with drugs in his or her system has been found to be twice as likely to be absent, four times as likely to have an accident, and five times as likely to file a worker's compensation claim.

Consider sending managers to a drug and alcohol awareness class. Have these managers write down their impressions of the classes and their recommendations for adopting a company substance abuse policy. Have a management "round table" with company officers, directors, and the managers who attended these classes. Discuss attitudes and experiences and get down to solving issues. Get your company legal counsel involved, too.

Analyze your product liability if one or more of your employees is working while under the influence. How many delivery vehicles do you have operating right now? Are heavy equipment, dangerous materials, or complicated procedures a part of your business?

Who is likely to be hurt if a substance abuser makes a few mistakes on the job? A member of the public at large? A customer? Another employee? You or your shareholders? Are you insured for it?

With these considerations in mind, you need to remember that there is a substantial body of evidence that substance abuse off the job — even intermittent, recreational drug use — sometimes affects the mental and physical abilities of the user on the job.

The issue of substance abuse is a sensitive one and one that presents a number of emerging legal questions, including employees' privacy rights. The area of substance abuse can also create economic concerns related to the cost of drug testing, drug counseling, and administering the substance abuse portions of the policy manual.

The difficult question is how does your company take action to prevent substance abuse and at the same time provide for the dignity, privacy, and welfare of its employees and the continued operation of the business?

When considering a substance abuse policy, be prepared to establish and prove the company's legitimate business interests (duties) to justify adopting and using a substance abuse policy. Where an employee's right to privacy is violated or he or she is disciplined, possibly terminated, for substance abuse, business interests will be balanced against the employee's interests in privacy and his or her job. Although safety concerns are paramount, the effects of substance abuse are pervasive and can affect overall employee morale and productivity.

Obviously, creating health and safety hazards and breaching company security measures or proprietary interests are among the most serious examples of misconduct. Use, possession, or sale of drugs and alcohol on the company premises may also justify significant discipline. However, arriving at work drunk once or twice a year may indicate a problem but not be significant when the employee is caught before the shift and not allowed to work that day.

If you can establish on-the-job impact of substance use or abuse, then your interests must be protected by disciplinary measures suited to the gravity of the violation (i.e., the interest to be protected). Where the on-the-job impact is minimal, no harsh or significant action should be taken, but a friendly warning may prevent a problem later.

Beware of a perceived double standard by your lower-level employees. Your disciplinary policy in this area should treat a supervisor or manager no better and no worse than anyone else.

Sometimes the implication of a double standard comes from actions rather than the written policy. Consider a manager's lunch where alcohol is served and which is sponsored by the company on the premises.

Concern must also be noted for employer-sponsored picnics, sporting events, and similar occasions. Company sponsorship of such activities may provide a sufficient link or nexus to impose liability on the company. This area may be addressed separately in the policy manual.

Regardless of your approach, define prohibited activities and apply discipline when the rules are violated. Then offer or suggest help from a third person or group.

Alcohol and drug abusers cannot help themselves. They need help from another source. Do not discipline just because of addiction. Discipline an employee for failing to follow rules which protect your legitimate business interests.

Spotting Substance Abuse

Drug detection training as part of a substance abuse sensitivity course is a good idea for all managers and supervisors.

The following types of behavior are noteworthy and two or more of these indicate a potential problem with drugs or alcohol. This list is not intended to be exhaustive.

- Chronic tardiness or early departure; long breaks or lunches;
- Equipment, money, or supplies under one employee's control are missing;
- Unexplained mood swings;
- High absenteeism rates, especially after weekends and holidays or in a pattern of several days in a row;
- Frequent trips to the bathroom or parking lot;
- Frequent accidents or excessive sick leave;
- Lethargy, inability to concentrate, forgetfulness, and lack of motivation (chronic);
- A pattern of denial, possibly coupled with threats when confronted with the behaviors listed above.

Supervisors/managers should be trained to intervene when work is first perceptively affected, even if substance abuse is not suspected right away. If you are lax or not evenhanded in these instances, then the marginal or unacceptable work or behavior only gets worse.

Your policy can legitimately require employees who are taking prescribed medication to report this to their supervisors/managers, especially if the type of medication could affect performance or mood, e.g. a muscle relaxant. Precautions about mixing such medications with alcohol is always prudent.

Quoting again from Robert Taggart's speech concerning Southern Pacific Transportation Company's experiences in this area: "It's incredible the amount of employees who had been forced into rehabilitation and have come back and said, 'My God, you saved my life.'"

Federal Law

The private employer's principal compliance problem in the federal legislative area is the Rehabilitation Act of 1973, 29 U.S.C. Sections 701-796(i). Generally, the law prohibits both federal contractors and federal employers from discriminating against persons who are disabled as long as they are otherwise qualified to do the job. The law requires an employer to reasonably accommodate someone who is protected under the Act. There are also affirmative action requirements.

As a result of amendments to the Act in 1979, current substance abusers are not protected. However, a prior abuser with a record of impairment as a result of addiction is considered within the protected class of persons. The Americans With Disabilities Act follows a similar interpretation. What this means is that a prior substance abuser who has "recovered" will be considered a disabled person.

State Law

Generally, you will find your state's disability discrimination laws follow to some extent the federal provisions. There will be some differences. Not all states will consider a substance abuser to be disabled.

Some states provide protection to the employee who wants to participate in a recovery program and keep his or her job. California has such provisions in its Labor Code (Section 1025–W28) which apply to alcohol rehabilitation. Employers who employ 25 or more people must reasonably accommodate such persons as long as their participation in an alcohol rehabilitation program does not cause an undue hardship for the employer.

The employer must make reasonable efforts to safeguard the employee's privacy. The employer can still fire, or refuse to hire, someone who can't perform the job or who is a safety risk. The law allows the employee to take time off without compensation and to take accumulated sick leave if available. Some states may also protect drug abusers.

A number of states have specific privacy guarantees protecting their citizens. Consider these guarantees and any other statutes pertaining to employee privacy when you draft your policy. Have your legal counsel help you with this.

Some states protect all medical information and strictly limit its use and disclosure, for example, California Civil Code Section 56 et seq. Information about urine tests or substance abuse falls into the protected category so you will have to pay attention to those laws in the use of such information. There may be other kinds of confidentiality provisions which legal counsel should summarize for you.

When you send an employee home for substance abuse on the job, state law may have an impact where you least expect it. In one Texas case, the employer sent an obviously intoxicated employee home. The employee drove his own vehicle to work. Driving home, the employee killed two people in an accident. The appellate court held that the employer had a duty to exercise reasonable care to control the employee when the employer knew, or should have known, of the great likelihood of harm to third persons when the employee drove home. The court emphasized that the employer does not have an absolute duty to insure safety.[1] Exercise good common sense.

Drug Testing

Medical screening, such as urine tests, blood tests, and breath tests, presents risks for an employer. This discussion is not intended to be an authoritative guide to applicable law in this area. However, consider these points:

- Government regulation is extensive in this area.
- This area is relatively new to common law courts, and decisions will be slow in coming and possibly conflicting, especially from state to state.
- The potential for liability is very great if you make any one of several errors.
- Before you select any practice or procedure, consult experienced legal, medical, and rehabilitative professionals and get good, practical, and accurate advice.

Policy Guidelines

Policy approaches to substance abuse can be categorized in three ways:

1. Pure discipline — This is probably the easiest approach in terms of designing a policy. One drawback to it is the waste of the company's investment in the training of an employee if you terminate him or her. Another negative result is the loss of morale and respect for management because of the response. This approach is most common among

smaller companies, usually with fewer than ten employees, where the work force is easily replaced.

2. Therapeutic — The approach is viewed more kindly by the employees, but it has drawbacks as well. A "revolving door" attitude develops when an employee can be "rehabilitated" one day, go back to the same abusive pattern for whatever reason, and be welcomed back to the rehabilitation program over and over again. It's an expensive way to handle what may be a lack of maturity.

3. Flexible intermediate approach — This approach is somewhere in between the two listed above. An employee should be subject to significant discipline for behavior which threatens health, safety, or the substantial proprietary interests of your company. Voluntary successful participation in a recovery program should be a mitigating factor, but discipline needs to be applied nonetheless. Some violations just can't be tolerated under any circumstances — like selling drugs on company premises or possession of a handgun at the work station. Termination is the only answer for such a violation. The therapeutic alternative seems appropriate for the employee who shows the first sign of substance abuse and who has not warranted significant discipline yet (e.g., marginal performance or some absenteeism).

One way to avoid lawsuits in this area is to preserve the dignity and privacy of the employee who is under scrutiny or in rehabilitation. Another way to keep out of court is to follow your established and announced procedure with no deviations unless discretion is allowed in the policy or is dictated by common sense.

Some courts regard a company policy or employee handbook as a contractual commitment to employees. You can say that you are free to change or revoke any policy or procedure. However, some courts will hold the company to the policy provisions at the time of an incident. Deviations from the policy which do not work to the employee's benefit are subject to rigorous scrutiny.

Here are some more guidelines regarding your company's substance abuse policy:

- Carefully identify your company's compelling business interests to justify your policy and ensure that they are capable of being proved in court.
- Make sure that you understand the federal, state, and local laws which apply to your company and that your policy meets these requirements. Enlist support of legal counsel and experienced health care professionals to develop checklists for you.
- Prepare a clear statement of your policy. It should contain a strong rationale for testing if you choose to implement it. Compelling business interests and the adverse impact of substance abuse should be underscored.

- Communicate the policy and its procedures, especially any testing and search provisions, well in advance of implementation. Give employees at least a 90-day notice. Hold company or departmental meetings to discuss your policy and get feedback. Where employee concerns and objections are valid, make required changes. If you have a union contract, advise the union bargaining agents about the change or adoption of the policy as soon as possible, if required by your contract. You may have to bargain for its inclusion, especially if more employee time is required by policy provisions.

- Modify your employment applications and forms to contain a notice of your policy, especially to highlight the testing and search provisions. If applicants will be screened, make sure this is adequately communicated in your advertisements. Secure consents to screening before it is done — at the time of application or at the time of hire. Then make a consent request at the time for testing.

- To be safe, require drug testing only after hiring an employee and condition continued employment on successfully completing the drug test. If you adopt this process, be certain to test all employees with the same job classification.

- Before you adopt a testing policy, consult with several laboratories or hospitals. Obtain their advice on drafting a policy and a formal, detailed testing procedure. Insist on references before you contract with a lab or hospital. Inquire about error rates, litigation problems, and real costs. Many hospitals and labs have developed written testing and rehabilitation policies which you can receive at no cost and revise to fit your situation. Insist on retesting for positives. Consider also allowing employees to retest the same sample at employee cost. Make sure your testing program involves the least intrusion into the employee's privacy and preserves dignity. Consider plant accidents or on-the-job injuries as part of your testing rationale and routinely test all employees involved in plant accidents. Publicize this.

- Create a filing system and documentation procedures which maintain strict confidentiality of the employee's medical or personal information. Use only an absolute "need to know" basis in revealing information. Have a procedure for verifying this information and a procedure for destroying the information that you no longer need to keep. Keep this research in a separate medical file apart from personnel files. Strictly limit access to this folder. Keep information on terminated employees until after the state or federal statutes of limitation have expired. Check with legal counsel for these time limits.

- Adopt a training program on sensitivity to substance abuse for all supervisors/managers, how to administer the policy, and what types of mistakes should be avoided at all costs to avoid substantial risk of liability.

- Prepare and use a legally adequate consent and release form drafted in easily understood English (and any required foreign language translations). Consider using this form as a part of the employment application. Require the form for testing, investigations, and searches. Awareness of a drug testing policy at the time of application may cause substance abusers to look elsewhere. Have your legal counsel review it for sufficiency.

- If you adopt a search policy as part of your program, make sure it is properly announced in detail, referenced in your employment forms, and followed to the letter. Seek to preserve dignity and confidentiality during a search. Require reasonable, rational facts, and carefully drawn inferences to justify all searches unless there is imminent danger to employees or the public at large.

- Refusals to be tested or refusals to consent to searches should be handled with the least intrusion possible. If an employee refuses to be tested for religious or privacy reasons, consider transferring that employee to a less sensitive or less risky department when that satisfies your business interests. If not, then treat refusals as a disciplinary matter and determine the response accordingly.

- Review all applications and questionnaires that you use regarding substance abuse and collection of personal data in general. Tailor these forms, and any pertinent policies and procedures already adopted, to require only the information necessary to the job requirements or the legitimate company needs.

- Adopt an employee assistance counseling program or contract for a rehabilitation program, either directly or through insurance benefits. At the very least, become familiar with the recovery programs in your area for substance abusers, as well as Alcoholics Anonymous (AA), Narcotics Anonymous (NA), etc. Participation should never be mandatory. Keep discipline separate from rehabilitation. If someone asks for help, be in a position to help. Give a referral, make a telephone call, and do whatever you can beyond that. You may be saving someone's life.

Drug-Free Workplace

Many employers have established a general policy regarding a drug-free workplace, and it may appear separately from the policy manual.

Such a policy is required for most federal contractors by the Drug-Free Workplace Act of 1988. The Act does not require drug testing.

Generally, these employers post this policy on an employee bulletin board and distribute it to new hires and current employees.

See Alternate Policy 3 for more information on following this approach.

Substance Abuse

Alternate Policy 1   2060.1

(COMPANY) recognizes that substances such as alcohol and drugs are used by individuals, sometimes to an extent that their abilities and senses are impaired. Our position regarding substance abuse is the same whether alcohol, marijuana, illegal drugs, prescription drugs, or controlled substances are involved ("substances").

This policy is implemented because we believe that the impairment of any (COMPANY) employee due to his or her use of substances is likely to result in the risk of injury to other employees, the impaired employee, or to third parties, such as customers or business guests. Moreover, substance abuse adversely affects employee morale and productivity.

"Impairment" or "being impaired" means that an employee's normal physical or mental abilities, or faculties, while at work have been detrimentally affected by the use of substances.

The employee who begins work while impaired or who becomes impaired while at work is guilty of a major violation of company rules and is subject to severe disciplinary action. Severe disciplinary action can include suspension, dismissal, or any other penalty appropriate under the circumstances. Likewise, the use, possession, transfer, or sale of any substance on company premises or in any (COMPANY) parking lot, storage area, or job site is prohibited. Violations are subject to severe disciplinary action. In all instances, disciplinary action to be administered shall be at the sole discretion and determination of the company

Employees who are taking prescription drugs shall report this to their supervisor/manager. This is for the protection of the employee and for safety purposes in case of an adverse reaction to the drug while at work, or so the employee is not falsely accused of taking an illegal substance.

When an employee is involved in the use, possession, transfer, or sale of a substance in violation of this policy, the company may notify appropriate authorities. Such notice will be given only after such an incident has been investigated and reviewed by the employee's supervisor, the personnel director, and the (PRESIDENT).

(COMPANY) is aware that substance abuse is a complex health problem that has both physical impact and an emotional impact on the employee, his or her family, and social relationships. A substance abuser is a person who uses substances, as defined above, for non-medical reasons, and this use detrimentally affects job performance or interferes with normal social adjustments at work. Substance abuse is both a management and a medical problem.

Substance Abuse

Alternate Policy 1 (continued)   2060.1

A supervisor/manager who suspects a substance abuse case should discuss the situation immediately with his or her supervisor/manager. Because each case is usually different, the handling and referral of the case must be coordinated with the supervisor/manager and the personnel director.

We have resources available to assist an employee who requests help with substance abuse. The employee must ask for help. The company will not require it. Should disciplinary action be pending against an employee who asks for help, the company will assist to the extent of its resources assuming that the employee remains employed. Nonetheless, regular disciplinary action will proceed. If the employee is terminated, the company will be unable to continue any program. Voluntary, successful participation in a recovery or rehabilitative program by an employee may be a mitigating factor in any disciplinary action, depending on the facts and circumstances of each individual case. In some cases, disciplinary action may be suspended, or the employee placed on probation pending a successful completion of a recovery program.

Employees who are placed on a rehabilitation program because of performance or behavior problems due to substance abuse are subject to dismissal for failure to successfully complete the program or change their performance or behavior.

Applicants who have a past history of substance abuse and who have demonstrated an ability to abstain from the substance, or who can provide medical assurance of acceptable control, may be considered for employment as long as they are otherwise qualified for the position for which they are applying.

Management has chosen to adopt an alcoholic beverage policy in keeping with the concern for and the risks associated with alcohol use. Alcoholic beverages shall not be served or used on (COMPANY) premises at any time. Alcoholic beverages have no part in and shall not be used in conjunction with any company business meeting.

Social activities, held off-premises and paid for on a personal basis are not affected by this policy. If management considers it appropriate, light alcoholic beverages may be served at company-sponsored events held off premises and for purely social reasons. The service must be managed in good taste and with good judgment. No alcoholic beverages should be served at any company event where children are present.

Substance Abuse

Alternate Policy 1(continued)   2060.1

The company is concerned with its employee's privacy, especially when matters regarding medical and personal information are involved. As long as the information is not needed for police or security purposes, the company shall maintain employee medical and personal information in confidence and release this information to authorized company personnel on a "need to know" basis. An exception to this policy is when the employee signs a release for the transfer of such information on forms acceptable to the company to designated persons or agencies.

Nothing contained in this section shall eliminate or modify the company's right to terminate any employee at any time for any reason.

Substance Abuse

Alternate Policy 2   2060.2

(COMPANY'S) (PERSONNEL DEPARTMENT) is responsible for assisting every employee who has personal problems which may, or do, impact his or her work performance or attendance at work. Such problems may include alcohol or drug abuse and psychological problems. Sometimes, the problems are multi-faceted and have family relationships as a cause. An example of this would be severely ill parents who cannot care for themselves.

Any psychological or physical problem which affects an employee's work performance or causes an abnormal work atmosphere is the concern of management.

The (PERSONNEL DEPARTMENT) maintains a referral service for employees with problems such as the ones mentioned above. Counseling and referrals are provided on a confidential basis as long as the employee is not pending any disciplinary action. Employees who admit that they might have an alcohol or drug problem will be assured of assistance as long as they accept the help provided, agree to abstain from the substance involved, and do not violate any company rules or prohibitions by misconduct related to alcohol or drug use or otherwise violate any company rules or prohibitions.

If an employee is terminated for any reason the employee assistance program shall cease and the company will not be obligated to provide further assistance.

Nothing contained in this policy shall eliminate or modify the company's right to terminate any employee at any time for any reason.

Substance Abuse

Alternate Policy 3   2060.3

(COMPANY) is committed to providing an employment environment that is safe and provides appropriate motivation to ensure a creative and productive work force. To this end, the company unequivocally endorses the philosophy that the workplace should be free from the detrimental effects of illicit drugs and alcohol. To ensure worker safety and workplace integrity, the illegal manufacture, possession, distribution or use of controlled substances or alcohol in the workplace by its employees or those who engage or seek to engage in business with the company is prohibited.

Each employee and new hire will receive a drug/alcohol abuse awareness form to be signed and dated by the employee and which shall indicate that the employee:

1. Understands and agrees to abide by the drug/alcohol-free workplace policy;

2. Has knowledge that disciplinary action, including termination, will be imposed for violation of this policy;

3. Consents to undergo a blood test and urinalysis to determine the presence of alcohol or drugs in the system. Any such testing will be on (COMPANY) time and expense and is mandatory. All test results will remain confidential between the company and the tested employees except as may otherwise be permitted or required by law. Circumstances which would make such tests appropriate include but are not limited to the exhibition of behavior normally associated with persons under the influence of drugs or alcohol, or involvement in an on-the-job accident or other work-related incident.

The signed and dated statement will be permanently maintained in the employee's personnel file.

All current employees will receive drug/alcohol abuse training. New hires will receive training within six months following the date of hire.

Training shall include information on drug/alcohol abuse, dangers of drug/alcohol abuse in the workplace, and available counseling and treatment services.

Smoking   2070

Comment

Health-conscious individuals are responsible for a change of attitude toward smoking both in public and, particularly, on the job. It is no longer acceptable to smoke at your work station. With increasing concerns at all levels about the negative effects of "second hand smoke", the increasing number of state and local anti-smoking laws and ordinances, smoking in the workplace may become a thing of the past.

Research continues to indicate:

- Absenteeism is higher for smokers than for non-smokers;
- Smokers have more accidents than non-smokers because they pay less attention to their work while smoking;
- Productivity among smokers is lower because they spend time smoking;
- Estimated costs to the company for each smoking employee range from $850 to $5,000 for a variety of reasons, including workers' compensation, janitorial service costs, damage to office furniture and draperies, and insurance claims.

As the policy is developed, consider the impact it will have on present employees who do smoke. Much of the dissatisfaction among present employees can be avoided if they are involved in deciding the necessary restrictions.

Since health and safety are so closely linked in the discussion of smoking, you will want to reinforce this in your policy. Consider:

- The exact nature of the hazards of smoking to your particular type of business;
- The effect of smoking on the smoker as well as the co-workers;
- The impact of smoking on productivity; and
- The ability to adequately ventilate smoking areas to protect non-smokers.

Include the company's rationale for the policy in the policy itself. Define areas in which smoking is forbidden, as well as permitted, and the disciplinary action to be taken if the policy is violated. You don't have to preach to your employees about the evils of smoking, but you do have the duty to create a healthy working atmosphere where everyone's rights are respected.

A strict company smoking policy often creates a monetary savings when your company negotiates health insurance rates.

Caution

A number of states prohibit discrimination against smokers. While such laws do not obligate an employer to permit smoking in the workplaces, they do prohibit an employer from regulating an employee's smoking away from the workplace or from failing to hire or promote an employee who smokes.

In a recent case, a decision of an employer with a non-smoking policy to terminate an employee who smoked away from the workplace was upheld. The employer's decision was based on poor personal hygiene of the employee. The employee and her clothing smelled heavily of smoke.

Smoking

Alternate Policy 1   2070.1

No smoking will be allowed in the office area at any time. This policy is for the health and safety of all employees. Smoking will be allowed only in the lunchroom, restrooms, and designated areas.

Your cooperation is requested, as this policy must be rigidly enforced to comply with the company health and safety requirements and to maintain proper insurance coverage for our building.

Smoking

Alternate Policy 2   2070.2

With the wide variation in space, ventilation, and general physical arrangements within (COMPANY) departments, a single policy cannot be established for the entire company. Each supervisor/manager, with the cooperation of smokers and non-smokers alike, will establish a department smoking policy regarding the following points:

1. Separation of smokers and non-smokers in the department;
2. The policy regarding smoking during any group meetings; and
3. The purchase of air purification equipment by employees, if necessary.

Each department policy will be clearly posted in the work area. All new employees will be given a copy of the policy. If a conflict arises, the supervisor will resolve it in accord with department policies and good judgment.

Smoking

Alternate Policy 3   2070.3

Because smoking is a danger to health and is a cause of material annoyance and discomfort to those who are present in confined places, (COMPANY) hereby declares the purposes of this policy are:

1. To protect the public health and welfare by regulating smoking in the office workplace;
2. To minimize the toxic effects of smoking in the office workplace by adopting a policy that will accommodate, as much as possible, the preferences of non-smokers and smokers alike.

If a satisfactory accommodation cannot be reached, smoking will be prohibited in the office workplace. This policy is not intended to create any right to smoke.

Any non-smoking employee may object to his or her supervisor/manager about smoke in his or her workplace. Using already available means of ventilation or separation or partition of office space, the supervisor or manager shall attempt to reach a reasonable accommodation, as much as possible, between the preferences of non-smoking and smoking employees. However, the company is not required to make any expenditures or structural changes to accommodate the preferences of non-smoking or smoking employees.

If an accommodation which is satisfactory to all affected non-smoking employees cannot be reached in any given office workplace, the preferences of non-smoking employees shall prevail and smoking shall be prohibited in that office workplace. Where (COMPANY) prohibits smoking in an office workplace, the area in which smoking is prohibited shall be clearly marked with signs.

The Smoking Policy shall be posted conspicuously in all workplaces and shall be given in writing to every prospective employee and new hire.

Every supervisor/manager who has questions or issues regarding implementation of this policy is requested to contact the (PERSONNEL DIRECTOR) for guidance and interpretation.

Smoking

Alternate Policy 4   2070.4

With the current evidence that smoking is dangerous and injurious to a person's health, employees are encouraged not to smoke.

However, (COMPANY) recognizes that the decision to smoke or not to smoke is a personal one. During working hours, our policy is to limit smoking to the restrooms, lunchroom, and in certain designated areas. Check with your supervisor.

Smoking

Alternate Policy 5   2070.5

There is no smoking permitted on company premises at any time.

Employment Classifications   2080

Comment

Most positions within any company are thought to require full time employees. Employment classifications should be defined to provide supervisors/managers with a guide in determining other alternatives in the selection of employees to meet company needs. The classifications will also be used by the personnel department and accounting in recordkeeping.

Two alternative employment status definitions are provided on the following pages. The work hours are given as an example and may not fit all companies — some companies have a 35 or 37.5 hour work week.

Caution

Do not use "permanent" or similar language in classifications. The use of this language may affect your right to discharge employees "at will." See the *Comment* portion of *Section 2160 — Termination*.

Collective bargaining agreements between an employer and a labor union representing an employer's employees may provide for additional classifications. Similarly, other provisions of a personnel policy manual may be superseded by a collective bargaining agreement with union employees.

Employment Classifications

Alternate Policy 1   2080.1

There are three classifications of employees:

1. Regular Full-time — An employee who works a normal 40-hour work week on a regularly scheduled basis.
2. Regular Part-time — An employee who works less than a normal work week, on either a regularly-scheduled basis or on an irregular basis.
3. Temporary — An employee hired for a period not exceeding three months and who is not entitled to regular benefits. An extension of a temporary work classification for an additional three-month period, or less, may be granted, if upon review by management, the assignment is clearly found to be necessary. A temporary employee may be full-time or part-time. In addition to the use of this classification for secretarial or clerical positions, it applies to students working part-time and those who work during the summer.

All employees are classified as exempt and non-exempt according to these definitions:

Salaried Exempt — Positions of a managerial, administrative, or professional nature or for outside sales, as prescribed by federal and state labor statutes, which are exempt from mandatory overtime payments.

Salaried Non-Exempt — Positions of a clerical, technical, or service nature, as defined by statute, which are covered by provisions for overtime payments.

Note: These definitions are illustrative in nature and are not intended as a statement of the law. Refer to the Comment preceding the policy on Overtime Compensation, Section 3060, the Fair Labor Standards Act, and applicable state law.

If you are uncertain as to your status, please contact your supervisor/manager.

Employment Classifications

Alternate Policy 2   2080.2

Positions within the company are generally designed to require full-time employees. In certain functions and during some seasons, work schedules and company needs may require the services of other than full-time employees. There are four classifications of employees at (COMPANY):

1. Full-time — An employee hired for an indefinite period in a position for which the normal work schedule is 40 hours per week.
2. Part-time — An employee hired for an indefinite period in a position for which the normal work schedule is at least 20 but less than 40 hours per week.
3. Temporary — An employee hired for a position for which the scheduled work week can range from less than 20 to 40 hours, but the position is required for only a specific, known duration, usually less than six months.

Temporary employees do not qualify for regular company benefits.

Provisions in the Fair Labor Standards Act divide all employees into two categories, exempt and non-exempt, with respect to eligibility for overtime payment. They shall be defined as:

Exempt — An employee considered to be either managerial, administrative, professional or outside sales.

Non-Exempt — An employee who devotes most of his or her hours in activities that are not managerial, administrative, professional or outside sales.

Note: These definitions are illustrative in nature and are not intended as a statement of the law. Refer to the Comment preceding the policy on Overtime Compensation, Section 3060, the Fair Labor Standards Act, and applicable state law.

If you are uncertain as to your status, please contact your supervisor/manager.

Employee Safety   2090

Comment

Employers have an obligation to provide a safe and healthful workplace environment for their employees. The employer's duty is the result of a complex of case law and federal and state statutes and regulations. Statutes such as the federal Occupational Safety and Health Act which is administered by the Occupational Safety and Health Administration (OSHA), and similar state statutes provide government agency authority for regulations which regulate and control many aspects of business operations and require reporting of occupational accidents and illnesses. Other federal and state acts, such as the Clean Air Act, Clean Water Act, Toxic Substances Control Act, and similar state acts, directly impact business operations and employee safety.

Many rules and regulations are industry-specific or relate specifically to certain types of equipment, machinery, materials, or substances used in particular workplaces. For example, federal legislations requires seat belts to be worn by employees operating automobiles or that helmets be worn by employees driving motorcycles while engaged in business on behalf of the company. Legal or other competent professional advice in this area is strongly encouraged due to the number and complexity of applicable rules and regulations.

Any policy concerning employee safety will have certain common elements. The policy must set forth the company's affirmative obligation to provide a safe and healthful workplace. Rules and regulations to govern an employee's conduct must be set forth. Post the rules and regulations conspicuously on an employee bulletin board, in addition to including them in the policy manual.

Establish adequate supervision to monitor compliance with company safety rules and regulations, to provide adequate training and instruction, and to foster suggestions and ideas from employees to improve company safety.

Finally, a reporting mechanism must be established to measure the effectiveness of a company's safety program and to ensure compliance with governmental reporting obligations. OSHA requires the posting of prescribed notices in a conspicuous place, the maintenance of a *Log of Occupational Injuries and Illnesses,* a *Supplementary Record*, and an annual *Statistical Summary of Occupational Injuries and Illnesses.* Although smaller employers may be exempt from reporting obligations, good practice would indicate that similar reporting practices be established.

In addition to stated policies, the employer must stay aware of technological advances which could produce additional protective clothing or devices for equipment and machinery to further promote safety and constantly monitor their business operations to develop safer business practices.

Hazards created by the presence of chemicals and toxic substances in the workplace have received much attention in recent years. Federal and state statutes mandate the reporting of chemicals present in the workplace as well as the establishment of means to educate and train employees of the hazards and ways to avoid danger.

Material Safety Data Sheets (MSDS) are required to be supplied by manufacturers along with manufactured products containing hazardous chemicals and substances. Information contained in the MSDS should provide much of the information needed to advise employees. In addition, these materials should be forwarded to fire department authorities along with information specifying the location of the hazardous substances.

Recognizing that good health and fitness promote a safe and healthful workplace, many employers provide instructional clinics or financial assistance for stop smoking classes, stress management, and other wellness or lifestyle training.

Several states now require the formation and use of safety committees designed to discover potential workplace hazards and unsafe work practices. The last two paragraphs of the *Employment Safety Policy* provide a framework for a safety committee. Check with your legal adviser to learn if safety committees are required in your state.

Employers should cross-reference this section with the following sections: *Equal Opportunity — Section 2010; Medical Evaluations and Interviews — Section 2050; Substance Abuse — Section 2060;* and *Smoking — Section 2070.*

A sample *Employee Accident Report Form*, to be completed by the employee, is included following the policy statement on employee safety. An accident report in narrative form should also be prepared by supervisory personnel charged with the responsibility of investigating each accident or illness report.

Finally, your business insurance carrier, state department of labor, or workers' compensation department may have programs to help you evaluate and alleviate safety risks. Often, these programs exist at little or no expense to the employer.

Employee Safety

Alternate Policy 1   2090.1

(COMPANY) strives to provide its employees with a safe and healthful workplace environment. To accomplish this goal, both management and employees must diligently undertake efforts to promote safety.

The company, through its supervisory personnel, shall develop and implement safety rules and regulations. This process will be ongoing and will require periodic safety audits. Safety audits will be undertaken to determine the necessity and feasibility of providing protective clothing, devices, or safeguards to make the workplace safe and healthful. The company shall also undertake the responsibility to educate employees as to hazards of the workplace and to train employees as to such hazards and the proper and safe method to perform job tasks.

Employees shall devote their full time skill and attention to the performance of their job responsibilities utilizing the highest standard of care and good judgment. Employees will follow all safety rules and regulations at all times including the use of protective clothing, devices, or equipment, attendance at all training sessions related to employee's job description, and follow the directions of warning signs or signals or the commands or directions of supervisory personnel.

Finally, all job-related injuries or illnesses are to be reported to your supervisor immediately, regardless of severity. In the case of serious injury, an employee's reporting obligation will be deferred until circumstances reasonably permit a report to be made. Failure to report an injury or illness may preclude or delay the payment of any benefits to the employee and could subject (COMPANY) to fines and penalties.

Safety rules and regulations will be issued or modified from time to time and shall be effective immediately. Rules and regulations will be distributed to employees and posted on the employee bulletin board. Safety first!

Employee Safety

Alternate Policy 1 (continued)   2090.1

Note: The following two paragraphs should be used only where required by state law or where a safety committee is otherwise desired. Check with your legal adviser.

The (PRESIDENT) shall select a safety committee which shall be composed of an equal number of employer and employee representatives. The term of each committee member shall be two years subject to earlier resignation or termination, provided, however, that one-half of the employer and employee representatives of the initial committee shall serve an initial term of one year to stagger the term and provide at least one experienced member on the committee at all times.

The committee shall select one of its members to serve as chairperson. The chairperson shall also provide a written agenda for all committee meetings. The committee shall hold regular meetings at least once each month except months when quarterly safety audits are made. Minutes of committee meetings shall be recorded and retained for three years by the company. Copies of minutes shall be posted for all employees, together with the names and departments of safety committee members.

The safety committee shall recommend to the (PRESIDENT) how to eliminate hazards and unsafe work practices. The (PRESIDENT) shall respond within 30 days following the receipt of committee recommendations.

Employee Accident Report Form

_____   _____   _____

Last Name   First   Initial   Social Security #   Department

_____

Address (Including City, State, Zip)

_____   _____

Telephone Number   Date of Birth

Time, Date, and Location of Accident: _____

_____

What injuries are being reported: _____

_____

How did accident occur? _____

_____

Witnesses to the accident: _____

_____

Treatment or first aid provided: _____

By signing below, employee consents to the release of medical charts, reports, X-rays, diagnoses, and other information to (COMPANY) or its authorized representatives from any health care provider rendering treatment or providing consultative or other services in conjunction with the diagnosis and treatment of the injury described above.

_____   _____

Employee's Signature   Date

(ADD NOTARIAL OATH OR AFFIRMATION)

Anniversary Date and Reinstatement   2100

Comment

In defining an employee's anniversary date, there are several dates that might be considered:

- The first day on the job;
- The date the employment offer is accepted by the applicant; or
- The date he or she signs the necessary company employment documents.

When deciding which date to choose as the anniversary date, consider the effect the date will have on the company's benefit programs, such as insurance or pension plan. It should also be easily interpreted by management and other employees. Naturally, the same date should be used for all employees, but the choice is important because employee morale and recordkeeping will be affected if your company has to change in midstream. The policy statement provided for consideration can easily be rewritten to reflect your company's decision on any of the three possible anniversary dates mentioned above or any others chosen.

Your company will want to determine the effect an employee's termination and later re-employment will have on that employee's anniversary date because of benefits related to time employed with the company. Reinstatement to the original anniversary date may imply some kind of "permanent" employment which may affect your right to discharge an employee later. When you consider company morale, however, it is worthwhile to accept this risk.

Regarding pension or retirement plans and striking employees, consult legal counsel to determine if *Alternative Policy 2* complies with the current law. Arguably it does, at least regarding strikes, because striking employees generally cannot be "terminated" but only "replaced."

Retirement plans often provide for reinstatement of a terminated employee's vested status if the employee is reinstated within one year following termination. In this event, an additional sentence should be added to the policy manual stating, "In the event of any inconsistency between this policy manual and any retirement plan maintained by the company, the terms and conditions of the retirement plan shall prevail."

Anniversary Date

Alternate Policy 1   2100.1

An employee's anniversary date is defined as his or her first day on the job with the company. Performance reviews will be completed annually on the employee's anniversary date. Although a salary adjustment never automatically follows a performance review, if a review cannot be completed prior to the employee's anniversary date and a salary adjustment is in order, it will be made retroactive to the anniversary date.

Note: The last two sentences are optional and can be omitted by the company that wants to specify periodic evaluation dates in a separate policy.

Reinstatement

Alternate Policy 2   2100.2

Employees who are reinstated into the company will maintain their original anniversary date for seniority purposes as well as for those benefit programs governed by the anniversary date. The policy will be as follows:

1. Layoff — Employees who terminate because of reduction in work force will maintain their original anniversary date for seniority purposes, if they are re-employed by (COMPANY) within one year after date of termination.
2. Voluntary resignation — Employees who voluntarily terminate their employment with (COMPANY) may maintain their original anniversary date, subject to management approval, if they are re-employed by the company within six months after date of termination. The company is under no obligation to rehire any such employee

Reinstatement

Alternate Policy 3   2100.3

Employees who are re-employed by the company after termination will lose their original anniversary date for all purposes and be assigned a new date corresponding to their first day on the job after re-employment. This policy shall not apply to layoffs or to an employee who was erroneously terminated for cause and later reinstated.

New Hire, Rehire, Relatives, Return to Work After Serious Injury or Illness and Early Return to Work   2110 – 40

Comment

The policy statements in the following sections define the consistent procedures your company will follow in the orientation of new hires, the processing of rehires, and the employment of relatives of present employees. Also included in the policy statement is the procedure to follow for employees who have been absent from work because of an injury or extended illness. The *Early Return to Work* policy would apply in cases when an employee can be assigned to a position where the tasks can be modified to fit the employee's recovery. Such a policy encourages the employee to make a rapid recovery and remain in close contact with company operations. At the time of initiating the policy, have the employees sign and date the policy to refresh their understanding of the conditions. With the exception of the policy on *Relatives,* alternate policies are not provided.

Avoid policies which restrict the hiring of spouses. Such policies may be found to discriminate because of sex. Similarly, a policy which seeks to bar employment of persons who are spouses of persons employed by a competitor may also be discriminatory. A policy restricting the hiring of family members employed by the company or a competitor seems to remove the discriminatory taint, but legal counsel should be consulted before drafting this policy.

For your convenience, the above issues have been segregated into separate policies to enable you to pick and choose policies for your manual. With minor modifications, these policies can be combined to form one policy.

New Hire

Policy   2110.1

The (PERSONNEL DIRECTOR) is responsible for having the new employee fill out all pre-employment forms, benefit applications, and enrollment forms; having the employee's picture taken for the company identification card; and providing basic information on pay and leave policies, benefits, parking situations, and working hours, on the employee's first day of work. Within the first week of employment, a new employee orientation will be conducted by the (PERSONNEL DIRECTOR).

Note: Delete the last sentence if your company has no structured orientation meeting.

Rehire

Policy   2120.1

Applications received from former employees will be processed using the same procedures and standards that govern all direct applications. The hiring manager/supervisor will review the former employee's performance records and the circumstances surrounding termination of previous employment with the company. This information will be provided to the staff responsible for screening and interviewing applicants. (COMPANY) is under no obligation to rehire former employees.

Relatives

Alternate Policy 1   2130.1

(COMPANY) permits the hiring of relatives of current employees, if the applicant is qualified and selected by the hiring manager/supervisor. The primary consideration for placement is the proximity of the relatives' work areas to each other. Only in extraordinary circumstances, with management approval, should an employee be directly or indirectly supervised by a relative. A relative is defined as any person related to the employee by blood, marriage, or adoption.

Relatives

Alternate Policy 2   2130.2

Relatives of (COMPANY) employees may apply and, if qualified, will be considered for employment except in certain sensitive areas, such as accounting, personnel, or research and development. Relatives will not be allowed to supervise or evaluate each other. Relatives will not work in the same department or under the same supervisor or manager.

A relative is defined as any person related to the employee by blood, marriage, or adoption in the following degrees: parent, child, grandparent, grandchild, brother, sister, brother-in-law, sister-in-law, aunt, uncle, niece, nephew, and first cousin.

Relatives

Alternate Policy 3   2130.3

It is the policy of (COMPANY) not to hire relatives of current employees or relatives of persons employed by competitors of the company.

Note: State and federal laws may restrict the ability of an employer to prohibit or restrict the hiring of relatives or significant others. Check with your legal counsel.

Return to Work After Serious Injury or Illness

Policy _____ 2140.1

As a joint protection to the employee and the company, employees who have been absent from work because of serious illness or injury are required to obtain a doctor's release specifically stating that the employee is capable of performing his or her normal duties or assignments. A serious injury or illness is defined as one that results in the employee being absent from work for more than (ADD NUMBER) consecutive weeks, or one which may limit the employee's future performance of regular duties or assignments.

(COMPANY) management shall ensure that employees who return to work after a serious injury or illness are physically capable of performing their duties or assignments without risk of re-injury or relapse.

If the cause of the employee's illness or injury was job-related, the employee's supervisor/manager will make every reasonable effort to assign the returning employee to assignments consistent with the instructions of the employee's doctor until the employee is fully recovered. A doctor's written release is required before recovery can be assumed.

***Note: Consult with your company counsel and federal and state laws
relating to leaves of absence before using this policy.***

Early Return to Work Policy and Procedure

Policy   2140.2

(COMPANY) is concerned about the health and good work habits of its employees. In the event you are injured and unable to perform your job, we want to assist in obtaining the best treatment and the return to your regular job as soon as possible. Whenever possible, (COMPANY) will provide modified work while you are recovering from your injury. The following information has been prepared to help you understand the procedures for notifying us concerning your condition and your work restrictions.

1. Inform your doctor that (COMPANY) does provide modified work and have your doctor provide you with physical limitations.

2. Return your work limitations to your supervisor immediately following your doctor appointment or at the beginning of your next work shift.

3. (COMPANY) will then provide a Job Analysis of a modified job which is within your work restrictions to your doctor for his/her approval if necessary.

4. Once your physician has approved the Job Analysis, (COMPANY) will provide you with a written job offer letter, describing the details of the light duty assignment when available.

5. Modified jobs are temporary and it will be the employee's responsibility to provide their supervisor with a current work status report following every doctor appointment.

6. If your physician does not release you to any work activities, then you will need to contact your supervisor on a weekly basis, either by phone or in person.

Failure to accept an offer for light duty assignment can be the basis for termination of employment.

I have read and understand this policy and procedure.

_____

Employee's Signature   Date

Performance Improvement   2150

Comment

This policy establishes a consistent program of progressive actions to help your employees and their supervisors discuss and resolve performance deficiencies or employee misconduct. If an employee's performance or conduct is not meeting the company's standards, he or she should be given adequate time and guidance to improve performance or conduct.

It is the employee's immediate supervisor/manager who assumes direct responsibility for counseling and guiding the employee. The supervisor/manager who faces these issues should be directed to seek guidance, assistance, and concurrence from the personnel department or higher management to ensure appropriate action and consistency.

Carefully draft this type of policy. Proven major violations of company policies or gross misconduct — fraudulent expense reports, stealing company property, or substantial conflicts of interest — may lead to immediate suspension or discharge. Draft this policy to give management sole discretion in deciding the appropriate level of discipline without having to resort to a structured, unyielding process of successive steps before discharge for major violations. In addition, the time and expense required to administer a highly structured review or counseling process, or both, may prove too much of a burden for smaller employers.

In recent years, courts have begun to erode the right of an employer to discharge at will. For example, recent court decisions and statutes have restricted the ability of employers to discharge an employee for off-duty use of tobacco products, sexual orientation, Olympic athletes, and reporting unsafe or unhealthy workplace conditions.

Remember that company policies are statements of rules and sometimes rights. To the extent employees are granted rights by company policies, or are erroneously led to believe that they have certain rights, the courts may likely recognize those rights in much the same way as courts recognize contractual rights and corresponding duties. Some courts look upon written policies, or consistently applied verbal policies, as part of a contractual relationship between employer and employee.

When you create a policy with a structured process of successive steps, or provide for some kind of an appeal procedure, you should follow it to the letter. If you make exceptions to the process for certain employees, without reserving the right to do so in the policy itself, your exceptions may be viewed as a breach of contract or a modification to your stated policies.

Language in the first paragraph of the following policy provides management with the flexibility necessary to avoid a structured process. It also reserves the right to disregard this policy and discharge at will when appropriate to do so. Companies desiring to maintain the structured process can remove the at will language and redraft this policy accordingly.

Another alternative to consider when deciding between flexibility and structure is to adopt two separate policies. One is for performance improvement and the second one is for misconduct. The first expresses confidence that the employee can improve his or her performance through the guidance and assistance of management. The second is reserved for cases where discipline must be used to discourage employees from inappropriate behavior.

Another common error to avoid is the long or short list of violations which may lead to some type of disciplinary action. To the extent that you try to specifically define and prohibit all types of misconduct, you may be limiting management's prerogatives rather than enhancing them. No list can be all-inclusive. It may be considered to be unless you state that the list is for purposes of example only and not exclusive.

Other companies may choose to disregard the following policy entirely in order to avoid the issues discussed here. Although this is acceptable, consider two points. First, management should conspicuously state its right to discharge at will. It would be better to have several consistent references to this right in several different policies or company communications. Second, a performance improvement policy is a method to preserve the company's costly investment of time and training in an employee who should be given reasonable guidance and time to become a more efficient and productive person. It also saves future recruiting expenses.

One other characteristic of the policy that follows is its emphasis that all corrective or disciplinary action be documented. Every employer should make documentation mandatory. Such documentation is extremely important, possibly as evidence, and certainly to refresh a supervisor's or manager's recollection of events that led to the discharge of an employee for cause.

Some employees, although discharged for proven cause, may justify filing a claim for unemployment compensation or an administrative claim or lawsuit that alleges discrimination or a wrongful discharge under various legal theories. In these situations, one of the first things a state agency or the attorneys will want to examine is the former employee's personnel file. It is better to be slightly overprepared than underprepared. Once documented, great care must be taken to preserve the file and its contents. All information pertaining to the employee, whether positive or negative, should be kept in his or her personnel file. Incomplete, missing or "doctored" files or records will almost certainly cause a company more harm than a completed, well-maintained file.

Before drafting your *Performance Improvement* policy, read the *Comment* and policies on *Termination* which follow this section.

Caution

Failure to comply with your performance improvement policy can result in a lawsuit by a disgruntled employee. In this case, what you do in practice may be more important than the policy language. Work with your legal counsel to draft a policy that will work for you.

Performance Improvement

Policy   2150.1

Performance improvement may be suggested whenever company management believes that an employee's performance is less than satisfactory and can be resolved through adequate counseling. Corrective counseling is completely at the discretion of company management. The company desires to protect its investment of time and expense devoted to employee orientation and training whenever that goal is in the company's best interests. The company expressly reserves the right to discharge "at will." Even if corrective counseling is implemented, it may be terminated at any step at the discretion of management. Management, in its sole discretion, may either warn, reassign, suspend, or discharge any employee at will, whichever it chooses and at any time.

The supervisor/manager, with assistance of the (PERSONNEL DIRECTOR), will determine the course of action best suited to the circumstances. The steps in performance improvement are as follows:

1. Verbal counseling — As the first step in correcting unacceptable performance or behavior, the supervisor/manager should review pertinent job requirements with the employee to ensure his or her understanding of them. The supervisor/manager should consider the severity of the problem, the employee's previous performance appraisals and all of the circumstances surrounding the particular case. The seriousness of the performance or misconduct should be indicated by stating that a written warning, probation, or possible termination could result if the problem is not resolved. The employee should be asked to review what has been discussed to ensure his or her understanding of the seriousness of the problem and the corrective action necessary. The supervisor/manager should document the verbal counseling for future reference immediately following the review.

2. Written counseling — If the unacceptable performance or behavior continues, the next step should be a written warning. Certain circumstances, such as violation of a widely known policy or safety requirement, may justify a written warning without first using verbal counseling. The written warning defines the problem and how it may be corrected. The seriousness of the problem is again emphasized, and the written warning shall indicate that probation or termination or both, may result if improvement is not observed. Written counseling becomes part of the employee's personnel file, although the supervisor/manager may direct that the written warning be removed after a period of time, under appropriate circumstances.

Performance Improvement

Policy (continued)   2150.1

3. Probation — If the problem has not been resolved through written counseling or the circumstances warrant it, or both, the individual should be placed on probation. Probation is a serious action in which the employee is advised that termination will occur if improvement in performance or conduct is not achieved within the probationary period. The (PERSONNEL DIRECTOR) and the employee's supervisor/manager, after review of the employee's corrective counseling documentation, will determine the length of probation. Typically, the probation period should be at least two weeks and no longer than 60 days, depending on the circumstances. A written probationary notice to the employee is prepared by the supervisor/manager.

The letter should include a statement of the following:

- The specific unsatisfactory situation;
- A review of oral and written warnings;
- The length of probation;
- The specific behavior modification or acceptable level of performance;
- Suggestions for improvement;
- A scheduled counseling session or sessions during the probationary period; and
- A statement that further action, including termination, may result if defined improvement or behavior modification does not result during probation. "Further action" may include, but is not limited to reassignment, reduction in pay, grade, or demotion.

The supervisor/manager should personally meet with the employee to discuss the probationary letter and answer any questions. The employee should acknowledge receipt by signing the letter. If the employee should refuse to sign, the supervisor/manager may sign attesting that it was delivered to the employee and identifying the date of delivery. The probationary letter becomes part of the employee's personnel file.

On the defined probation counseling date or dates, the employee and supervisor/manager will meet to review the employee's progress in correcting the problem which led to the probation. Brief written summaries of these meetings should be prepared with copies provided to the employee and the (PERSONNEL DIRECTOR).

Performance Improvement

Policy (continued)   2150.1

At the completion of the probationary period, the (PERSONNEL DIRECTOR) and the supervisor/manager will meet to determine whether the employee has achieved the required level of performance and to consider removing the employee from probation, extending the period of probation, or taking further action. The employee is to be advised in writing of the decision. Should probation be completed successfully, the employee should be commended, though cautioned that any future recurrence may result in further disciplinary action.

4. Suspension — A two or three day suspension without pay may be justified when circumstances reasonably require an investigation of a serious incident in which the employee was allegedly involved. A suspension may also be warranted when employee safety, welfare, or morale may be adversely affected if a suspension is not imposed.

In addition, and with prior approval of the (PERSONNEL DIRECTOR), suspension without pay for up to three consecutive working days may be imposed for such proven misconduct as intentional violation of safety rules, fighting, or drinking alcohol on the job. These examples do not limit management's use of suspension with or without pay in other appropriate circumstances, such as the need to investigate a serious incident. In implementing a suspension, a written counseling report should set forth the circumstances justifying the suspension. Such a report shall become part of the employee's personnel file.

Note: Suspension is a disciplinary action and is not normally reserved for performance deficiencies.

5. Involuntary Termination — The involuntary termination notice is prepared by the supervisor/manager with concurrence of, and review by, the personnel department. The employee is notified of the termination by the supervisor/manager and will be directed to report to the personnel department for debriefing and completion of termination documentation. Involuntary termination is reserved for those cases that cannot be resolved by corrective counseling or in those cases where a major violation has occurred which cannot be tolerated.

Performance Improvement

Policy (continued)　　　　　　　　　　　　　　　　　　　2150.1

Note: Those companies that desire to maximize flexibility and preserve the right to discharge at will should delete this last sentence and the remainder of this policy.

The following definitions and classification of violations, for which corrective counseling, performance improvement, or other disciplinary action may be taken, are merely illustrative and not limited to these examples. A particular violation may be major or minor, depending on the surrounding facts or circumstances.

1. Minor violations — Less serious violations that have some effect on the continuity, efficiency of work, safety, and harmony within the company. They typically lead to corrective counseling unless repeated or when unrelated incidents occur in rapid succession. Here are some examples of minor violations:
   - Excessive tardiness;
   - Unsatisfactory job performance;
   - Defacing company property;
   - Interfering with another employee's job performance;
   - Excessive absenteeism;
   - Failure to observe working hours, such as the schedule of starting time, quitting time, rest and meal periods;
   - Performing unauthorized personal work on company time;
   - Failure to notify the supervisor/manager of intended absence either before or within one hour after the start of a shift; and
   - Unauthorized use of the company telephone, Internet or equipment for personal business.

2. Major Violations — These more serious violations would include any deliberate or willful infraction of company rules and may preclude continued employment of an employee. Here are some examples of major violations:
   - Fighting on company premises;
   - Repeated occurrences of related or unrelated minor violations, depending upon the severity of the violation and the circumstances;
   - Any act which might endanger the safety or lives of others;
   - Departing company premises during working hours for personal reasons without the permission of the supervisor/manager;
   - Bringing firearms or weapons onto the company premises;

Performance Improvement

Policy (continued)   2150.1

- Deliberately stealing, destroying, abusing, or damaging company property, tools, or equipment, or the property of another employee or visitor;
- Disclosure of confidential company information or trade secrets to unauthorized persons;
- Willfully disregarding company policies or procedures;
- Willfully falsifying any company records;
- Failing to report to work without excuse or approval of management for three consecutive days;
- Bringing software into the company and installing it on company computers without authorization; or
- Violating the terms set out in the Internet Policy.

Termination   2160

Comment

Terminations are very costly to an organization in the following ways:

- Employee Turnover — The company's investment in training the employee and grooming him or her to be a valuable and active part of the company work force is lost.
- Corrective Counseling — The amount of rehabilitation time invested by management in assisting the employee in a performance improvement program is, to some extent, wasted.
- Dismissal — The amount of time spent by management to define appropriate action for employee discipline is non-productive.
- Layoff — Company morale and productivity are reduced as everyone becomes anxious that they may be the next to receive a layoff notice.

Terminations, however, are inevitable within any organization. You should develop clearly stated procedures that are flexible enough to handle the various forms of termination.

In deciding on the policies and procedures for terminations, you should be aware of certain legal traps. Discussion of these traps in conjunction with this policy does not mean that you should include an exhaustive list of "dos and don'ts" into an already lengthy policy.

Failing to recognize these traps could certainly affect your company's profits. You could face the legal cost of defending a lawsuit or administrative proceeding, and the potential for court judgments or fines against the company or its officers. Consult with an expert both at the time of writing this policy and if a termination appears to involve some potential for legal entanglement. You and your personnel director should consider a seminar, led by an authoritative professional, for your managers on these issues. The following comments are not a complete discussion of all the legal issues related to terminations.

Many states have statutes which require that final wages be paid to a terminated employee on the final day of work. Some make the failure to pay final wages a crime or subject to a penalty.[1]

Some states also have statutes that govern the payment of final wages to an employee who voluntarily terminates. For instance, the time of payment may depend upon the amount of notice given by the employee.

States may also have statutes requiring special treatment for employees in special occupations who are laid off.[2]

In most cases, state law requires that pay for vested vacation time and vested sick leave be included in the final paycheck. Some statutes specifically prohibit the forfeiture of vested vacation pay upon termination whether or not for cause.[3]

"Vested" generally means that the time off is permanently credited to the employee and is readily available or convertible to money. Consult the local statutory and case law, especially regarding the issue of when vacation pay vests. In some states, notably California, vacation pay has been held to vest as the services are performed and is equivalent to wages.[4]

Another issue is raised when the employee owes the company money (e.g., for a travel expense advance) and is terminated before repayment. Can the employer legally deduct this money from the final paycheck? Most employers are surprised to learn that most states prohibit this practice unless the employee has signed a written consent to this practice before the money is advanced to the employee. Obviously, state laws will differ on this issue.

Employers should also be advised to consult state and federal laws regarding anti-retaliation laws. Generally, the laws prohibit an employer from disciplining or discharging an employee just because he or she filed a discrimination claim, a labor grievance, or a workers' compensation claim, to name a few protected activities. Many laws make such retaliation a crime and impose fines or imprisonment or both for violations.

Carefully review your state's list of unlawful employment practices as you prepare your policy manual. Also, the National Labor Relations Act[5] (NLRA) protects employees from discrimination — discharge or other disciplinary reprisals — for engaging in protected "concerted activity." This phrase "concerted activity" generally includes the exercise of the employee's statutory rights under the NLRA.

However, an activity that is concerned with the terms or conditions of employment and is of mutual concern to a group of employees, probably two or more, will be protected. Protection is granted regardless of whether or not there is a collective bargaining agreement in existence. The situation is generally not as one-sided as it may first seem. For instance, an employer can discipline or discharge an employee who engages in an unprotected strike or work stoppage.

Give special consideration to the termination of an employee for theft, fraud, or other crimes committed on company premises. In such cases, the use of suspension, which is a provision of *Performance Improvement — Section 2150*, should be considered for the following reasons:

- The need to make a more thorough investigation is warranted;
- Other employees, especially informers, may need some protection;
- Company property may be vandalized or removed in retaliation; and
- False accusations can lead to claims for false imprisonment, defamation, or invasion of privacy.

Although all terminations should be handled in a confidential manner, this is especially true when the cause of termination is crime-related.

The best approach is to reveal the circumstances of the termination to only those staff members who must know, e.g., personnel director, director of security. Otherwise, the terminated employee may sue you and the company for defamation or invasion of privacy.

A recent case in California held that public posting of an employee's termination established a prima facie case of invasion of privacy under the California Constitution.[6] If you use the threat of reporting the matter to the police as leverage for the employee's resignation, you may be charged with extortion.

By now you have read the *Comment* to the *Performance Improvement* policy — *Section 2150*. The erosion of the employer's right to discharge an employee at will has been occurring in many states for some time. This is occurring in California despite a state statute which clearly sets forth the "employment at will" doctrine.[7] Other states probably have similar laws.

Several legal concepts have emerged to hold employers liable for wrongful discharge of an employee. Listed below are some of these legal concepts.

- Public policy — The employee was told to do an illegal act, refused, and was fired.[8] Similarly, employees who report their employers to government agencies for such things as safety violations, contract fraud, and others may find protection under various whistle blower statutes.
- Intentional infliction of emotional distress — Conduct by an employer considered to be outrageous could result in liability to the employer.[9] Recent examples of what is often referred to as "outrageous terminations" include escorting long-time employees off the premises with security guards and making personal comments to the terminated employee or others.
- Retaliatory discharge — The employee was terminated after signing a union membership application.[10]

- Breach of written contract — A contract that provided for permanent employment as long as the employee operated in a competent, profitable, and efficient manner.[11]
- Bad faith, malice, or ill will — The employee was discharged for refusing to date the foreman.[12]
- Exercising a statutory right — The employee was discharged for filing a workers' compensation claim.[13]
- Breach of oral contract — This claim was based on a promise of permanent employment, as long as employee's work is satisfactory, and further oral assurances made by the company that termination would occur only for good cause.[14]
- Breach of implied covenant of good faith and fair dealing in an oral contract — An employee with 18 years seniority was terminated and the company failed to follow its grievance procedure.[15]
- Implied agreement to discharge for only good cause — It was found upon the termination of a corporate officer, who had been employed for 32 years and received commendations and promotions without derogatory performance appraisals, was given assurances of continued employment.[16]
- Breach of contract — The employee policies and handbook, when considered together, were evidence of "good cause only" discharge policy. The court held that these company communications became part of the employment contract which was admittedly oral.[17]
- Discrimination — An alarming increase in claims based on discrimination, especially in the areas of sex, age, and disability have been filed in recent years. Under several recent disability-related claims, employees have successfully argued that the behavior which led to termination was so aberrant that the employer should have known the employee was disabled.

For example, an employee discharged for bringing a gun to work successfully sued for wrongful discharge. The employee's conduct was poor judgment related to a chemical imbalance. The employer had a duty to accommodate this employee. Similarly, employers have been called to task for wrongfully discharging employees who the employer knew or should have known suffered from such things as attention deficit disorder stress or depression. Employees perceived as disabled, although not, have successfully maintained wrongful discharge claims. Such things can include obesity, facial scars, non-contagious diseases, etc. On April 5, 1995, the Wall Street Journal identified the pitfalls an employer faces when terminating a potentially violent employee.

Fortunately, for employers, the pendulum seems to be swinging back toward a more moderate analysis in discrimination cases, especially those involving disability. For example, recent cases have noted that employers need not provide stress-free workplaces or restructure a job in order to change its fundamental requirements. The ability to work with stress and work as part of a team can be essential requirements of a job.

Without question, it is not always easy to identify and distinguish a stress disorder which could be considered a disability from personality traits such as immaturity, bad temper, or poor judgment which are not disabilities. In addition, courts are increasingly holding that misconduct or violation of clearly stated company rules can be grounds for discipline, including termination, regardless of disability status. Included within this emerging trend are unpredictable absences by employees. At some point , the number of absences creates a basis for discipline without regard to disability status.

In addition to the ADA claims discussed above, look for claims of invasion of privacy, violation of anti-bias laws, negligence if the employee becomes violent, and more.

It's a jungle out there. Work with your attorney.

Anytime an employee takes an action which he or she is legally entitled to take, such as filing statutory claims for benefits or making a charge of discriminatory practices, the employee is protected from discharge or discipline for doing so. Many federal and state statutes provide such protection. If the employee is subsequently discharged or disciplined for some misconduct warranting it, be prepared to present documentary evidence to support the independent reason for the discharge or discipline.

In 1995, the U.S. Supreme Court determined in *McKennon v. Nashville Banner Publishing Co.* that an employer may utilize prior undisclosed wrongdoing on the part of a terminated employee as a defense to a charge of wrongful termination or discrimination.[18] The prior wrongdoing does not extinguish the employee's claim, but it can serve to reduce the damage award.

Under the "after acquired evidence" theory, an employer who discovers wrongdoing on the part of an employee, such as lying on a job application or inappropriate post-hire conduct, may be able to use the conduct as a defense to a wrongful termination or discrimination claim. However, the after acquired evidence must be such that had the employer known about it, the employer wouldn't have hired or would have terminated the employee in the first place.

Your company policies and procedures, when read together, should not be able to be interpreted as promising permanent or long-term employment. This book tries to avoid this interpretation in these policies and procedures, but no one can predict how a judge or jury will interpret a particular set of facts. If possible, your employment application and your policies should conspicuously state the employment-at-will doctrine.

If you adopt an appeal procedure, make sure it is followed. At a minimum, any appeal procedure should provide the employee with a right to know the charges or alleged misconduct, to hear the evidence against him or her, to present documentary and oral evidence on his or her behalf before a neutral decision maker, and to have a sufficient time to prepare for this hearing.

If a corrective counseling policy is adopted, follow it, and ensure that the process is documented. If your termination policy provides examples of misconduct, which will lead to discipline or immediate discharge, do not try to make the list all-inclusive. State that the examples of misconduct are not limited to those listed. Above all, you must treat all employees fairly and even evenhandedly and apply your written policies consistently.

Examine all company communications and any other personnel or benefit-related documents for the flaws cited above. You should also adopt a mandatory policy of no promises of long term or permanent employment by anyone to anyone. Even the use of the words "career opportunity" in employment ads or personnel requisitions is suspect.

Avoid the words "fair cause," "good cause" or any such implications that can defeat the employment-at-will doctrine. Remember also that the words and actions of supervisors can give rise to unintended rights or benefits in favor of employees. Make certain that supervisory personnel understand the policy manual and act in a manner consistent with it.

Some employers believe that taking all of the above steps, especially emphasizing the right to discharge at-will in various documents, may damage employee morale or cause good prospective employees to go elsewhere. This may occur unless you diplomatically word your company communications to set a softer tone. If you feel this way, then adopt policies that reflect your own style of management. If you desire some type of appeal or grievance procedure, draft one that is fair to both sides. You may not prevent a wrongful discharge lawsuit from being brought, but you can at least show that the termination process was fair and that the employee was afforded those rights and still lost.

Several common themes appear in these cases. First, a representation of some kind was made by someone with apparent supervisory authority. Representations include statements in a policy manual, verbal promises or assurances, or past conduct of an employer in response to similar situations. What you do is as important as what you say. Make certain that your managers understand the policy manual and act consistently with it.

Second, don't discharge an employee for exercising a statutory right. Third, don't engage in conduct which by all objective standards is outrageous or would tend to shock the conscience of a judge or jury.

The disciplinary or termination process must be confidential. When you terminate someone, do so privately. Explain in detail exactly why the person is being terminated and use your documentation as backup. Explain the appeal or grievance process to the employee, and let the employee exercise those rights. You can be polite, but firm. Stick to your carefully thought-out policy.

Two policies regarding terminations are provided on the following pages. The right to discharge at-will is included in the second policy. The first policy could be interpreted to mean that the employer can only discharge "for cause" (e.g., substandard performance, misconduct) or layoff. No appeal or grievance procedure is provided in either policy. It is probably better to consult someone familiar with local law before finalizing such a procedure.

If you decide to use the second policy and reserve your at-will rights, make sure any corrective counseling or performance improvement policy also contains the same appropriate language or is tailored to achieve this result.

Due to the high cost of terminations, many companies now evaluate each employee termination through an exit interview. The interviews may be a source of vital information that can eventually reduce employee turnover and increase productivity and profit. A sample Exit Interview Guide follows the policies presented in this discussion.

Without question, case law and statutory law, which impact terminations and the related issue of plant closings, continue to evolve. Consult your legal counsel as you prepare your policy manual and periodically afterwards to keep your manual current with any changes in law.

Termination

Alternate Policy 1   2160.1

Terminations are to be treated in a confidential, professional manner by all concerned. The supervisor, department manager, and personnel department must assure thorough, consistent, and evenhanded termination procedures. This policy and its administration will be implemented in accordance with the company equal opportunity statement.

Note: *You may choose to include the preceding sentence in a separate guide for supervisory personnel and eliminate it from the policy manual.*

Terminating employees are entitled to receive all earned pay, including vacation pay.

Note: *If you do not have a "vested" vacation policy you will want to delete or modify the preceding sentence in accordance with local law.*

Only employees with 15 or more years of service with the company, as explained in the policy, *Sick or Personal Leave — Section 4040*, are qualified to receive sick or personal leave payout.

Note: *The preceding sentence must be consistent with your sick or personal leave policy and local law.*

Employment with the company is normally terminated through one of the following actions:

1. Resignation — voluntary termination by the employee;
2. Dismissal — involuntary termination for substandard performance or misconduct; or
3. Layoff — termination due to reduction of the work force or elimination of a position.

Resignation

An employee who wants to terminate employment, regardless of employee classification, is expected to give as much advance notice as possible. Two weeks or ten working days is generally considered to be sufficient notice time. If an employee resigns to join a competitor, if there is any other conflict of interest, or if the employee refuses to reveal the circumstances of his or her resignation and the future employer, the manager may require the employee to leave the company immediately rather than work during the notice period. This is not to be construed as a reflection upon the employee's integrity but an action in the best interests of

Termination

Alternate Policy 1 (continued)   2160.1

business practice. When immediate voluntary termination occurs for the above reasons, the employee will receive pay "in lieu of notice," the maximum being two weeks of pay based upon a 40-hour work week at the employee's straight-time rate or salary.

Dismissal

1. Substandard Performance — An employee may be discharged if his or her performance is unacceptable. The supervisor/manager shall have counseled the employee concerning performance deficiencies, provided direction for improvement, and warned the employee of possible termination if performance did not improve within a defined period of time. The supervisor/manager is expected to be alert to any underlying reasons for performance deficiencies such as personal problems or substance abuse. See *Section 2060*. The (PERSONNEL DIRECTOR) must concur in advance of advising the employee of discharge action. Documentation to be prepared by the supervisor/manager shall include reason for separation, performance history, corrective efforts taken, alternatives explored, and any additional pertinent information.

2. Misconduct — An employee found to be engaged in activities such as, but not limited to, theft of company property, insubordination, conflict of interest, or any other activities showing willful disregard of company interests or policies, will be terminated as soon as the supervisor/manager and personnel director have concurred with the action.

Note: See Performance Improvement — Section 2150 for a list of other examples.

Termination resulting from misconduct shall be entered into the employee's personnel file. The employee shall be provided with a written summary of the reason for termination. No salary continuance or severance pay will be allowed.

Layoff

When a reduction in force is necessary or if one or more positions are eliminated, employees will be identified for layoff after evaluating the following factors:

1. Company work requirements;
2. Employee's abilities, experience, and skill;
3. Employee's potential for reassignment within the organization; and
4. Length of service.

Termination

Alternate Policy 1 (continued)   2160.1

The immediate supervisor/manager will personally notify employees of a layoff. After explaining the layoff procedure, the employee will be given a letter describing the conditions of the layoff, such as the effect the layoff will have on his or her anniversary date at time of call-back — the procedure to be followed if time off to seek other employment is granted — and the company's role in assisting employees to find other work. The employee and the personnel director, after consultation with the employee's supervisor/manager, will follow one of the following procedures:

1. The employee will receive at least two weeks advance notice of termination date.
2. The employee will be terminated immediately and will receive one week of pay for each year of employment with the company in lieu of notice, up to a maximum of four weeks. The payment will be based on a 40-hour work week at the employee's straight time rate or salary.

Note: Your policy may be silent on such a determination which leaves it up to management to decide, but the determination must be made evenhandedly.

Termination Processing Procedures

1. The supervisor/manager must immediately notify the (PERSONNEL DEPARTMENT) of the termination so that a termination checklist can be initiated. The (PERSONNEL DEPARTMENT) will direct and coordinate the termination procedure.
2. All outstanding advances charged to the terminating employee will be deducted from the final paycheck by the payroll department.

Note: Some states limit this procedure in the absence of a signed written agreement entered into prior to the advance, so check local law.

3. On the final day of employment, the (PERSONNEL DEPARTMENT) must receive all keys, ID cards, and company property from the employee.
4. The (PERSONNEL DEPARTMENT) shall conduct an exit interview with the employee.

Note: A sample Exit Interview Guide is provided at the end of this section.

5. The employee will pick up his or her final payroll check from the (PERSONNEL DEPARTMENT) at the time of the exit interview. The final check shall include all earned pay and any expenses due the employee.

Termination

Alternate Policy 2   2160.2

Terminations are to be treated in a confidential, professional manner by all concerned. The supervisor/manager, and personnel department must assure thorough, consistent, and evenhanded termination procedures. This policy and its administration will be implemented in accordance with the company equal opportunity statement.

Note: You may choose to include the preceding sentence in a separate guide for supervisory personnel and eliminate it from the policy manual.

Either the employee or employer can terminate the employment relationship with the company at any time and for any reason. The company subscribes to the policy of employment at will. Continued employment with the company is at the sole and exclusive option of company management. Permanent employment or employment for a specific term cannot be guaranteed or promised in the absence of a specific written contract of employment between an employee and the company.

Note: It is recommended that the two preceding sentences be inserted in a conspicuous place at the beginning of the company employment application.

Terminating employees are entitled to receive all earned pay, including vacation pay.

Note: If you do not have a "vested" vacation policy, you will want to delete or modify the preceding sentence in accordance with local law.

Unused sick or personal time will be forfeited.

Note: Check your sick or personal leave policy and local law.

Employment with the company is normally terminated through one of the following actions:

1. Resignation — voluntary termination by the employee;
2. Dismissal — involuntary termination by the company for any reason at any time with or without cause; or
3. Layoff — termination due to reduction of the work force or elimination of a position.

Termination

Alternate Policy 2 (continued)   2160.2

Resignation

An employee desiring to terminate employment, regardless of employee classification, is expected to give as much notice as possible. Two weeks or ten working days is generally considered to be sufficient notice time to find a replacement.

Should an employee resign to join a competitor, if there is any other conflict of interest, or if the employee refuses to reveal the circumstances of his or her resignation and the future employer, the manager may require the employee to leave the company immediately rather than work during the notice period. This is not to be construed as a reflection upon the employee's integrity but an action in the best interests of business practice. When immediate voluntary termination occurs for the above reasons, the employee will receive pay "in lieu of notice," the maximum being two weeks of pay based upon a 40-hour work week at the employee's straight-time rate or salary.

Employees terminating voluntarily are entitled to receive all earned vacation pay.

Note: If you do not have a "vested" vacation policy, you will want to delete or modify the preceding sentence in accordance with local law.

Unused sick or personal time will be forfeited.

Note: Check your sick or personal leave policy and local law.

Dismissal

An employee may be dismissed at any time, for any reason, with or without cause, at the sole and absolute discretion of company management. In the case of dismissal, the company may, at its sole discretion, give some notice of its intent to dismiss an employee, but the company is not required to give any such notice.

Layoff

When a reduction in force is necessary, or one or more positions are eliminated, the company will, at its sole discretion, identify the employees to be laid off. The company may give two weeks notice to the laid off employee, but it reserves the right to substitute two weeks

Termination

Alternate Policy 2 (continued)   2160.2

severance pay in lieu of notice. Such pay will be based upon a 40-hour work week at the employee's straight-time rate or salary.

Termination Processing Procedures

1. The supervisor/manager must immediately notify the (PERSONNEL DEPARTMENT) of the termination so that a termination checklist can be initiated. The (PERSONNEL DEPARTMENT) will direct and coordinate the termination procedure.
2. All outstanding advances charged to the terminating employee will be deducted from the final paycheck by the payroll department.

Note: Some states limit this procedure in the absence of a signed written agreement entered into prior to the advance, so check local law.

3. On the final day of employment, the (PERSONNEL DEPARTMENT) must receive all keys, ID cards, and company property from the employee.
4. The (PERSONNEL DEPARTMENT) shall conduct an exit interview with the employee.

Note: A sample Exit Interview Guide is provided at the end of this section.

5. The employee will pick up his or her final payroll check from the (PERSONNEL DEPARTMENT) at the time of the exit interview. The final check shall include all earned pay and any expenses due the employee.

Termination

Alternate Policy 3   2160.3

An employee may be terminated at any time with or without notice and for any reason whatsoever.

Exit Interview Guide

Note: An exit interview, properly conducted, can give an employer information about the climate within the company, company morale, and the attitude of employees toward their supervisors, management, and fellow employees. It is important to build rapport by asking non-threatening questions similar to the following:

1. Which responsibilities did you like most about the job? Which responsibilities did you like least?

2. What did you like most about the department you were assigned to?

3. What did you think about the way the manager handled complaints?

4. What type of working conditions are most conducive to your best productivity?

5. What do you see as the future of this company?

6. What impressed you about this company when you first accepted your position? Has this impression changed? If so, how? Why?

7. When you first joined the company, was your training helpful for what you were actually doing six months later?

8. What type of job are you going to? What are you looking for in that position that you feel is not present in this company?

9. What kind of work do you like to do best? Were you doing that kind of work in your job here?

10. What points would you want to make if you could tell top management how you felt about this organization?

11. How do you feel about the contribution you have made to this company?

12. Tell me what your feelings are about the benefit program offered by this company?

Note: In analyzing the responses, watch for patterns that may provide helpful information for the employee selection process. The responses may also provide suggestions for improvement in the general organizational or personnel areas.

Employment Disputes   2170

Comment

Although the law is unsettled in this area, employers increasingly require that employees arbitrate any dispute or claim which is based on the employment relationship. For example, if an employee believes that he or she has been discriminated against, arbitration will be required to determine the validity of the claim and assert and assess any appropriate remedy or relief. As a general rule, arbitration is an alternate dispute resolution process which is quicker and less expensive than litigation.

Federal law and state laws may vary regarding whether or not arbitration can be required, especially where a violation or state or federal constitutional right is asserted. At this time, the legality of these provisions is in question. In addition, some states may require that a separate arbitration provision be signed by the employee rather than simply being placed in a policy manual. Similar treatment can be expected for non-compete provisions which are not covered in this book.

The policy which follows selects arbitration under the rules of the American Arbitration Association. Consult with the state law in your state to determine what arbitration procedures may be available and to determine whether you wish to use the American Arbitration Association or some other arbitration service.

Arbitration of Employment Disputes

Policy   2170

Any dispute or claim that arises out of or that relates to employment with (COMPANY), or that arises out of or that is based on the employment relationship (including any wage claim, any claim for wrongful termination, or any claim based on any employment discrimination or civil rights statute, regulation or law), including tort or harassment claims (except a tort that is a "compensable injury" under workers' compensation law), shall be resolved by arbitration in accordance with the then effective commercial arbitration rules of the American Arbitration Association by filing a claim in accordance with the filing rules of the American Arbitration Association, and judgment on the award rendered pursuant to such arbitration may be entered in any court having jurisdiction thereof.

Internet Usage Policy   2180

Comment

The importance of being able to communicate electronically in today's business world requires a substantial investment on the part of a company. The purpose of these investments is to help the company and employees perform their job in a more efficient manner. The company's facilities that make this possible include costs for telecommunications, networking and additional software and mass storage. This communication involves fellow employees, customers, as well as to seek information from the worldwide web.

Existing company policies that apply to your normal business behavior also apply when you are using the Internet. Issues of confidentiality take on critical importance when it comes to the Internet. The Internet provides a new level of communication enabling all levels of company employees to make statements for the company. When a company employee sends a message or communicates through a public forum as an employee, it is natural for the recipient of that message or communication to understand it to be a company position or message. In fact, as will often be the case, it may just be a personal opinion.

Access to the Internet enables users to download a wide variety of software products for a fee as a shareware or for free. Often you are required to fulfill all license and copyright obligations of software that you download for your own use. These software downloads become the property of the company.

Internet Miscellaneous

Comment

It is advisable that your users sign a statement that they understand the terms of the Company Internet Policy. A sample acknowledgment letter follows.

Internet Usage

Policy   2180

This policy is designed to define expectations for what is acceptable when using company Internet resources. Internet usage at (COMPANY) is provided to you as result of a company investment and it is expected that you use these resources for business purposes. Examples of appropriate usage include the following:

1. Communicating with fellow employees, customers, prospects and suppliers regarding business matters.

2. Researching topics that are relevant to your specific job requirements.

3. Conducting other business activities, such as working with the manager assigned to company website (e.g. posting job opportunities, describing company products, etc.).

Special care is to be taken in disseminating company confidential information over the Internet. When employees are in doubt about dissemination of information, they should contact (MANAGER) for written approval to release the information. Security and confidentiality needs to be of high concern for all company employees. It is inappropriate to make comments regarding the market for the company's products, its profitability or product margins.

All software downloaded from the Internet becomes the property of the company. Employees are not allowed to download copyrighted software from the Internet. In any cases where an employee downloads copyrighted software they assume full responsibility for their action and absolve the company from their unauthorized action.

All files that are downloaded must first be scanned for possible infection. Any employee who knowingly tries to propagate the Internet or internal resources with infected viruses or Trojan Horses will be subject to termination.

The company has installed a variety of systems to thwart intrusion by outside hackers. It is extremely important that these systems integrity be maintained. Any user who tries to override these security measures will be subject to termination.

All communication and Internet visits made during business hours are considered public information. Employees of (COMPANY) are not allowed to visit sites that are considered "obscene." The (COMPANY) has the right to view all private files that have been downloaded and to monitor Internet and e-mail communications.

Internet Usage

Policy (continued)   2180

It is a violation of company policy to store, view or print graphic files that are not directly related to an employee's job or business activity of the company. Examples of these misuses might include downloading games, jokes, audio files, animation's or movie segments.

All (COMPANY) employees are expected to honestly disclose who they are when they send e-mail, register accounts or when conducting other Internet transactions.

Sample Internet Usage Acknowledgment Letter

I acknowledge the (COMPANY) Internet Usage Policy. I have read the policy in full and fully agree to abide by all its terms. I understand that the company may monitor my personal use of the Internet and that my communications are not considered private. All communications may be recorded and stored for archival retrieval. I understand that if I violate the terms of this policy, my employment could be subject to termination or even civil prosecution.

_____

Employee's Signature   Date

Footnotes

2010 — Equal Opportunity

1. 42 U.S.C. (United States Code) § 2000e-2000e-17.

2. 42 U.S.C. § 1981.

3. 29 U.S.C. § 206.

4. 29 U.S.C. § 201–219.

5. 29 U.S.C. § 621–634.

2050 — Medical Evaluations and Interviews

1. Coffee v. McDonnell-Douglas Corp., 8 Cal.3d 551, 105 Cal.Rptr. 358 (1972).

2. Mrachek v. Sunshine Biscuit, Inc., 308 N.Y. 116, 123 N.E.2d 801 (1954).

2060 — Substance Abuse

1. Otis Engineering Corp. v. Clark, 668 S.W.2d 302 (Tex. 1983).

2150 — Performance Improvement

1. McKennon v. Nashville Banner Publishing Co., 115 S Ct. 879 (U.S. 1995)

2160 — Termination

1. Cal. Lab. Code § 201, 203.

2. Cal. Lab. Code § 201, 201.5, 201.7.

3. Cal. Lab. Code § 227.3.

4. Saustez v. Plastic Dress-up Co., 31 Cal.3d 774, 183 Cal. Rptr. 846 (1982).

5. 29 U.S.C. § 158(a)(1).

6. Payton v. City of Santa Clara, 132 Cal. App.3d 152, 183 Cal. Rptr. 17 (1982).

7. Cal. Lab. Code § 2922.

8. Tameny v. Atlantic Richfield Co., 27 Cal.3d 167, 164 Cal. Rptr. 839 (1980).

9. Agis v. Howard Johnson Company, 371 Mass. 140, 355 N.E.2d 315 (1976).

10. Glenn v. Clearman's Golden Cock Inn, Inc., 192 Cal. App.2d 793, 13 Cal. Rptr. 769 (1961).

11. Drzewiecki v. H & R Block, Inc., 24 Cal. App.3d 695, 101 Cal. Rptr. 169 (1972).

12. Monge v. Beebe Rubber Co., 316 A.2d 549 (N.H. 1974).

13. Frampton v. Central Indiana Gas Co., 297 N.E.2d 425 (Ind. 1973).

14. Rabago-Alvarez v. Dart Industries, Inc., 55 Cal. App.3d 91, 127 Cal. Rptr. 222 (1976).

15. Cleary v. American Airlines, Inc., 111 Cal. App.3d 443, 168 Cal. Rptr. 722 (1980).

16. Pugh v. See's Candies, Inc., 116 Cal. App.3d 311, 171 Cal. Rptr. 917 (1981).

17. Toussaint v. Blue Cross of Michigan, 408 Mich. 579, 292 N.W.2d 880 (1980).

18. 115 S. Ct. 879 (U.S. 1995).

Chapter 3

Compensation

Introduction

The monetary rewards that your employees receive in exchange for their intellectual, emotional, and physical efforts have a significant effect on your company's success. Although the non-monetary factors of a job contribute greatly to employees' job satisfaction and productivity, the effect of compensation can't be ignored.

The challenge in the development of the policies for this section of your policy manual is to provide a fair and equitable compensation package. This package should enable you to provide quality products or services at competitive prices and stimulate your employees to exert that effort which results in quality production. The policies discussed in this chapter permit your company to attract and maintain outstanding employees. Your compensation package must ensure a profit for your company.

Compensation is also a source of conflict, especially where employees within the same classification compare and contrast what their fellow employees are being paid. As a result, the confidential nature of compensation should be stressed.

Equal Pay   3010

Comment

As noted earlier in *Section 2010 — Equal Opportunity*, federal and state statutes require equal pay for comparable work for men and women performing similar services. Failure to do so can result in a claim based on wage or sex discrimination.

Non gender-based pay systems such as a seniority or merit system do no violate equal pay laws. In addition, employees working twenty hours or less per week or temporary employees are not generally covered under equal pay laws. A general policy statement concerning equal pay follows.

Keep in mind you have a right to pay different rates to employees who have different levels of responsibility, workloads or working conditions. The employee's gender cannot be the determining factor for the wage base. In summary, base your test on four basic factors: 1) skill-level required, 2) effort expected, 3) responsibility, and 4) working conditions.

Equal Pay

Policy   3010.1

(COMPANY) will not pay wages to any employee at a rate less than the company pays employees of the opposite sex for work which is substantially equivalent requiring comparable skills.

This policy is to be construed in accordance with applicable federal and state laws and regulations.

Job Descriptions   3020

Comment

A well-defined description for each position within your company is a valuable asset. Taken as a whole, position descriptions are similar to a blueprint. They define the parts of a company's organization and detail every part's specifications. The specifications include job qualifications, assigned duties, responsibilities, knowledge, coordination, reporting requirements, and physical working conditions. Management's analysis and review of all the company position descriptions may also uncover overlapping duties. It will also identify employee responsibilities that might be more effectively assigned to another position.

A good position description should define all essential tasks to be accomplished. It helps the employee understand what the job entails and what the company expects of him or her. A position description encourages high employee productivity and is a tool which provides the standards to measure an employee's performance. This is especially true when the employee is involved in creating the position description, as suggested in Alternate Policy 1 on the following page.

A complete set of position descriptions will assist management in structuring or restructuring the company organization. They are also a basis for determining employee classifications and compensation levels. They help your company comply with various federal laws, such as the Fair Labor Standards Act, the Equal Pay Act, Title VII, and the Americans with Disabilities Act because they contain essential information which helps determine the following:

- The essential function of a particular job;
- Exempt and non-exempt classifications;
- Equal pay for equal work; and
- The existence of artificial employment barriers.

All of your position descriptions should be in the same format. Personnel responsible for developing them should receive similar training and follow the same guidelines. The position descriptions should provide a balanced and integrated picture of your organization and each one should be reviewed periodically and updated when necessary. This will ensure that they accurately describe each employee's responsibilities and his or her relationship to others within the organization. For your convenience, a sample Job Description Form follows Alternate Policy 2.

Job Descriptions

Alternate Policy 1   3020.1

The purpose of job descriptions at (COMPANY) is to define the duties and set requirements for filling the job. Within three months after every employee has filled a position, a personalized job description detailing the unique features of the job and establishing the employee's job objectives will be prepared by each supervisor using input from the employee. The previous job description will be used as a model in defining the present employee's position. A supervisor shall review an employee's job description when he or she requests it.

All job descriptions shall include the following information:

1. Title of position;
2. Assigned organizational unit (e.g., payroll, marketing);
3. Position classification number;
4. Job summary or overview;
5. Position qualifications (essential qualifications including job experience, skills, and education); and
6. Major duties and responsibilities.

These position descriptions are used to compare our positions with the positions of other companies for salary surveys. Position descriptions are also one of the factors used in setting the pay scale of positions within our company.

Management shall review all position descriptions annually to ensure equity and consistency within and across job families and functional lines.

Job Descriptions

Alternate Policy 2   3020.2

Job descriptions are available in the (PERSONNEL DEPARTMENT) for all positions in the company. The items included in each position description are the following:

1. Job identification;

2. Essential job qualifications;

3. Summary statement;

4. Assigned responsibilities or duties; and

5. Supervisor or rater.

Position descriptions are used to determine employee selection, job requirements, performance appraisals, organizational structure, and the relative worth of jobs in relation to each other.

Company management annually reviews all company positions to ensure equity and consistency in our human resource system.

Job Description

Job Title: _____ Job Code: _____

Department: _____ Date: _____

Written by: _____

Approved by: _____

Pay Scale: _____ Exempt: _____ Non-Exempt: _____

Essential Job Qualifications: _____

_____

_____

_____

_____

Summary Statement: _____

_____

_____

_____

Assigned Responsibilities or Duties: _____

_____

_____

Supervisor: _____

Workday, Payday, and Pay Advances   3030–50

Comment

Time worked is defined by the Fair Labor Standards Act (FLSA) and by the laws or regulations of most states. Under federal law, work not requested but "suffered or permitted" is compensable. That means that if an employer knows or has reason to believe that an employee is working, the employer must pay for the time worked.

Having a rule or policy that no overtime will be permitted is not sufficient. The employer must also make certain that the policy is being enforced.

Meal periods are compensable time unless the employee is completely relieved from his or her work. Rest periods are compensable time regardless. See the *Comment* to *Meal and Rest Periods — Section 3070.*

Preparatory or concluding activities are compensable if they are an integral part of the employee's principal activity — cleaning up around a machine before leaving. However, preparatory or concluding activities are not compensable if they are allowed for the employee's convenience only, e.g., washing up.

Travel to and from work is not compensable time. However, an employment agreement or a collective bargaining contract can vary the rules regarding travel and preparatory and concluding activities.

A discussion of who is or is not covered by the Fair Labor Standards Act is contained in the *Comment* to *Overtime Compensation — Section 3060.* Most states have laws regarding what is or is not time worked. Typically, these will parallel the FLSA.

Your policy should define what hours will be considered as the company workday, for example, 8:00 AM to 5:00 PM. If your company has two or more shifts, it would be appropriate to define them as well, either in this policy or in a separate policy on shifts. You may want to use *Shift Premium — Section 3120*, for this purpose. Also, you should define your company pay periods.

Frequency of paydays is regulated by state law for most employers. One exception is under the Davis–Bacon Act which applies to employers who hire mechanics and laborers working on federal building construction contracts, including alterations and painting. Under that law, employers must pay weekly. Typically, state laws or regulations will require an employer to pay all employees at a specified frequency — weekly, biweekly, or monthly. Exceptions to the general rule may also be provided for certain employee classifications, e.g., executive or management employees may only have to be paid once a month instead of twice a month. Obviously, you can pay more frequently than the law requires. However, there is usually a specific law or regulation pertaining to terminated employees.

State legislation will also set limitations on how long you can postpone payment for work performed earlier. For example, in California, work that is performed between the 1st and 15th of the month must be compensated between the 16th and 26th of the same month. Work performed between the 16th and the end of the month must be compensated between the 1st and 10th of the following month.[1] You will usually be required to post a notice of the company paydays and the time and place of payment in a conspicuous place on the premises.[2]

For every employee, you must maintain complete and accurate records of all hours worked daily and weekly, pay rates, time off with and without pay, time of day and day of work week that begins and ends, total daily or weekly straight-time earnings, overtime compensation, additions to or deductions from gross earnings for each pay period, total wages paid each pay period, dates of those payments, and the inclusive dates of each pay period.[3]

You should also have a record of every employee's name, Social Security number, address, sex, and occupation. Every employee must receive an itemized statement of gross wages, all deductions, net wages, inclusive dates of the pay period, employee's name or Social Security number, and the employer's name and address for every pay period.

The majority of companies pay on a biweekly basis with time cards or time sheets being submitted to the payroll department three to five days prior to payday. Typically, employees are responsible for recording and reporting their hours worked.

The sample Time Sheet located after the alternate policies on workdays requests the very basic information of time-in for the morning, time-out at noon, time back after lunch, and time-out at the end of the day. Columns are provided for calculating regular and overtime hours. Dates and times are recorded on a semi-monthly period. The employee's and supervisor's signatures certify the hours worked and approved. The check number provides an audit trail for the accounting department.

A legend might be added at the bottom of the time sheet, designating "R"— regular, "S"— sick, "H"— Holiday, and "V"— Vacation. These letters can be used in identifying hours for each pay period.

Advances in pay may be authorized by this policy, if it is your desire to make this benefit available to your employees. Some companies prohibit it. Other companies allow for it in emergency situations only. Rarely do companies provide this benefit without any limitations. Collecting and accounting for a pay advance can be a headache for your payroll department and a burden on an employee. Abuses are hard to prevent, and errors can be demoralizing.

If you grant an advance pay benefit, be sure that you have a previous written, signed, and dated authorization from the employee to justify the later deduction. It should also authorize you to deduct the full remaining balance from the employee's last paycheck. It would be best to inform the employee, on the authorization itself, how much will be deducted from his or her future paychecks.

If the employee terminates or doesn't come back to work, you are probably stuck if his or her last paycheck is insufficient to cover what is owed. If you prohibit pay advances, you may still want to consider vacation pay advances which involve less risk. A sample Payroll Advance Request Form follows Alternate Policy 1 on Payroll Advances.

For your convenience, the issues discussed above have been segregated into separate policies to allow you to pick and choose policies for your manual. With only minor modifications, these policies can be combined to form one policy.

The Payroll Change Notice, following the Payroll Advance Request serves as documentation for any changes in payroll status for the payroll department and the employee's personnel file.

Workday

Alternate Policy 1   3030.1

A workday begins at (ADD START TIME) and ends at (ADD FINISH TIME) with (ADD NUMBER) hour off for lunch. Each workweek consists of (ADD NUMBER) hours, and generally includes work performed Monday through Friday.

However, the nature of our business sometimes demands workday or workweek hours different than those set forth above. Variation to the schedule will be made or approved by department managers.

Workday

Alternate Policy 2   3030.2

Specific workday and workweek hours for each employee will be determined from time to time by the appropriate department manager based on the operational needs of the company.

(COMPANY) will attempt to notify employees of any changes in workdays or workweek hours two weeks in advance of the effective date of any such change.

Time Sheet

Name: _____ Week(s) ending: _____ 19____

Date	Time in	Time out	Time in	Time out	Regular Hours	Overtime Hours

TOTAL HOURS (Regular and Overtime): _____

Employee's Signature: _____

Supervisor's Signature: _____

Check #: _____

Payday

Alternate Policy 1   3040.1

Our employees are paid every two weeks, 26 times annually. The first payday of the year will be on the first (DAY) of the month, with each successive payday being on alternate (DAY).

Time cards are to be submitted to your supervisor/manager by close of business the Friday preceding the company payday. Pay is for the two work weeks preceding the next payday.

Payday

Alternate Policy 2   3040.2

The company paydays are the 5th and 20th of each month. Employees are to submit their time card or time sheet to their supervisor/manager three working days prior to the 5th and 20th of the month.

For paydays that fall during the weekend, checks will be distributed on the Friday prior to the payday. If a company holiday falls on the 5th or 20th, employees will receive their payroll check on the last workday prior to the holiday.

Pay Advances

Alternate Policy 1   3050.1

An employee pay advance is a temporary cash advance of an amount no more than (ADD
DOLLAR AMOUNT), repayable in (ADD NUMBER) pay periods. The pay advance is interest
free and is granted only in the event of an employee emergency. The determination to grant
or reject an advance request is made at the sole discretion of (COMPANY). The advance is
obtained by filling out a payroll advance request and submitting it through the employee's
supervisor/manager to the payroll department for processing. Requests for additional
advances will be processed only after the initial advance is repaid.

*Note: A Payroll Advance Request Form is included on the following page. All
arrangements for mailing or depositing employee paychecks must be made in
advance and in writing with the payroll department.*

Pay Advances

Alternate Policy 2   3050.2

It is our policy to decline all requests for early paychecks or pay advances for personal
reasons. Pay advances in the event of vacation or legitimate business reasons (e.g., temporary
duty assignment) may be requested through the employee's supervisor/manager to the
(ACCOUNTING DEPARTMENT).

Payroll Advance Request

Employee Name: _____

Date of Advance: _____ Request Advance Amount: $ _____

Agreement:

In consideration of the above advance pay given to me by (COMPANY), I hereby irrevocably authorize the (COMPANY) Payroll Department to deduct the above advance amount in equal installments from the net earnings payable to me for the (ADD NUMBER) pay period(s) immediately following the date of receipt of the advance amount. I understand that each deduction shall be (ADD DOLLAR AMOUNT). I fully understand and agree that the total of all payroll deductions for repayment of this advance shall be equal to the total amount advanced.

I further understand and agree that my acceptance of the advance amount and this authorization for payroll deduction shall in no way be construed as a contract for my continued employment with (COMPANY). In the event of my termination of employment with (COMPANY), whether voluntary or involuntary, prior to the total recovery by (COMPANY) of the amount advanced to me, I authorize (COMPANY) to deduct the full remaining balance of this advance from my final paycheck. In the event my final paycheck is insufficient to repay the advance, I recognize my absolute and irrevocable obligation to fully repay any remaining balance to (COMPANY) after my final paycheck has been credited against the advance amount owed and to pay reasonable attorney fees incurred by (COMPANY) in the event collection efforts are required.

Signatures:

_____   _____
                Employee   Date

Approved by:_____   _____
                Supervisor   Date

_____   _____
                Payroll Department.   Date

Payroll Change Notice

Sample Form

To: Payroll Department

Please enter the following change/s in your records to take effect _____

Date & Time

Employee _____

Social Security No. _____

Clock No. _____

The Change/s

✓ Check all Applicable Boxes	From	To
■ Department		
■ Job		
■ Shift		
■ Rate		
■		

Reason for the Change/s

■ Hired	■ Transfer	■ Length of Service Increase	■ Retirement
■ Re-hired	■ Merit Increase	■ Re-evaluation of Existing Job	■ Layoff
■ Promotion	■ Union Scale	■ Resignation	■ Discharge
	■ Demotion	■ Probationary Period Completed	

■ Leave of Absence from _____ until _____
Date   Date

■ Other (Explain) _____

Change Authorized by_____ Date _____

Overtime Compensation   3060

Comment

In establishing a company policy for overtime compensation, you must consider federal and state legislation and regulations governing wage and salary practices. Some of the legislation is generally reviewed below. However, before you establish a company policy in this area, seek expert assistance from federal or state, or both, agencies or an attorney to ensure compliance with all applicable laws.

The Fair Labor Standards Act of 1938 (FLSA) covers four areas: minimum wage, equal pay, overtime, and child labor standards. These comments only apply to the general rules regarding overtime compensation and typical exemptions from those provisions.

Generally, the FLSA applies to the employer-employee relationship and not to the employer-independent contractor relationship. The primary factor in determining the employment relationship is the amount of control the employer has over the employee, but the test is liberally construed in favor of finding the employer-employee relationship. An employer who incorrectly characterizes a relationship as an independent contractual one can incur significant liability, including personal liability, for Social Security and federal and state unemployment taxes which were not withheld. Other tests may be used, and consultation with your attorney is recommended.

If the employee-employer relationship exists and if either the employee or the employer is subject to the FLSA, compliance is required. In order to be subject to the FLSA, either the employee or the employer must be engaged in interstate commerce. If the employee is so engaged, then only he or she is covered by the FLSA. If the employer is covered, then all of the employees are covered whether they are individually engaged in interstate commerce or not.

Some businesses are specifically named in the Act as covered, e.g., clothing or fabric laundering, cleaning, or repairing. You should seek expert advice if you are in doubt about whether the FLSA applies to your company or your employees.

The Act requires that all employees who work in excess of a 40-hour workweek must be paid at a rate of one and one-half times their "regular rate" for all hours worked in excess of 40. "Regular rate" is defined in the Act. Each workweek stands alone and hours may not be averaged over two or more work weeks. Once an employee's workweek has been established, it may be changed but only if the change is not designed to avoid paying overtime.

The FLSA defines a number of distinct employee classification exemptions, even if those employees are engaged in interstate commerce or the employer is covered. The more commonly used exemptions are: executive, administrative, professional, and outside sales. Remember, the Act specifies more than these four, and it would be wise to check if one of these covers some or all of your employees. The Act and its accompanying regulations provide certain tests and examples to assist employers in determining whether or not particular employees are exempt. The regulations are complex and not capable of brief description. Review the regulations or consult your legal adviser.

Generally, if an executive, administrative, or professional employee performs certain enumerated duties and responsibilities and is paid a salary of $250 per week or more, the employee is exempt from mandatory overtime compensation. However, certain employees paid a salary of less than $250 per week, but at least $155 per week, who meet the additional duties and responsibilities required by the regulations, will also be exempt.

The exemption for outside salespeople is detailed in a series of federal regulations. Generally, a salesperson must be employed to make sales or take orders, not to provide service. He or she must be customarily and regularly doing such sales work away from the employer's place of business. Additionally, work other than that described above, or incidental to it, such as writing sales reports or attending sales meetings, must not exceed 20% of the workweek hours of non-exempt employees. The outside salesperson is exempt if he or she meets these requirements.

The burden of proof falls on the employer claiming an exemption. Use caution and consult an expert in this area for specific advice relating to coverage and exemptions. Do not try to delineate the definition of exempt and non-exempt classifications in your policy without expert assistance, unless you do so in the most general of terms. See the policy, *Employment Classifications — Section 2080.* In recent years, many employees thought to be exempt by their employers have successfully claimed back overtime pay. This can result in significant expense to the employer.

Other federal laws besides the FLSA also regulate wages and hours. These laws, however, apply only if you have a federal government contract or subcontract, and only if the value of the contract exceeds a specified limit — usually very low. They include The Walsh–Healy Act ("goods," $10,000+); The Davis–Bacon Act (construction of public buildings or alterations, $2,000+); The Contract Work Hours Standards Act (construction; expands the FLSA coverage for overtime to all hours in excess of eight in one day in addition to those in excess of 40 in one week); and The Service Contract Act (services, $2,500). Generally, the terms, conditions, and requirements of the applicable laws will be referred to in the documents which solicit bids or proposals for the particular contracts or in the contracts themselves.

Caution

All of these laws carry penalties to encourage compliance. Civil suits by the employee or the government are specified. Certain willful violations are crimes and may result in heavy fines or imprisonment of officers and directors. Officers and directors may have personal liability for unpaid amounts as well. If you violate the laws that apply to federal government contractors, you may have these fines or judgments withheld from future contract payments, and you may be barred from future contracts for a specific period of time. Keep detailed records and hours worked by all employees.

Naturally, you also will have to comply with state laws and regulations in this area, and all states have legislation on wages and hours. For example, you may find that your state requires all employers to pay overtime to employees who work in excess of 8 hours in any given day as well as for the hours worked over the 40-hour standard work week. Some states, such as California, require double time for all hours over 12 in one day or on holidays. Sometimes, the exemptions parallel the federal laws and sometimes not. Some states have special industrial or job classification standards and exemptions, in addition to those provided by the FLSA.

Even though some states require overtime compensation to be paid for all hours over eight in one day, exceptions may be available under state law. One interesting exception available under California's regulations is when an employer, or his or her employees, wants to institute a 10-hour day, four days per week. If two-thirds of the affected employees agree in writing to such a workweek, the employer does not have to pay overtime for the ninth and tenth hours of each day as long as the employees have at least two days off between work weeks. Of course, if one or more of the employees works more than 40 hours in one week, or more than 10 hours in one day, the law requires payment of overtime compensation. Later, if two-thirds of the affected employees vote to curtail the 10-hour day, the employer must comply.

You may conclude that wage and hour legislation and restrictions are intertwined, overlapping, and complex. They are. And this is without touching on other related legislation such as the minimum wage and child labor laws.

Where can you go for help? The U.S. Department of Labor or the local state employment office will provide informal advice. They will also send printed information upon request. There is also a procedure for requesting a formal written opinion from the applicable state agency or the local office of the U.S. Department of Labor, Wage and Hour Division. You should also work closely with your legal counsel.

The FLSA and state laws will require you to keep accurate and detailed employment records on wages or salary paid, hours worked, overtime paid, and deductions — to name a few. Contact your local wage and hour office (state and federal) for a detailed list of the records you must maintain and the length of time that you must preserve them. Also, see the *Comment* to the policy, *Payroll Deductions — Section 3110*.

The law requires that non-exempt employees be paid overtime in applicable situations. The exempt employee is not as fortunate. However, nothing prevents you from providing your exempt employees with some recognition of overtime in appropriate circumstances. Several examples of this recognition are listed in the discussion in the introduction to Chapter 4. You may want to include some of these benefits in your overtime policy for exempt employees. Note the provision on exempt overtime in Alternate Policy 2.

Compensatory Time

Many employers reward non-exempt employees with compensatory time off in lieu of overtime pay. This can prove to be a costly mistake for the employer. Most states restrict the ability of a private employer to provide compensatory time off, especially when it is not made available during the business week in which the overtime is worked. Government employees may be eligible for compensatory time, usually at a rate equal to 1 1/2 hours of compensatory time for each hour of overtime worked.

Overtime Compensation

Alternate Policy 1   3060.1

Non-exempt salaried employees will be paid at the rate of one and one-half times their regular hourly rate of pay for all time worked in excess of 40 hours in any one workweek.

Note: Some state laws require overtime after eight hours in one day for public employees.

Overtime is never at the employee's discretion. It shall only be incurred and paid at the request of the company through the employee's supervisor/manager. Supervisors/managers shall ensure that no unauthorized overtime hours are worked.

Overtime Compensation

Alternate Policy 2   3060.2

Non-exempt employees will be paid at the rate of one and one-half times their regular rate of pay for the following:

1. Hours worked in excess of 40 in a single workweek.
2. Hours worked on official company holidays.

Note: Be sure to correlate this statement with your policy on holidays and holiday pay.

Non-exempt employees will receive double their regular rate of pay for:

1. Hours worked in excess of 12 in a single workday.
2. Hours worked in excess of eight on the seventh workday and following consecutive workdays.

Note: State law on these matters is assumed, unless the employer desires this higher overtime pay even though no requirement exists.

If a non-exempt employee receives shift premium, his or her regular rate of pay includes that premium.

Exempt employees may be eligible for overtime compensation, in appropriate circumstances, for hours worked in excess of a 40-hour workweek. However, managers are encouraged to recognize necessary exempt overtime by allowing compensatory time off to be taken at a time and under conditions mutually agreed upon between the exempt employee and his or her manager. Overtime compensation for exempt employees, other than compensatory time off, must be approved in advance by the (VICE PRESIDENT). Managers making such a request should provide the (VICE PRESIDENT) with a written memorandum stating the reasons for such overtime, the maximum hours requested and the dates that overtime shall be worked.

Note: See general definitions of exempt and non-exempt employees, Employment Classifications — Section 2080.

Meal and Rest Periods   3070

Comment

Both federal and state laws and regulations impact your company's meal and rest period policies.

Often the state laws and regulations will parallel, and sometimes overlap the federal. The federal law in question is the Fair Labor Standards Act (FLSA). It requires that all rest periods be paid time. Meal periods are not paid time if the employee is relieved of all of his or her duties. If the employee is required to eat at his or her desk or machine, then that time must be paid. A meal period of at least 30 minutes is sufficient, although shorter periods may qualify under special circumstances. Some states such as New York require longer periods. Generally, an employer is not required to let an employee leave the premises for meals.

State laws and regulations must be researched to determine any additional standards, restrictions, or requirements in this area. Local law will prevail even if your business is not subject to the FLSA. For guidance regarding coverage, see the *Comment* to *Overtime Compensation — Section 3060*.

The following comments are based on California State Regulations which are probably representative of other states. You should determine your specific local requirements and whether or not your business is subject to them.

Meal Period

If an employee works more than five hours, there must be at least a 30-minute meal period. The meal time need not be paid as long as the employee is relieved of all duties. The meal period can be waived by mutual consent of the employee and employer for employees working six hours or less per day.

Rest Period

Not all state laws require a rest period. However, as a rule, there must be a rest period of at least 10 minutes for every four hours worked at the middle of each four hour period. Employees working fewer than four hours per day are exempt from rest period requirements. There must be a ten minute rest period for every two hours worked beyond the normal eight hour shift. These rest periods are part of regular time worked or overtime hours, or both. The following alternative policies suggest a thirty-minute or an hour meal period and provide slight variations in the wording of the rest period policy.

Meal and Rest Periods

Alternate Policy 1   3070.1

Meal Period — The normal workday is eight hours, commencing at (ADD START TIME) and ending at (ADD CLOSING TIME) with a one-hour unpaid lunch period beginning at noon.

Employees who begin their workday before noon and continue to work past 7:00 PM will be granted an unpaid 30-minute meal period between 5:00 PM and 7:00 PM

Rest Period — Non-exempt employees are permitted two paid 10-minute rest periods. Rest periods are to be scheduled as near the middle of the morning and afternoon as possible.

Note: This policy describes the meal period as unpaid. However, if the employee performs work-related tasks during the meal period, the meal period must be compensated.

Meal and Rest Periods

Alternate Policy 2   3070.2

Meal Period — The required lunch period for all employees is 30 minutes. It may be taken at any time between 11:00 AM and 1:30 PM with the approval of your supervisor/manager.

Rest Period — Each employee is allowed two paid 10-minute rest periods, one for every four hours worked. For every two hours of overtime worked, an additional 10-minute rest period is allowed.

Flextime   3080

Comment

"Flextime" has been introduced into the labor scene to allow employees more control over their work environment. It has many variations, some of which include flexible scheduling and compressed workweeks. Broadly defined, flextime is an arrangement established by management to allow employees to work full time at hours convenient to them.

Before you initiate flextime, consider the impact on management. It may be wise to allow department managers or supervisors to decide if their workload or production schedule will be amenable to flextime. Next, the employees' opinions should be heard. Consider instituting flextime for a trial period only, such as three or six months. Then evaluate both management and employee feedback to see if everyone's expectations are being met. If you decide to continue it, let the employees and their managers readjust their schedules if necessary. Repeat the whole process periodically.

Flextime is not for every company. Its greatest success has been in service companies rather than companies having a production line. Flextime reduces the hours a company or department will be fully staffed, but it expands the number of hours for service. Management's work time may be increased unless supervisors/managers coordinate their schedules to ensure supervisory coverage. Higher employee morale and an increase in the level of trust between employer and employee can outweigh these disadvantages. If your company adopts a flextime policy, you must ensure company records accurately reflect the work time of each employee for purposes of the Fair Labor Standards Act as well as state law.

The flextime policies presented below are only two of several variations. One alternative is to let the employee and supervisor work out the employee's schedule giving consideration to that department's needs. A second alternative, although not flextime, is giving a few hours per week of merit or personal time off with pay. Encourage employees to use this time for short personal absences, such as a doctor's appointment, or to make up for being late to work.

Another alternative is a compressed schedule — a four-day workweek of ten hours per day. The Fair Labor Standards Act and many state labor laws or regulations will allow such a compressed schedule, without having to pay overtime, if a certain high percentage of employees vote for the schedule. These laws or regulations also give the employees the option to terminate it by a vote.

Flextime

Alternate Policy 1   3080.1

Flextime allows our employees optional starting and quitting times to coincide with their personal preference. The flextime employee is expected to be responsible and is trusted to begin and end work without direct supervision.

Available flextime schedules are as follows:

Begin Work	Conclude Work
8:00 AM	4:30 PM
8:15 AM	4:45 PM
8:30 AM	5:00 PM
8:45 AM	5:15 PM
9:00 AM	5:30 PM
9:15 AM	5:45 PM
9:30 AM	6:00 PM

The employee and supervisor/manager are to select a work schedule which ensures effective functioning of the department and is convenient for them.

Once a mutually convenient work day schedule has been chosen by the employee and supervisor/manager, the schedule becomes "fixed" and is to be adhered to without deviation. However, the employee normally may be allowed to change his or her schedule once every six months subject to the supervisor/manager's approval.

Flextime

Alternate Policy 2 3080.2

Employees are given the opportunity to schedule their own working hours within the limitations set by the company to meet its goals and objectives. The only requirement is that the full time employee must work eight hours each day and must arrive and leave within specified two-hour periods. Arrival time can be any time between 6:30 AM and 8:30 AM. Departure time can be anytime between 3:00 PM and 5:00 PM after eight hours of work.

Note: This allows for a minimum of 30 minutes for lunch.

The employee is expected to adhere to the general guidelines on a voluntary basis and to continue to meet job commitments and responsibilities. Another of the responsibilities is consideration of the needs of the work group and avoiding any disruption of others when arriving or departing from the work station.

The employee must accurately fill out his or her time sheet each day. The supervisor/manager is responsible for fair administration of this flextime policy.

Performance Review and Salary Merit Increases   3090

Comment

One of the most researched and discussed management concerns is an equitable and valid performance review process. Often in frustration, after lengthy management discussions on how to properly initiate a performance review process, the company will do nothing or implement a meaningless, vague, or subjective review process.

The challenge to your company is to establish a performance review process that is workable, equitable, ongoing, and as objective as possible. As your organization grows, it must be able to assess its individual and group achievements, as well as recognize and reward those individuals responsible for your company's success.

Performance reviews should provide employees with feedback on their performance. It should offer an opportunity for them to discuss ways of improving their performance and to discuss and establish future employment goals.

For management, performance reviews can:

- Identify a need for employee or department training or both;
- Provide information for person power and organizational planning;
- Reinforce or suggest modifications to the company employee selection process; and
- Improve employee morale when above average performance or extra effort is recognized and rewarded.

Research of the literature indicates that numerous techniques have been tested in search of a better method of performance appraisal.

Some of the methods include:

- The narrative descriptive review where reviews are conducted in response to essay-type questions related to establishing and accomplishing specific employment goals;
- The rank method whereby employees in a work group are rank-ordered by some universal factor or factors, e.g., overall performance;
- A checklist or rating scale; and
- The management by objectives approach.

Federal legislation and court rulings, primarily in the equal employment opportunity area, have identified the following red flags to be aware of in considering your company performance appraisal process.

1. The rating criteria and standards selected must be job-related.

2. Supervisors/managers must have been able to consistently observe the employee in performing assigned tasks.

3. Supervisors/managers must use the same rating criteria.

4. Employees must be rated against standards rationally related to the group to which they functionally belong.

5. Criteria used in rating employees must not be vague or completely subjective and must not unfairly depress scores of protected classes, e.g., women, minorities, disabled.

6. The importance of training supervisors/managers to conduct performance reviews should not be overlooked — all raters must understand what the rating criteria mean and have the interpersonal skills to effectively conduct the performance reviews.

Before management adopts any performance review process, there must be agreement on what standards will be used for ratings or performance appraisal. The process and standards must be fair and just to the employee as well as for the company. Once again, communication is a key to the process. Let your employees know what the process is and by what standards they will be measured. Allow them to make suggestions for improvement of both.

At a minimum, include the following information in your company policy:

- Criteria to be used in the performance review;

- How employee performance will be measured (against what standards);

- Who will do the appraisal(s);

- When the appraisal(s) will be done;

- What feedback will the employee receive;

- Can the employee give input to the process and when;

- What assistance the company will provide in improving performance; and

- The rewards for above-average performance.

We further suggest that your company strive to establish a "coaching" relationship when initiating the performance review process. Although the performance review is intended to be a positive process, sometimes it is not. Every supervisor/manager must be encouraged to evaluate every employee accurately. Where an employee's performance is poor, the appraisal should indicate this clearly and unequivocally. Substandard performance, or even average performance, should not be described in such a way that the employee believes that his or her performance is better than that. Emotions or time constraints must not be allowed to affect or undermine the review process. If an employee is terminated for poor performance, but all of his or her previous appraisals were good or vague, the employee may cause you great difficulty in a wrongful termination lawsuit.

Finally, there are many possible combinations of performance review policies and review forms which can be created. Which type of form will work best for you depends to a certain degree upon your management style and the nature of your employees. For example, a review process which focuses largely on planning goals and objectives may have little relevance to certain job categories, such as clerical or warehouse jobs. These employees may benefit more from a review process which focuses more immediately on productivity and evaluates such skills as quality and quantity of work produced, attitude, and teamwork.

Why is this important? A large majority of wrongful termination claims revolve around a previous positive performance review. How, it is argued, could such a good employee have been fired? Don't fall into this trap. Train your supervisor/manager to be objective and honest in completing reviews.

Three alternate policies follow. Each of the alternate policies include a form for a review process which is closely tailored to the policy which precedes it. With minor language changes, however, any of the forms which follow could be adapted for use with any of the alternate policies. To minimize confusion to the reader, the form which follows Alternate Policy 1 is captioned Employee Work Plan and Performance Appraisal/Criteria for Appraising Demonstrated Performance. Following Alternate Policy 2, you will find a policy called Performance Appraisal. A form labeled Performance Review Outline follows Alternate Policy 3.

Because many combinations of policies and forms can be created, you are also provided with three additional forms which follow the Performance Review Outline. The first two forms are called Employee Performance Review and Employee Work Update. Both of these forms are similar to ones which follow the alternate policies. The Employee Work Update is intended for use by employees and supervisors/managers to be used as a diary to record work-related matters between scheduled reviews. The update would be used to refresh the employee's and supervisor/manager's memories prior to the review.

The final form is the Company Evaluation Form. Its purpose is to provide employees with an opportunity to review the company, their individual work department, their supervisor/manager, and their fellow employees.

The use of this form fosters two-way communication and enables management to learn what its employees feel about the company. If you used this form, don't use it at the same time the employee performance review is undertaken. You may also wish to consider making the employee's signature optional to promote candor and preserve anonymity.

Performance Review and Salary Merit Increases

Alternate Policy 1   3090.1

Note: If salary merit increases are not to be utilized in conjunction with performance reviews, the words "and salary merit increases" should be deleted.

(COMPANY) has adopted a management by objectives approach to performance appraisal. Each employee is given the opportunity to set individual written goals. He or she will be evaluated based on how well these goals have been met. Three months after an employee joins the company, the supervisor/manager and employee will meet to establish employment goals consistent with the business objectives of the company and the employee's department. The first performance review will occur near the end of the next three months, preferably on a date agreed to in writing. All future employee performance reviews will be scheduled at six month intervals and noted in the preceding appraisal report.

It is the supervisor's/manager's responsibility to develop and maintain a work environment in which employees can openly discuss performance and develop plans. The employee will be notified in writing ten days in advance of the performance review date. Also included in the notification will be the time, place, and the discussion topics for the employee to prepare for the review. The employee, as well as the supervisor/manager, is to bring the following to the review meeting:

1. A summary statement of the progress made toward meeting his or her employment goals;

2. Examples of job-related areas demonstrating greatest strengths and identifying areas where additional training is needed;

3. An outline of job-related tasks in which the employee can participate in to improve performance;

4. A recommendation of job responsibilities and goals to be established for the next six-month period;

5. A summary of overall employment performance.

The Employee Work Plan and Performance Appraisal/Criteria for Appraising Demonstrated Performance form which follows this policy is to be used for the performance review. The Employee Work Plan and Performance Appraisal portion of this form serves as a planning tool by which employees and their supervisor/managers set forth specific examples of job performance. The Criteria for Appraising Demonstrated Performance portion of the form is

Performance Review and Salary Merit Increases

Alternate Policy 1 (continued)   3090.1

used to evaluate overall employee performance based on the specific examples referred to on the Employee Work Plan and Performance Appraisal portion. Employees and their supervisor/manager should complete both portions of the form.

The supervisor/manager is responsible for establishing a relaxed atmosphere at the performance review and encouraging two-way communication. The discussion should be conducted in a positive manner, in complete privacy, and with no interruptions. The supervisor/manager shall verify that the employee is familiar with his or her job duties, previous goals, and the appraisal criteria or factors. At the conclusion of the performance appraisal, the employee will be requested to sign the appraisal verifying that he or she participated in the evaluation. The employee should be encouraged to submit comments about the appraisal which will become part of the record. A date for the next appraisal shall be agreed upon and noted on the appraisal form. The employee must be given a signed copy of the appraisal. The appraisal is then submitted for review by the next level of management.

(COMPANY) believes that pay increases should be related to an employee's performance. Following performance reviews, the supervisor/manager will rank the employee's performance according to his or her relative level of contribution to the company. Factors will include how well the employee has met the objectives agreed upon in the last review, whether it be the initial meeting or the following six-month review; and the employee's level of contribution to the success of the department/division relative to other employees. The supervisor/manager will rank all department/division employees in one of four groupings:

1. Outstanding
2. Very Good
3. Good
4. Marginal
5. Unsatisfactory

A decision relating to the employee's merit increase in pay will be made by the supervisor/manager after the review and ranking process has been completed. Any merit increase in pay will be retroactive to the date of performance appraisal. The supervisor/manager will forward a merit increase recommendation with the appraisal to the next level of management. Merit increases in pay are neither automatic nor periodic. They are reserved for employees who show skills improvement and higher than average performance. Information about rates of pay and merit increases in pay, if any, are deemed to be confidential matters between the company and each employee and are not to be discussed among employees.

Note: If performance or merit pay isn't to be included, delete the three preceding paragraphs.

Performance Review and Salary Merit Increases

Alternate Policy 2   3090.2

All employees of (COMPANY) will participate in a performance review with their supervisor/manager based on the following schedule:

1. Twice a year during (MONTH) and (MONTH)

Note: Typically, the review should be approximately six months after employee is hired and every six to twelve months thereafter. Executive or management employees may only require a yearly review.

2. As often as is warranted by the job situation and the employee's performance.

The performance review will be completed in writing after the completion of an interview between the employee and his or her supervisor/manager. The employee is encouraged to share in the review process by adding written comments to the evaluation form.

The employee is also encouraged to:
- Inquire about his or her performance from time to time;
- Accept additional responsibilities and show initiative;
- Review opportunities for advancement within the department or job classification;
- Ask for assistance in developing a goal-oriented path for advancement within the department or company;
- Learn about training available to assist the employee in skills improvement, promotion, or lateral transfer.

The supervisor/manager will determine if a merit increase is warranted at the time of the performance review. It is (COMPANY) policy to reward employees with merit increases in salary for dedication in their work, extra effort, and better-than-average performance. Management does not award merit increases on an automatic basis or at any pre-set interval. Merit increase recommendations must be approved by the next level of management and submitted to the personnel department for final review and approval. All approved merit increases will be made retroactive to the first workday of the week of performance review. Information pertaining to rates of pay and merit increases in pay, if any, are deemed to be confidential matters between the company and each employee and are not to be discussed among employees.

Note: If performance or merit pay is not to be included, delete the preceding two paragraphs

Performance Review and Salary Merit Increases

Alternate Policy 3   3090.3
___

All employees will participate in a performance review process. The process provides greater employee participation in personal growth and a greater degree of employee self-management. Thirty days after each employee joins (COMPANY), the employee will draft objectives to be met in the position within the next 90 days. The employee's manager will complete a similar list, and the two will meet and agree on the performance objectives to be achieved at the end of 120 days. An important part of this performance planning will be prioritizing the objectives. The employee or manager may request an interim progress review at anytime during the following 90 days.

The 120-day evaluation shall consist of reviewing results and achievements against the established objectives, reviewing the priorities, and establishing the next set of objectives for future evaluations. The focus for the evaluation will be on how closely the employee is meeting his or her potential in the assigned position. The required terminology to be used in the evaluation will be "exceeded," "achieved," or "below" with respect to the standards set in the defined objectives.

Here are some performance factors that should be considered in the development of employee objectives:

- Organizational skill
- Planning skill
- Decision making
- Job commitment
- Knowledge of field
- Communications
- Teamwork

Employee Work Plan and Performance Appraisal

(COMPANY) has adopted a management by objectives approach to performance reviews. Both employees and their supervisors/managers should respond in writing to the specific issues raised below prior to the scheduled review. Employees will be notified at least ten days prior to the scheduled review. At the review, the employee and his or her supervisor/manager will discuss and compare each other's response to the issues. The first page should be considered a planning tool to prepare for the review session. Employees and their supervisors/managers should record specific examples of employee conduct and performance. The criteria listed on the reverse side is used to evaluate the employee's overall performance.

1. Major responsibilities of the job _____

_____

2. Specific accomplishments since last performance appraisal _____

_____

3. Specific examples of work quality _____

_____

4. Specific examples of work quantity_____

_____

5. Specific examples of employee's judgment in work performance_____

_____

6. Specific examples of employee's initiative in completing assigned tasks_____

_____

7. Specific examples of employee's teamwork with fellow employees_____

_____

_____

_____

Employee Work Plan and Performance Appraisal (continued)

8. Specific examples of employee's dependability in completing tasks _____

_____

_____

9. Achievement of employee's goals _____

_____

10. Summarize employee's performance _____

_____

11. Action to be taken to improve performance _____

_____

12. Employee's goals for next six months. _____

_____

13. Employee comments — employee may put additional comments on a separate sheet.

_____

_____

_____

_____

_____

_____

Criteria For Appraising Demonstrated Performance

1. Work quality — reliability, accuracy, neatness of work _____

_____

2. Work quantity — amount of work produced_____

_____

3. Judgment — ability to make sound decisions in performing work tasks_____

_____

4. Initiative — interest shown in job, dedication, willingness to complete tasks, and accept
   additional work_____

_____

_____

5. Teamwork — relationship with fellow employees in department/division _____

_____

_____

6. Dependability — reliability and responsiveness in completing assigned tasks _____

_____

_____

7. Achievement of goals and objectives by employee — express as 100%, 50% etc. _____

_____

I am signing this performance appraisal to indicate that my supervisor and I have met to discuss
the above comments.

_____   _____
Employee's Signature   Date

_____   _____
Manager's Signature   Date

Performance Appraisal

Employee's Name: _____ Job Title: _____

Supervisor's Name: _____ Performance Review Date: _____

The following scale should be used in evaluating the employee's performance when compared to the norm of his or her position.

Outstanding — Employee consistently meets, and in many instances exceeds, established standards and desired results;

Very Good — Employee consistently meets established standards; sometimes exceeds, and never falls short of desired results;

Satisfactory — Employee meets established standards; usually meets and seldom falls short of desired results; and

Development Needed — Employee meets established standards in some instances but lacks consistency; seldom exceeds and frequently falls short of desired results from time to time.

Performs Job Skills:	Outstanding	Very Good	Satisfactory	Development Needed	Comments
Knowledge of Work:					
Ability to Organize:					
Quality of Work:					
Quantity of Work:					
Communication:					
Teamwork:					
Meets Deadlines:					
Dependability:					
Judgment:					
Attitude:					
Problem Solving:					

Areas needing improvement: _____

Performance Appraisal (continued)

Areas where improvement has been made _____

_____

_____

Objectives met since last review _____

_____

_____

Objectives set for next evaluation period _____

_____

_____

Summary of evaluation_____

_____

_____

Employee comments: (Separate sheet may be attached.)_____

_____

_____

_____

_____

_____

Employee Signature   Date

_____

Manager Signature   Date

Performance Appraisal Definitions

The following definitions should assist you in completing the Performance Appraisal Form:

Term	Definition
Performs Job Skills	Ability to perform assigned job tasks.
Knowledge of Work	Technical knowledge of job and related work.
Ability to Organize	Effectiveness in planning own work.
Quality of Work	Accuracy of work; freedom from errors.
Quantity of Work	Output of work; speed.
Communication	Effective communication with manager and others.
Teamwork	Ability to work together within the department.
Meets Deadlines	Timeliness in performing work; deadlines.
Dependability	Reliability in carrying out assignments conscientiously.
Judgment	Ability to obtain and analyze facts and apply sound judgement.
Attitude	Positive attitude and enthusiasm to work and others.
Problem Solving	Ability to develop more efficient means to job tasks.

Performance Review Outline

All employees participate in a company-wide review process. Prior to each review, both the employee and his or her supervisor/manager will draft responses to the criteria described below. The review will consist in part of a comparison of the responses prepared by the employee and the supervisor/manager. Both parties will also work together to develop new objectives and priorities to achieve prior to the next scheduled review.

Employee Objectives:

1. _____

2. _____

3. _____

Results to Achieve:_____

_____

Priorities: _____

_____

Interim Review (list dates):

1. _____

2. _____

3. _____

Change in Objectives:_____

Change in Priorities:_____

Performance Evaluation: _____

Results and Achievements:_____

_____

New Objectives and Priorities:_____

_____ Next Review Date: _____

_____
Employee's Signature   Date

_____
Manager's Signature   Date

Employee Performance Review

Please respond in writing to the questions listed below. Space has been provided for your response. If you need additional space to answer questions, you may attach a separate sheet.

The initial review will be conducted at the end of 90 days following the date your employment began. For that review, you should only complete Item 1. You and your supervisor/manager will work together during the review to complete the remainder of the form. For employees who have completed the initial review, you should complete all of the items except Item 1.

1. During the past three months you've had the opportunity to learn more about the company and your individual job responsibilities. Do you feel that you have a full understanding of your job responsibilities? Please list your job responsibilities, as you understand them.

2. What are your personal employment goals?

3. Would you like more or less responsibility?

4. Would you like different responsibilities? If so, what?

Employee Performance Review (continued)

5. For your job, what are your greatest strengths? _____

_____

_____

6. How can the company utilize your strengths more effectively? _____

_____

_____

7. Please identify any areas where you feel you need additional training: _____

_____

_____

8. What can the company do to help you in these areas? _____

_____

_____

9. What goals have you established for yourself to accomplish before your next review?

_____

_____

_____

10. How would you evaluate your overall employment performance and accomplishment of employment goals since your last review? _____

_____

_____

_____

_____

Employee Signature   Date

_____

Manager Signature   Date

Employee Work Update

The purpose of this form is to assist employees and managers in preparing for performance reviews. This form works similar to a diary. As an event occurs which might be relevant for review purposes, make a note of the event and the date on this form. This information will refresh your memory at review time.

Name of Employee _____

1. Major responsibilities of the job: _____

_____

2. Specific accomplishments since last review: _____

_____

3. Specific examples of work quality: _____

_____

4. Specific examples of work quantity: _____

_____

5. Specific examples of employee initiative in completing assigned tasks: _____

_____

6. Specific examples of employee judgment: _____

_____

7. Specific examples of employee teamwork: _____

8. Specific examples of employee dependability: _____

9. Specific examples of employee attitude: _____

_____

10. Specific examples of employee creativity: _____

_____

11. Goals achieved since last review: _____

_____

12. Specific examples of employee communication skills: _____

_____

13. Any other matters which are relevant for review and reflect on employee skills and ability:

_____

Company Evaluation Form

Note: *Complete this company evaluation form at a time separate and apart from the employee evaluation. The responses should not impact an employee's evaluation. The purpose of this form is to provide employees with the opportunity to participate in the review process by evaluating the performance of their department manager, their department, in general, and employees within their department. In some circumstances, employees will be asked to review the manager of a different department and that department where the departments have a significant overlap with one another.*

Please respond to the following statements of fact by indicating the numbered response that most closely applies.

1 = You strongly agree with the statement.

2 = You moderately agree with the statement.

3 = You moderately disagree with the statement.

4 = You strongly disagree with the statement.

The Company:

1. Is quality-oriented: _____

2. Promotes teamwork and cooperation: _____

3. Has created a positive work environment: _____

4. Shows consideration and respect for its employees: _____

Are there any specific instances which impact on any of your answers above? Please explain:

_____

_____

Do you have any specific suggestions or comments concerning the company as a whole?

_____

_____

If _____ were different, the company would be a better place to work.

Company Evaluation Form (continued)

My Department:

1. Department (please list your department):_____

2. Is quality-oriented: _____

3. Works as a team: _____

4. Meets its deadlines: _____

5. Maintains a positive work attitude: _____

Are there any specific instances which impact on any of your answers above? Please

explain: _____

_____

Do you have any specific suggestions or comments concerning your department?

_____

_____

If _____ were different, my
department would be a better place to work.

My Manager:

1. Clearly communicates what is expected of me: _____

2. Listens to me: _____

3. Promotes teamwork and cooperation: _____

4. Distributes workload fairly: _____

5. Is a good motivator: _____

6. Encourages employee feedback: _____

7. Shows consideration and respect for employees: _____

Company Evaluation Form (continued)

Are there any specific instances which impact on any of your answers above? Please explain:

_____

_____

Do you have any specific suggestions or comments concerning your manager?

_____

_____

Employees Within My Department:

1. Have a positive work attitude: _____

2. Are supportive of one another: _____

3. Contribute fairly to department workload: _____

4. Are dependable: _____

5. Work well together: _____

6. Communicate effectively: _____

Are there any specific instances which impact on any of your answers above? Please explain:

_____

_____

Do you have any specific suggestions or comments concerning the employees within your department?_____

_____

Signature:_____(optional)   Date:_____

Please return to (VICE PRESIDENT) on or before _____

Salary Administration 3100

Comment

One of the greatest challenges in today's business is the management of human resources for optimum yield rather than for minimum cost. All managers must ensure that:

- Employee power is not misused;
- Everyone does a full day's work for a full day's pay;
- Accidents are held to a minimum;
- Employee turnover is minimized; and
- Time and materials are not wasted.

In the management of a wage administration program, human resource accounting puts a specific dollar asset value on an individual's or a department's specific contributions to the company. For managers to remain effective in human resource accounting, job descriptions must be reviewed and updated regularly.

Employee evaluations must be frequent and the supervisor must help the employee work closer to potential through realistic and supportive appraisal. The company must also continue to be aware of pay survey information and significant changes.

To emphasize that pay is tied to productivity, some managers question the assumption that performance appraisals are to be conducted in conjunction with merit pay reviews. One faction of management continues to argue that linking appraisals with salary increases is an effective way of rewarding excellent employees while notifying poor performers that their work is substandard.

On the other hand, there is an equal number of managers who believe performance reviews should be completed periodically with the discussion of salaries held separately. By separating appraisals from salary increases, these managers contend that they focus an employee's attention on the importance of achieving long-term goals rather than receiving monetary awards.

Your company may choose to include information about salary administration in a separate manual provided to department managers who have the responsibility of budgeting the company's compensation package rather than including the language in the policy manual. Similarly, smaller companies may utilize only one or two persons in establishing a compensation package. In this case, this section should be eliminated.

Salary Administration

Alternate Policy 1   3100.1

The management staff will meet during the first quarter of each year to budget the company's compensation package. They will establish a compensation pool for:

1. Pay increases;

2. Monies to be allocated to the continuation and expansion of the company benefits program; and

3. Monies to be budgeted for the addition of new employees.

Department managers will meet with the fiscal officer to establish the percentage of monies to be allocated to each department for annual pay increases. Pay increases are not granted on an automatic basis but only on the basis of demonstrated performance and documented contributions to the company. A performance appraisal is one of several criteria which will be used to support the department manager's recommendation for salary adjustment and adjustment amount. Other criteria include, but are not limited to, the actual amount of money allocated to the department, pay survey data, and impact of an individual on company profit and loss. Recommendations will be submitted to the president for final approval. Salary adjustment letters will be distributed during the month of June and become effective July 1.

Salary Administration

Alternate Policy 2   3100.2

It is (COMPANY) policy to award annual merit increases to employees for their dedication to the growth of the company, based on their skills, improvement, and outstanding performance. Every employee is eligible for a merit increase. However, merit increases are not automatic. Following the employee's performance review, the manager will rank the employee's performance according to his or her relative level of contribution to the company. Factors will include, without limitation, how well the employee has met the objectives agreed upon in the last review and the employee's level of contribution to the success of the department relative to other employees. Employees will be ranked as 1) Outstanding; 2) Very Good; 3) Good; and 4) Marginal. The manager will forward a merit increase recommendation with the appraisal to the president for final approval. Any merit increase will be retroactive to the date of the performance appraisal.

Payroll Deductions 3110

Comment

As an employer, you have certain obligations to federal, state, and local governments regarding the withholding of taxes from the salaries of your employees and the payment of various payroll taxes to the government. Your obligations, the procedures to be followed, and the reporting requirements imposed are discussed in *IRS Circular E — Employer's Tax Guide*. The state and local jurisdictions have their own publications describing requirements and procedures.

Federal income taxes are withheld on all wages paid to an employee above a certain minimum. This minimum is governed by the number of withholding allowances claimed by the employee on *IRS Form W-4*. Every employee is required to fill out a *W-4*. Social Security taxes apply to all wages earned by an employee during a year up to a maximum amount. This amount and the tax rate increase from year to year, so you need to check the current amount and the rate each year. The percentage deduction from the employee's wages is matched by an additional tax paid by the employer. Federal unemployment taxes are paid by the employer based on a set formula. The rates vary from time to time with new legislation. As an employer, you are, in effect, an agent of the government in collecting income, Social Security, and federal unemployment taxes. This is also true for state and city income taxes and any other state or local employment tax, such as disability insurance.

Any officer or other executive who has the responsibility to withhold and pay these taxes, and fails to do so, may become personally liable for the taxes, if the company cannot pay. This obligation is aggressively enforced.

Every employee should receive an itemized written statement from the employer for every pay period. The statement should contain all of the information specified in the *Comment to Workday, Payday and Pay Advances — Sections 3030–3050*.

Every employer who withholds taxes is also required to provide every employee with an annual *Wage and Tax Statement — Form W-2* for the calendar year. The *W-2* must be provided to each employee by January 31st of the following year, or earlier if the employee terminates. Copies of all employee *W-2s*, including a summary form (*W-3*), must be filed with the IRS by the last day of February.

Usually, the state or local jurisdiction will allow combined reporting of applicable state or local deductions using the federal forms.

You should also report other employee payroll deductions which relate to the company fringe benefit package, if these costs are paid by the employee.

A policy is usually necessary to explain to your employees the types of deductions that will be made from their payroll check. You should also refer to any voluntary deductions for contributions to a stock plan, pension plan, or credit union, if applicable to your company.

Payroll Deductions

Policy   3110.1

The following mandatory deductions will be made from every employee's gross wages: federal income tax, Social Security FICA tax, and applicable city and state taxes.

Every employee must fill out and sign a federal withholding allowance certificate, IRS Form W-4, on or before his or her first day on the job. This form must be completed in accordance with federal regulations. The employee may fill out a new W-4 at anytime when his or her circumstances change. Employees who paid no federal income tax for the preceding year and who expect to pay no income tax for the current year may fill out an Exemption From Withholding Certificate, IRS Form W-4E. Employees are expected to comply with the instructions on Form W-4. Questions regarding the propriety of claimed deductions may be referred to the IRS in certain circumstances.

Other optional deductions include the portion of group health insurance not paid by the company, which is deducted from each payroll check. Other voluntary contributions, such as credit union and pension plan, are also deducted each pay period.

Every employee will receive an annual Wage and Tax Statement, IRS Form W-2, for the preceding year on or before January 31. Any employee who believes that his or her deductions are incorrect for any pay period, or on Form W-2, should check with the (PAYROLL DEPARTMENT) immediately. Your supervisor/manager will give you time to do this during the workday.

Shift Premium   3120

Comment

The intent of a shift premium policy is to provide an incentive to employees, as well as additional compensation, for working non-daytime shift hours on a regular basis. The premiums stated in each alternate policy, as well as the shift times, are for example only.

Many factors should be considered in determining what level of premium will be sufficient incentive to work each shift as well as economical with respect to productivity.

Experimentation may be counterproductive to good morale. You may want to consult a compensation analyst for a study of your particular situation and his or her recommendations.

Shift Premium

Alternate Policy 1   3120.1

Employees working non-daytime shifts are paid a premium above their base rate for all hours worked. This premium pay will be included in pay received for any paid leave including vacation, sick leave, and holidays. It will not be considered for purpose of the profit-sharing program or stock purchase plan. Premiums will not be included in severance pay or pay in lieu of notice.

Note: The preceding sentences should coordinate with the welfare plan documents that your company has adopted.

The following premiums will apply to the shift indicated:

1. A 10% premium of the base pay rate for night shift (3:00 PM to 11:30 PM);

2. A 5% premium of the night shift pay rate for graveyard shift (10:00 PM to 6:30 AM).

Shift Premium

Alternate Policy 2   3120.2

Employees are paid a premium rate for hours worked that are not considered the normal daytime shift. The rates are established as follows:

1. A 7.5% premium of the base rate for second shift (3:00 PM to 11:30 PM);

2. A 15% premium of the base pay rate for third shift (10:00 PM to 6:30 AM).

Paid time off is reimbursed at the regular daytime shift rate without premiums.

Footnotes

3030-3050 — Workday, Payday, and Pay Advances

1. Cal. Lab. Code § 204.
2. Cal. Lab. Code § 207.
3. 29 C.F.R. § 516.2(a).

Chapter 4

Employee Benefits

Introduction

Employee benefits today can no longer be considered fringe. Once known as fringe benefits and accounting for 2 to 3% of the payroll cost, their security and non-tax advantages are significant to the employee. Their cost is significant to the employer. Many employees view the benefits package as a matter of entitlement with no appreciation of the costs involved. Employers should try to make employees aware of the cost of these programs.

In developing the company employee benefit program, the challenge is to provide a package of policies that will enhance employee morale and lead to greater productivity. Obviously, you have to pay for these objectives. Employee benefit packages today frequently exceed 50% of direct labor cost, and this rate is projected to climb steadily over the coming years. However, the cost is justifiable for the resulting high morale and greater productivity.

Another challenge to your organization is to keep abreast of the types of benefits provided by other companies and to update your benefit package to provide an attractive and competitive compensation program. Today's employees are better educated, better informed, and more aware of economic incentives than in previous years. They want and expect to share their views and opinions with management.

Also, times of inflation and relatively high mobility increases the communication among employees in comparing benefit packages from company to company. Consider a survey of your employees to determine their opinions and preferences about the types of benefits potentially available. Creativity and flexibility in the development of benefit programs will provide a strong allegiance between the company and its employees. Company-provided benefits and services can be used as an important marketing tool to attract and retain quality personnel.

The compensation package developed for middle management employees is usually comprised of the same benefits received by their subordinates with some trickling down of benefits from top management. Remember, that exempt middle management employees share a considerable amount of the responsibility for a company's success but do not share in the same benefits which top management reserves for itself. There appears to be some justification to recognize middle management's contribution in ways other than what the non-exempt employee has come to expect.

Here are some of the compensation alternatives you might consider for exempt employees:

- Larger amounts of life insurance proportional to base pay
- Opportunities to attend professional meetings
- Receipt of company subscriptions to professional newspapers, magazines, and journals
- Occasional use of a company car
- Special parking places
- Club memberships
- Free tickets to entertainment events
- Use of special corporate entertainment facilities
- Bonus plans
- Time off or use of company resources, or both, to write a paper for presentation to a professional organization
- Opportunities to select special challenging organizational assignments
- Opportunities to take a guest to professional meetings at company expense
- Stock options
- Free child care or child care allowance

Employers that provide certain benefits to their employees will have to comply with the requirements of the Employee Retirement Income Security Act, commonly known as ERISA. The act deals with two kinds of employee benefit plans: pension plans and welfare plans. Pension plans include tax-qualified retirement plans, profit-sharing plans, employee stock ownership plans (ESOPs) and individual retirement accounts (IRAs). Welfare plans include health insurance, long-term disability, group life, and accidental death insurance plans. Some of the ERISA requirements are discussed under two sections: *Insurance — Section 4010,* and *Pension, Profit-Sharing, and Retirement Plans — Section 4130.* Many employee benefits are considered to be additional compensation, such as vacation and sick leave pay, and are not pension or welfare plans under ERISA.

A related issue to consider is what benefits, if any, to provide to your sales staff. Often, this issue is preceded by a determination of whether your sales staff is considered to be employees or independent contractors. Employees are generally eligible for some or all of the benefits made available to other company employees. Independent contractors are not. Although the key determinant is the amount of control exercised by the employer, each state imposes its own tests for unemployment and workers' compensation purposes.

Remember that different benefit programs may have different income tax consequences to you and to the employee. Check with your legal adviser to develop a policy which will work best for you.

Insurance   4010

Comment

The Consolidated Omnibus Budget Reconciliation Act, or COBRA, requires companies with 20 or more employees to offer the same group health benefits, including dental and vision coverage, that is provided for current employees to:

- Employees who have been terminated for other than gross misconduct or laid off or who have quit voluntarily;
- Employees whose hours have been reduced;
- Widowed or divorced spouses of employees;
- Employees eligible for Medicare; and
- Children of employees who lose dependent status.

Under COBRA, as soon as employees become eligible for group health benefits, they and certain dependents are entitled to continued coverage at the employee's expense for up to 36 months after the qualifying event. Employers are also responsible for notifying all individuals who qualify for continued coverage of their eligibility. Companies can charge former employees, and their dependents requesting continued coverage, 100% of the cost of providing such benefits, plus a 2% surcharge. In addition, COBRA does not obligate the employer to continue the group health plan. The plan may be terminated at any time as long as it is terminated for all employees.

Terminated employees have 60 days to decide if they want to continue receiving health benefits under COBRA. It is wise to provide the eligibility notice to the employee in writing upon termination. The notice should inform the employee about the 60-day period for coverage continuation, the premium amount, the due date for premiums, and any other facts regarding COBRA or their continued coverage.

Employers who fail to comply with regulations will not be allowed to deduct any health plan contributions. Employers can also be fined up to $100 per day if they do not meet notification requirements. There can be other penalties as well for individual company officers.

Be aware of this act and how it might affect you as you select and offer insurance to your employees. Many states have similar requirements which will apply to smaller companies as well. Consult with a knowledgeable insurance specialist before making definite commitments on a plan. Many insurance companies or brokers can provide information and forms necessary to comply with COBRA.

An insurance plan is usually developed within companies to provide a number of compensation components. Each of these components may have a variety of features.

Some of these may be made available only to certain employees or certain groups of employees, if you have fewer than 25 employees.

Your policy should provide:

- A brief and general statement about the coverage;
- An indication of the portion of the premium costs the company will underwrite;
- An identification of the length of time new employees must wait for coverage to begin; and
- A discussion of employee conversion privileges.

Because of the complexity of insurance compensation components, it is wise to refer the employee to the detailed insurance brochures, the Summary Plan Description (SPD) or to the group policy.

Employers offering a health benefits plan to their employees may also be required to offer a membership in a qualified health maintenance organization (HMO) as an alternative in certain situations.

The circumstances under which this alternative becomes a requirement are found in The Health Maintenance Organization Act of 1973 and the regulations that interpret that Act. Basically, if you employ 25 full-time or part-time employees and are subject to the Fair Labor Standards Act, the HMO Act applies to you. If you receive a timely and complete request for inclusion from at least one qualified HMO, your company will probably have to include the HMO as an alternative to its health benefits plan. If you receive such a request, contact an expert in the health law field for advice. An HMO request does not occur often, but it's important to be aware of the law.

The insurance components covered by this policy are considered welfare plans under ERISA. One requirement under ERISA for all small businesses is the preparation of a Summary Plan Description (SPD) for each welfare plan. The SPD must be distributed to all employees who are covered by the plan. It must contain certain required information about the welfare plan, including an ERISA Rights Statement. These items are specified by U.S. Department of Labor Regulations.

Many insurance companies or brokers will provide these SPDs for the company. Ask them to prepare the document for each of the plans you are buying as part of their services. It is quite a savings of time and money.

The SPD must be given to each covered employee within 120 days of plan adoption and for new employees, 90 days after they are covered.

Once a company has 100 or more employees, ERISA requirements become more numerous and complex. Basically, these requirements involve several reports which must be filed annually with the U.S. Department of Labor and a Summary Annual Report which must be given to each covered employee every year.

Consult an expert in this area — most competent insurance companies or brokers can assist you — or contact the U.S. Department of Labor for information regarding ERISA requirements. The IRS also has detailed regulations concerning welfare plans, and compliance with them is essential to ensure deductibility of the expenses of these plans. Your tax adviser is a source of information about these requirements.

Finally, state law should also be checked. As in other areas, state law may provide coverage requirements which differ from federal law requirements.

Two alternative policy statements are provided on the following pages. One is very brief and refers the employee to the Summary Plan Description booklets and to the personnel department for assistance on specific insurance questions.

The second statement provides a more detailed explanation of the company insurance program. Please note the second alternative is not intended to qualify as an SPD. Due to the variety of plans available, the second policy is more of a rough outline to be tailored for the specific insurance components the company makes available.

Insurance

Alternate Policy 1   4010.1

(COMPANY) recognizes the needs of employees for financial protection in the event of illness or injuries that result in medical expense and loss of income. Providing adequate, cost-effective medical, (DENTAL), (DISABILITY), and (LIFE) insurance protection is a concern of the company. The company has selected several plans designed to meet the employees' needs. All are financially subsidized by the company to keep the employee's cost to a minimum. Certain coverage are offered at no cost to the employee.

*Note: **Whether or not coverage for dependents is provided and at whose cost should be addressed by using one of the following: "Coverage of dependents of employees is also available at the expense of the employee requesting coverage," or "Coverage for dependents of employees is available at no cost to the employee subject to the terms of the insurance plans."***

The plans offered are somewhat complex. For this reason, the Summary Plan Descriptions (SPD) or brochures which describe each plan should be referred to for specific information. A staff member in the personnel department is available to answer specific insurance questions. During new employee orientation, the cost, coverage, eligibility requirements and conversion privileges of each plan will be explained in detail. You will be provided a copy of the Summary Plan Description for each plan that you elect after you or your dependents become covered. The terms and conditions of the insurance policy, itself, will control over any inconsistent descriptions contained in this manual.

(COMPANY) reserves the right to change insurance companies or to modify or terminate eligibility requirements, benefits, or coverage at any time.

Insurance

Alternate Policy 2   4010.2

(COMPANY) provides group life insurance, group health insurance, and a group disability program for its employees at no cost to the employees.

Note: See Note to Alternate Policy 1 on preceding page.

The health insurance program includes hospital, accidental injury, and dental benefits. For specific questions on coverage of the programs, contact the insurance representative in the (ACCOUNTING DEPARTMENT). The company benefit programs are explicitly defined in legal documents, including insurance contracts, official plan texts, and trust agreements. In the event of a conflict between these documents and this policy, the formal language of the plan document and not the informal wording of this policy must govern. All of these official documents are readily available in the (ACCOUNTING DEPARTMENT).

Note: Tailor to specific policy definitions and classes of employees.

Eligibility

1. The employee is eligible for coverage on the (31st) day after his or her first day on the job.
2. Dependents of the employee are eligible for participation in the group medical and dental insurance program at no cost to the employee if the following is true:
   a. The employee is a full time employee.
   b. The employee elects dependent coverage when enrolling in the plan.
   c. The dependent satisfies the following definition:

Group Life Insurance

1. The following amounts will be paid to the employee's designated beneficiary or legal representative upon his or her death.

2. Accidental Death and Dismemberment.

Group Health Insurance

1. Hospital Benefits	4. Dental Benefits
2. Physician's Benefits	5. Psychiatric Benefits
3. Accidental Injury Benefits	6. Disability Benefits

Vacation   4020

Comment

Vacations are an integral part of the overall fringe benefit package. Although vacation policies vary widely, the trend in recent years has been to liberalize vacation entitlements. Many organizations provide a vacation package similar to this:

- One week after six months to one year of service;
- Two weeks after one to three years of service;
- Three weeks after three to ten years of service;
- Four weeks after ten years of service.

Vacations provide employees with paid time away from their jobs to give them an opportunity to recreate, rest, and relax. To minimize the disruptive effect of many employees requesting vacation in the summer months, companies may consider offering a bonus (e.g., $50) for each week of vacation taken in months other than May through September.

Another innovative idea to consider is a vacation banking plan, enabling employees to trade all or part of their unused vacation for a cash equivalent. This is collected at the end of the year, upon termination, or upon retirement from the organization.

The argument against this plan is that employees should be encouraged to take their vacation so that job burn-out and absenteeism for health-related reasons are avoided and productivity and safety are promoted. Some employers actually state their preference for employee vacations in their policies.

Federal law does not require employers to provide "vested" vacation time or even paid vacations. Some states, by law, may require a certain minimum vacation time — paid or unpaid — or even a permanent credit for vacation time not taken (vesting). Generally, the right to paid vacation time, whether or not the time is vested, is a result of an employment contract, a collective bargaining agreement, or the company's policy.

Some states recognize paid vacation time as a form of deferred wages and consider it vested in proportion to length of service. In those states, paid vacation time not taken by the employee, just like final wages, must be paid to a terminating employee. Likewise, an employer may be prohibited by state law from enforcing a policy of forfeiture of vested vacation pay.[1] Consult your state law for such provisions.

Almost every employer provides paid vacation, and many employers have a policy for vesting. Variations exist as to when the vacation time is actually earned — anniversary date, beginning of the calendar or company fiscal year, per pay period. The date that paid vacation is actually earned, and whether or not it is vested, is often an issue when an employee terminates and demands payment for paid vacation time not taken. Draft your vacation policies clearly and specify exactly when an employee's vacation entitlement is earned. However, this still may not protect you from having to pay terminating employees for pro rata vacation not taken if your state prohibits forfeiture of vested vacation pay.

In some industries, vacation plans are "funded," and employers are required to pay a set amount into a trust fund set up to provide paid vacation time. If this applies to a particular employer, he or she is required by law to make these payments or suffer a penalty. These types of funded vacation plans are subject to ERISA, and state law should be consulted for additional requirements.

Alternate policies are provided in this section. The first provides for a three-month waiting period before any vacation may be taken. Each policy presents variations in both accrual rates and carry-over of earned vacation days into the next year. There is no guarantee that either policy will protect you from having to pay terminating employees for vacation not taken. That depends on your state law.

An alternative paragraph which clearly provides for vested vacation time is provided after Alternate Policy 2. It can be used, with modifications, in either policy model.

Vacation

Alternate Policy 1   4020.1

Vacation benefits are based on the employee's next anniversary date which occurs in the current calendar year. The schedule is as follows:

Anniversary Date in Calendar Year	Vacation Entitlement as of January 1 of Calendar Year
1st through 4th	2 weeks
5th through 9th	3 weeks
10th through 19th	4 weeks
20th through 24th	5 weeks
25th or more	6 weeks

The employee's anniversary date is established according to the policy in Section 2100. To be eligible to take vacation, the employee must be in active pay status. Vacation is not vested, and a terminating employee will not be paid for vacation not taken. Vacation not taken during the calendar year is forfeited.

Note: The preceding two sentences are optional and may conflict with state law and should be researched.

New employees become eligible to take vacation after they have worked three consecutive months. Those reporting on the first working day in January are entitled to two weeks of paid vacation. Those reporting after the first working day in January through the first working day in July are entitled to one week of paid vacation. New employees reporting for work after the first working day in July are not entitled to paid vacation until the following year. Part-time employees are not entitled to paid vacation. Employees who are not entitled to paid vacation may request permission from their supervisor/manager to take up to one week of unpaid vacation time.

The employee's supervisor/manager is responsible for scheduling vacations. Vacation entitlement is administered by the (PERSONNEL DEPARTMENT). Employees are responsible for planning ahead for vacation and working out a complete schedule with their supervisor/manager. Normally, two-weeks advance notice of vacation is expected and necessary to ensure scheduling of work. Employees who desire to take more than three weeks of vacation at one time should give their supervisor/manager more than two weeks advance notice.

Vacation

Alternate Policy 2   4020.2

Vacation accrual begins with the first month of hire. Monthly accrual rates are determined by the employee's anniversary date, according to the schedule that follows. A new employee accrues the entire 6.67 hours of vacation time for the first month of service regardless of the day of the month the employee is hired. An employee must be in active pay status on the last working day of the month to accrue vacation for that month.

Vacation time accrues at a rate of 6.67 hours each month of full time service (ten days for every twelve months) up through the first five years of continuous employment. Accrual rates thereafter are as follows:

Years Completed	Hours Accrued Per Month	Yearly Total
5	10.00	15 days
15	13.34	20 days
20	15.00	22.5 days
25 and over	16.67	25 days

If the employee's 5th, 15th, 20th, or 25th anniversary date is on or before the last working day of the month, the employee will accrue the higher rate for that month. Vacation is not earned while an employee is on a leave of absence. Part-time employees earn vacation at half the accrual rates above.

Employees may take total "available" vacation at any time throughout the year. All vacations must be scheduled in advanced with the employee's supervisor/manager.

Employees may carry over accrued vacation, but all vacation hours carried over from one calendar year must be used by the end of the following year, or they will be forfeited.

Note: This last sentence may conflict with the law of your state.

Vesting Clause

Alternate Policy 3   4020.3

An employee's vacation time vests when it is accrued and can be carried over to future calendar years if not taken. This means that the earned vacation is permanently credited to the employee.

An employee cannot take more than 25 consecutive days of vacation (excluding Saturdays, Sundays, and holidays) in any one calendar year without the approval of the (PERSONNEL DIRECTOR).

Upon termination, the employee's accrued, but not taken vacation hours, will be added to the final paycheck using the employee's then-current straight-time hourly rate for conversion.

Holidays   4030

Comment

This policy designates the number of holidays which will be observed by the company and explains related scheduling and pay practices. Most companies now provide employees with nine to twelve paid holidays a year.

The most commonly observed holidays for federal employees are: New Year's Day, Martin Luther King, Jr.'s Birthday, Presidents Day, Memorial Day, Independence Day, Labor Day, Columbus Day, Veterans Day, Thanksgiving Day, and Christmas Day. Other holidays to be considered might include Good Friday, Presidential Election Day, and an additional day at Thanksgiving and Christmas. States have various special state holidays, and local statutes and regulations should be consulted prior to selecting the company holidays.

Two alternate policies are presented in this section, one providing specific holidays and a second providing the employee with a choice of floating holidays, in addition to specific company holidays.

Specific dates can be identified by a company memorandum issued once a year to every employee, or the policy itself can be modified year by year.

Holidays

Alternate Policy 1   4030.1

(COMPANY) provides (ADD NUMBER) paid holidays each year. The company is officially closed on these days:

Note: Select from or add to the paid holidays listed below.

January 1*	New Year's Day
February	President's Day
March/April	Good Friday
May	Memorial Day
July	Independence Day
September	Labor Day
October	Columbus Day
November	Thanksgiving Day
November	Day after Thanksgiving
December 24th**	Christmas Eve (office closes at noon)
December 25th*	Christmas Day
December 31st**	New Year's Eve (office closes at noon)

*If these holidays fall on Saturday, the preceding Friday will be a holiday. If they fall on Sunday, the following Monday will be a holiday.

**If these holidays fall on weekends, one-half day off will be observed on the last work day preceding the holiday.

Holidays

Alternate Policy 2   4030.2

(COMPANY) provides ten designated paid holidays each year. Eight of these are scheduled and identified on the company bulletin board, and two are "floating" holidays to be determined by the employee and approved by his or her supervisor. The eight scheduled holidays are as listed below:

Note: Tailor number of designated paid and floating holidays to your specific policy.

New Year's Day	Martin Luther King Jr.'s Birthday
Memorial Day	Independence Day
Labor Day	Thanksgiving
Day after Thanksgiving	Christmas

Weekend Holidays

When a recognized holiday falls on a Saturday, it will be observed on the Friday before the holiday. Recognized holidays that fall on a Sunday will be observed on the following Monday.

Eligibility for Holiday Pay

Employees must work the last scheduled day before a holiday and the first scheduled working day following the holiday to be eligible for holiday pay unless time off on these days has been excused with pay (e.g. vacation and sick leave). Only regular full time employees are eligible for full holiday pay. Temporary employees are not eligible for holiday pay.

Part-time employees are entitled to an equal number of company holidays, but they shall receive pay for only the number of hours they would have regularly worked. Scheduled work on holidays is discouraged since the purpose of holidays is seen by the company as a provision for employee relaxation. If an employee is required to work on a scheduled holiday, the employee will be paid for hours worked at his or her regular pay in addition to holiday pay.

If a designated holiday falls within an employee's vacation period, the holiday is not considered a vacation day. Employees may take religious holidays not designated as a company holiday either as a floating holiday or without pay. Prior approval in advance must be obtained from the employee's supervisor/manager.

Sick or Personal Leave   4040

Comment

Companies recognize an employee's need for income protection to reduce the financial burden during temporary periods of sickness or injury. Many companies which provide sick or personal leave, stress in the policy or new employee orientation that, unlike vacation leave, sick leave is not earned by the employee but is granted.

Whether it is called "sick leave" or "personal leave," the time is generally thought of by employers as being provided for an employee who is temporarily incapacitated, not free time just because it is provided in the benefit package. Some companies allow an employee to take personal leave without being incapacitated, but limit the number of consecutive days of leave, e.g., five consecutive days during a twelve-month period.

To encourage employees not to abuse this privilege, a number of innovative ideas are offered by companies. These include allowing an employee who has not used sick or personal leave during the year to receive paid leave time between the Christmas and New Year's holidays, or allowing an employee with perfect attendance during the month to receive an extra day's pay for that month (sometimes referred to as well pay). Other organizations buy back unused sick leave time at the end of the year by paying their employees for each day of sick leave not used. Some companies also vest sick or personal leave and will allow the employee to accumulate all unused portions of this leave to be ultimately cashed out if and when the employee terminates. Although federal law does not require sick or personal leave, state law may regulate this area or specify certain minimum entitlements.

Employees are more likely to call in sick when they believe that their attendance doesn't matter, when working conditions are stressful, or when they feel taken for granted. Your company's attention to the following points in administering a sick leave policy will have a positive effect on attendance.

- Ensure that all employees know the sick leave policy and that the company sticks to the policy.
- Managers should set the company example. Coming to work in spite of allergies or a sprained wrist will let employees know that the same level of commitment is expected from them.
- Employees calling in sick should be required to talk directly to their supervisor. The supervisor can stress that they will be missed and

express hope that they will recover quickly. An employee who is required to talk directly to a supervisor in such a case is more likely to have a good reason for calling in sick.

- Supervisors should talk with employees following absenteeism to reinforce that they were missed. Such personal attention is important for team spirit.

- Encourage employees who are feeling pressure or stress on the job to talk to their supervisor about it. Encourage supervisors to be better listeners.

Small companies encounter higher costs because of employee absenteeism. They usually pay sick leave for that day and someone else must assume two persons' responsibilities or work goes undone. Creative incentive programs for perfect employee attendance for a six-month, one-year, or two-year program might include cash bonuses, vacation trips, or dollar credits to purchase merchandise from a catalog.

Sometimes sick leave is combined with vacation (becoming earned and vested) and called time off with pay. This time is then available to the employee at his or her discretion with a supervisor's approval.

Caution

Few areas of law have changed so quickly or dramatically over the last several years as the laws which impact leaves of absence, particularly family and medical leave. The laws and regulations are extremely complicated and, if they apply, they take precedence over any inconsistent provisions in your policy.

No leave policy should be adopted without careful review by company counsel. In the policies which follow, *Section 4040* can be considered whenever state or federal leave laws do not apply. For medical and family leaves described in *Sections 4060 — 4090*, be careful to comply with applicable state and federal laws.

Finally, be careful to make sure your leave policy is applied in harmony with ADA requirements, workers' compensation and similar laws.

Sick or Personal Leave

Alternate Policy I   4040.1

A regular full-time employee will receive 40 hours of sick leave after six months of continuous employment. A regular part-time employee will be credited with an appropriate prorated number of hours. After the first six months of employment, sick leave is accrued monthly at a rate of 6.67 hours for a full-time employee and at a prorated amount for a part-time employee. Sick leave is accrued on the last workday of the month. Employees must be in an active pay status on the last day of the month to accrue sick leave for that month.

It is in the best interests of an employee who is ill or injured that the employee not remain at work. It is the supervisor's or manager's responsibility to send the employee home if the employee is incapacitated.

Time for routine doctor or dentist appointments is not to be charged to sick leave. Employees are encouraged to make such appointments before arriving for work or after leaving work for the day, if possible. If time off is required for such appointments, arrangements should be made in advance with the employee's supervisor or manager. The employee must use accumulated sick leave in conjunction with income protection plans or other sources of disability income to achieve full pay for as long as possible. However, at no time can the combination of these exceed normal earnings.

An employee is expected to notify his or her supervisor/manager at the beginning of each work day during illness or injury. Exceptions to this include a serious accidental injury, hospitalization, and when it is known in advance that the employee will be absent for a certain period of time.

Sick or Personal Leave

Alternate Policy 1 (continued)   4040.1

A Medical Release Statement is to be submitted to the employee's supervisor/manager for review before the employee returns to work in the following situations:

1. Five or more consecutive workdays of absence due to illness or injury;

2. In all cases of work-related injury when the employee has been unable to work after the time of the injury; or

3. When returning from medical or maternity leave of absence.

In the case of a work-related accident or injury, the company will compensate an employee for any lost work hours beginning on the date of the accident or injury and for the next (ADD NUMBER) hours of scheduled work time lost as a result of that accident or injury. The employee's sick leave is not to be used for this purpose. The employee must then use accumulated sick leave in conjunction with workers' compensation or other disability income to achieve full pay for as long as possible. However, at no time can the combination of these exceed normal earnings.

Unused sick leave will be forfeited upon termination. No employee will be allowed to overdraw sick leave beyond (ADD NUMBER) hours without approval in writing from the (PERSONNEL DIRECTOR). Such approval will only be granted on the condition, in writing and signed by the employee, that overdrawn sick leave will be deducted from the employee's final paycheck upon termination.

Sick leave is not earned while an employee is on a leave of absence.

Note: *If state or federal leave laws apply, or if your business is subject to the ADA, this policy may conflict with these laws. Because of the complexity of this area, consult with company counsel in developing an appropriate policy.*

Sick or Personal Leave

Alternate Policy 2   4040.2

Sick or personal leave equivalent to ten days per year, earned at a rate of 6.67 hours per month, is granted to all full-time employees. Part-time employees will earn sick or personal leave at half of the full-time rate. Temporary employees are not eligible for sick or personal leave.

Sick leave is earned on the last workday of the month for all employees on active pay status that day. An employee beginning employment earns the entire 6.67 hours of sick or personal leave for the first month, regardless of when he or she starts work. An employee who is on leave of absence does not earn sick leave.

Sick or personal leave is vested by the company on behalf of the employee as it is earned. This means that the leave is permanently credited to the employee, and the dollar equivalent of any unused leave will be paid to the employee when, and if, he or she leaves the company. The vested leave time payout may not exceed a total of four months equivalent salary for the employee.

Note: The last sentence is optional and may conflict with the law of your state.

If it is necessary for an employee to request sick or personal leave in excess of the amount earned, the employee's supervisor/manager has the authority to approve up to 40 hours in excess of the accrued amount. All excess sick or personal leave will be applied toward the employee's future accrual of sick or personal leave. The dollar equivalent of sick or personal leave owed to the company will be deducted from the employee's final check when an employee terminates.

Note: Some states may require a previously-written authorization for this deduction signed by the employee prior to granting excess sick leave.

An employee is to contact his or her supervisor/manager when sick or personal leave is needed because of illness. It remains the employee's responsibility to keep the supervisor/manager informed as to his or her condition and when he or she will return to work. A medical statement from the employee's doctor may be requested by the company when an employee is absent from work for more than five working days.

Note: If state or federal leave laws apply, or if your business is subject to the ADA, this policy may conflict with these laws. Because of the complexity of this area, consult with company counsel in developing an appropriate policy.

Leave of Absence and Military Leave   4050

Comment

An employee may encounter a situation which requires a temporary, but extended absence from work. As a rule, brief absences of not more than 10 working days should normally be considered as personal leave, unless the absence falls into a medical or military category as defined in the policies below. Generally, family or medical leave described in the next section or a leave of absence applies to a period of more than 10 days and less than 90 total days. Typically, the employee on leave of absence is not entitled to fringe benefits while in this non-pay status. This differentiates leave of absence from sick or personal leave or vacation.

Federal law requires that military leave be granted for a maximum length of five years.[1] The law basically guarantees that the employee will be re-employed by the employer, and requires the employer to do so, if the employee is inducted or voluntarily enlists in any of the armed services of the United States. It also protects those who are in the reserves or state national guard when they are called into federal service or ordered to initial training or periodic duty.

State law often prescribes non-discriminatory, temporary leaves of absence for employees to participate in required training or duty with the National Guard or Reserves. Some states make it a crime to discharge or discriminate against anyone because of military service.

Maternity leave and disability leave related to pregnancy are covered by Title VII, which applies to all employers who employ more than 15 employees and who engage in interstate commerce. Most states also have laws regarding pregnancy-related leave which cover most employers who are not subject to Title VII. Additional requirements beyond the requirements of Title VII may also be imposed.

Title VII requires employers to treat pregnant women, and those with related medical conditions, the same as other employees for all employment-related purposes. This includes all fringe benefit programs and especially duration of leave, availability of extension, accrual of seniority, and reinstatement. Title VII requires equality of treatment, not preferential treatment. See the discussion under *Pregnancy Leave — Section 4090, Parental Leave — Section 4080,* and *Family Medical Leave — Section 4070.*

Arbitrary, mandatory leave policies are prohibited by federal and state laws. Some state laws require the employer to permit a pregnant employee to transfer to less strenuous or hazardous work under certain conditions.[2]

You do not need a separate maternity leave or pregnancy disability policy. Treat all pregnancy-related leaves as you would any other medical leave of absence or disability leave. Consult with legal counsel or your state employment office to ensure that you draft your policy according to state laws regarding this type of leave. Your state may have additional requirements regarding pregnancy-related leave which will necessitate specific mention in your policy.[3]

Whether reinstatement to the same or a similar position is required after leave is another concern. Title VII says equality is required and no more. If your leave of absence or disability policy does not guarantee reinstatement, you do not have to guarantee reinstatement after a pregnancy-related leave under federal law. However, some states may require reinstatement or some kind of preferential recall for a pregnant employee. State law may also specify that a woman requesting pregnancy leave is entitled to use her full amount of accrued paid leave (vacation, sick, or personal leave) before commencing the pregnancy leave period required by state law.

If you decide not to have any leave of absence or disability policy, be careful. A lack of such policies could have an impermissible disparate effect on one gender, e.g., demotions or terminations, if there are no business needs to justify the disparity. Also, if you give preferential treatment to a pregnant employee, such as longer disability leave or leave of absence, without being required to do so by state law, you may violate federal or state discrimination laws or regulations with regard to other employees.

Leave of Absence and Military Leave

Alternate Policy 1   4050.1

Leave of absence is time off in a non-pay status. An employee must submit a request for leave of absence in writing to his or her supervisor/manager. Managers will forward the request for final approval to the (PERSONNEL DEPARTMENT) accompanied by the supervisor's/manager's recommendation. The employee is expected to request leave of absence with as much advance notice as possible. Leaves of absence will not be granted for periods less than two weeks in duration. Vacation or sick leave should be used for such absences.

The reason for leave should fall into one of the following categories:

1. Medical (including pregnancy-related)

2. Military

3. Personal

The employee has the responsibility to keep the (PERSONNEL DEPARTMENT) advised of the leave situation and to contact his or her supervisor/manager at least two weeks before the expiration of the approved leave to discuss return to work. I

If the employee desires voluntary termination, this should be reported as soon as possible. The company will make a reasonable effort, consistent with good business practices and company needs, to reinstate an employee to the same position he or she previously occupied, or to a similar position, following a leave of absence.

However, in the case of leaves over (ADD TIME PERIOD), the company cannot guarantee that the same or a similar position will be available at the time an employee desires to return to work, or thereafter. If this situation occurs, the company reserves the right to offer the employee a lower-level position, if one is available at the appropriate salary for such a position.

An exception to this rule occurs when an employee is guaranteed re-employment rights under federal or state laws.

Leave of Absence and Military Leave

Alternate Policy 1 (continued)   4050.1

How to Determine Benefits

1. Holidays — To be paid for a holiday, an employee must be in active pay status the day before and the day after the holiday. Employees are not eligible to receive pay for any holiday during the leave period.

2. Vacation — No vacation hours are earned during the leave period. Employees requesting a leave of absence for medical or military reasons may choose to use all earned vacation before beginning leave of absence. Employees requesting personal leave of absence must use all earned vacation before beginning leave of absence.

3. Sick or Personal — No sick or personal hours are accumulated during the leave period. Permissive or mandatory use of accumulated sick or personal leave is governed by the rules in paragraph 2, above.

4. Insurance — The company will continue the employee's insurance benefits on leave of absence approved for medical reasons only. In the case of military leaves, insurance benefits will be continued for up to ten working days per year, starting with the day military leave begins.

5. Profit-Sharing — An otherwise eligible employee will be entitled to profit sharing while on leave of absence in accordance with the rules of the profit-sharing plan and related policy. If the leave began before eligibility was established, eligibility will be postponed until the employee returns to work.

Note: If the company has a stock bonus plan, stock option plan or retirement plan, a statement similar to Item 5 should be included for each.

Notwithstanding the above, an employee on leave of absence who fails to return to work will be terminated effective his or her last day of work or paid leave (vacation, sick, or personal), whichever is later.

Leave of Absence and Military Leave

Alternate Policy 2   4050.2

A leave of absence is time off in a non-pay status. Upon receipt of a formal written request for leave of absence from regular full time employees, management will determine whether a leave of absence will be granted. The types of leaves granted are personal, educational, public service, and military.

The leave classifications are defined as follows:

1. Personal — Personal leaves are granted to employees having special personal need for an extended period of absence. Each case must be evaluated on its own merits and consider:

   a. The reason for the request;

   b. The amount of time required; and

   c. The employee's length of service and past record.

Normally, personal leaves are granted for periods of up to 90 days.

2. Educational — To encourage the academic development of deserving employees, educational leaves of absence may be granted. Employees must have (ADD NUMBER) year(s) of active service with the company for each year of leave. If the educational leave is for completion of a college bachelor's degree, the employee must also have a minimum of (add number of UNITS OF COLLEGE CREDIT and/or YEARS OF COLLEGE CREDIT). The employee's record, career objectives, and the applicability of the major area of study to the company's needs must be considered in determining whether educational leave will be granted. Typically, educational leave will be granted for one year and may be renewed for an additional year at the option of the company.

3. Public Service — Leaves of absence for public service may be granted to employees to permit participation in special community projects or political campaigns or to accept a governmental elective or appointive position. Employees must have a minimum of (ADD NUMBER) year(s) of active service with the company for such leave to be considered.

4. Military — To protect the employment rights of employees entering the armed forces of the United States and to ensure conformance with the applicable federal laws, a leave of absence must be granted to all employees, except temporary, who enter military service for active duty as a result of the following:

   a. Initial enlistment in the armed services of the United States;

   b. Initial training period in the National Guard;

Leave of Absence and Military Leave

<u>Alternate Policy 2 (continued)</u> 4050.2

c. Being ordered to active military service as a member of the Reserves or National Guard for an indefinite period or for a periodic training period up to ten working days; and

d. Any service requirements under the Selective Service Act.

Return to Work

The employee assumes responsibility for keeping the company periodically advised of the need for continuing leave of absence status. He or she should contact the supervisor/manager at least two weeks prior to expiration of the leave to discuss return to work. Following leave of absence, the company will make every reasonable effort, consistent with company needs, to reinstate an employee to the same position he or she previously occupied, or to a similar position. However, the company cannot guarantee that the employee will be reinstated to the same or a similar position. If the same or a similar position is not available, the company reserves the right to offer the employee a lower-level position at the appropriate salary for such a position.

Note: Check your state law regarding pregnancy-related leaves for any reinstatement requirements.

If this is not acceptable to the employee, the employee will be terminated. Exceptions to this rule are employees who are granted military leave of absence. They are entitled to full re-employment rights subject to the governing federal and state laws. Employees who do not return to work after leave of absence will be terminated effective on the last day of work or paid leave whichever is later.

Benefits

Medical, dental, and life insurance coverage continues for 90 days. Thereafter, coverage may be converted to an individual contract at the employee's expense. Holiday pay is not available to employees during leave of absence. Vacation and personal or sick leave is not accrued during the leave of absence.

Profit-sharing contributions continue based on actual earnings during the plan period and in accordance with the terms and conditions of the plan. Pension plan information is provided in the Summary Plan Description or the plan documents for a definite statement of the employee's entitlements, or see the (PERSONNEL DIRECTOR).

Leave of Absence and Military Leave

Alternate Policy 3   4050.3

It is (COMPANY) policy to support the United States, and in that regard, those of its employees who are members of the armed forces or military reserves. The company will grant such unpaid leave as may be required in order to enable its employees to comply with required reservist activities.

Such leaves will be granted in accordance with applicable laws and regulations of the United States, and such laws and regulations will control such matters as re-employment or continuation of benefits.

Note: This policy can be added to either Alternative Policy 1 or Alternative Policy 2.

Medical Leave of Absence   4060

Comment

The policies which follow are similar in many respects to the alternate policies in *Section 4050. The Medical Leave of Absence* policy is more specific. It deals solely with leaves attributable to matters such as illness, injury, or maternity. As a general rule, one would not use policies set forth in *Sections 4050* and *4060* in the same manual without first deleting any references to medical leaves of absence set forth in *Section 4050.* Similarly, if you determine to use only Section 4060 you may wish to add to it the paragraphs entitled "Benefits" found under either Alternate Policy 1 or 2 of Section 4050.

Whether their policy is formal or informal, most employers provide for leaves of absence. The most common form of leave is related to the occasional illness of an employee or employee's child. Other types of leave involve such things as death of a family member, family leave, parental leave, pregnancy leave, military leave, and jury duty. In some states, a brief leave may be required to permit employees the opportunity to vote. In the following sections, each of these leaves is profiled, and sample policies provided.

Some of these leaves are required by federal or state law. Whether or not these laws apply often depends upon the number of employees of a particular employer. Calculating the amount of leave which an employee may be entitled to is not always an easy process. In some instances, leave granted under different statutes can be applied by an employee to extend the length of a leave. In addition, federal or state laws or regulations may require that specific forms or notices be utilized. Consult with your business attorney to help you in these areas. Ask your attorney to show you the correct forms and procedures initially and you can take over responsibilities from there.

Although certain forms of leave required by federal or state law may not apply to your business, you may find it necessary to adopt a leave policy in order to attract good employees. As a result, you may wish to consider the policies which follow.

Medical Leave of Absence

Policy   4060.1

Upon written application by an employee who has at least (ADD NUMBER) months of continuous service with the company, (COMPANY) will grant to the employee for an appropriate period of time a leave of absence without pay for illness or pregnancy subject to the requirements set forth below. The company reserves the right to request a certificate or statement from the employee's physician establishing the employee's physical need for the leave of absence. An employee returning to work from a leave of absence in the case of illness or pregnancy will present a certificate or statement from the employee's physician indicating that the employee is able to return to work.

An employee need not apply for an illness or pregnancy leave of absence if the absence will not exceed five working days. However, the employee must notify his or her department manager no later than the day of such absence.

The following requirements will be applicable to employees on all types of leaves of absence:

1. An employee on any leave of absence shall not return to work prior to the expiration of his or her leave without the prior written consent of the company.

2. An employee who does not return to work at the end of his or her leave of absence will be considered to have voluntarily resigned from employment with (COMPANY).

3. If an employee returns to work within eight weeks after the leave of absence begins, the company will return the employee to employee's previous job, if the job exists and if the employee remains qualified and able to perform the work in such job.

4. If an employee returns to work more than eight weeks after the leave of absence begins, the company shall not be required to return the employee to any job within the company.

5. An employee who accepts other employment while on any leave will be deemed to have voluntarily resigned his or her employment with the company.

6. Group insurance participation for employees on a leave of absence will continue during the leave but will terminate the first day after the day on which the leave of absence ends, but in no event later than eight weeks following the date of commencement of the leave, if the employee has not returned to full time employment by that date.

7. The time that an employee is on leave of absence will be counted as time worked for determining whether or not the employee is entitled to other company benefits, subject, of course, to the specific provisions of any health insurance policy, retirement plan or other benefit package. Similarly, an employee's length of service will continue to increase while the employee is on leave of absence.

Note: This policy will conflict with any applicable state or federal medical leave laws. Consult with your company counsel for guidance in this complex area.

Family Leave, Parental Leave and Pregnant Employees   4070 — 4090

Comment

Family and Medical Leave Act requires larger employers to give mile workers unpaid leave for a family or medical emergency. As a general rule, the act applies to employers with 50 or more employees within a 75 mile radius. These employers are required to offer workers up to twelve weeks of unpaid leave following child birth or adoption, to care for a seriously ill child, spouse or parent, or in case of an employee's own serious illness. During the leave period, employers are required to continue health care coverage, and upon expiration of the leave, guarantee that employees will return to either the same job or a comparable position.

The law does not apply to employees who have not worked at least one year and who have not worked at least 1,250 hours or 25 hours a week in the previous twelve months. Employers can also exempt from the application of the law key employees, defined as the highest paid 10% of the work force and whose leave would cause economic harm to the employer. Employers may request a doctor's certification to verify a serious illness, and employers can require a second medical opinion. Employers are permitted to substitute an employee's accrued paid leave for any part of the twelve week period of family leave.

For employees required to take intermittent leave for planned medical treatment, employers will be required to permit these employees to transfer temporarily to an equivalent alternate position.

Family leave regulations adopted by the U.S. Department of Labor now apply. The regulations are complex. Among other things, the regulations distinguish and provide special rules for chronic and non-chronic diseases, provide new forms for employers and employees, and describe when an absence can be considered leave. The regulations also provide that for COBRA insurance coverage purposes, an employee who takes leave but fails to return from it is deemed to be eligible for COBRA benefits on the day he or she fails to return or otherwise announces he or she won't return. For a copy of these regulations, contact the U.S. Department of Labor at (202) 219-8727.

Similar state laws may apply to businesses with fewer than 50 employees. Generally, an employee can choose between inconsistent state and federal provisions, entitling the employee to the most favorable treatment. Check your state law to determine if the state or federal leave act applies to your business.

Family Leave

Policy   4070.1

The company provides an unpaid family medical leave for up to twelve weeks within a two year period subject to the following terms and conditions. For purposes of this policy, a "year" is determined by looking back twelve months from the date the leave is requested to determine how much leave has been taken in that period.

Employees taking a family medical leave of absence shall make a reasonable effort to schedule medical treatment or supervision so as to minimize any disruption to company operations. If a serious health condition is anticipated, employee shall provide at least 30 days written notice, prior to taking leave, explaining the reason for the leave. If a serious health condition is not anticipated, employee should make an oral request for leave at least 3 days prior to the leave.

For the purposes of this policy "serious health condition" means:

- An illness of a child of the employee requiring home care; or
- An injury, disease or condition that according to the medical judgment of the treating physician:
- Poses an eminent danger of death;
- Is terminal in prognosis with a reasonable possibility of death in the near future; or
- Is any medical or physical condition requiring constant care.

(COMPANY) may require certification from a health care provider as to the need for the leave. Employees may choose to use accumulated vacation or sick leave time. For any serious health condition that is not life threatening or terminal, no family medical leave is allowed during any period of time when another family member is taking family medical leave or is otherwise available to care for the family member.

During the leave, the regular position of the employee shall be considered vacant for the period of the leave, and the employee will not be removed or discharged as a consequence of the leave. Benefits do not continue or accrue during the leave period. However, the company will continue health care coverage for the employee during the leave.

At the conclusion of the leave period, the employee shall be restored to his or her former position or an equivalent job without loss of seniority or service credits accruing under any benefit plan as of the date the leave commenced. If the company is unable to restore the employee to his or her former job or an equivalent due to the company's circumstances,

Family Leave

Policy (continued)   4070.1

the employee shall be reinstated to any position that is available and suitable. The company is not required to discharge any other employee in order to reinstate the employee.

Family leave provisions are not applicable to employees who have not worked at least one year and who have not worked at least 1,250 hours, or 25 hours a week, in the previous twelve months.

Note: *State and federal laws may differ regarding which employers are required to provide leave, which employees are eligible for the leave , the duration of the leave, and an employee's right to reinstatement. Because of the complexity of the laws in this area, consult with your company counsel before using this policy.*

Parental Leave

Policy   4080.1

Company shall provide unpaid parental leave for its employees. Employees seeking parental leave shall provide a request in writing at least 30 days in advance of the anticipated date of delivery or adoption if the necessity for the leave is foreseeable. The notice shall be binding upon the parents unless:

- The birth is premature;

- The mother is incapacitated due to the birth such that she is unable to care for the child;

- The employee takes physical custody of a newly adopted child at an unanticipated time and is unable to give 30 days advance written notice; or

- In cases of premature birth, incapacity or unanticipated taking of physical custody of an adopted child, employee shall give the company written notice of the revised dates of parental leave within 7 days following the birth or taking of custody.

(COMPANY) may require certification from a health care provider as to the need for the leave. Employees may choose to use accumulated vacation or sick leave time. Any parental leave shall not exceed twelve weeks in length and shall consist of all or that part of the time between the birth of the employee's infant and the time the infant reaches twelve weeks of age, or in the case of a premature infant, until the infant has reached the developmental stage equivalent to twelve weeks as determined by an attending physician or all or part of the twelve week period following the date an adoptive parent takes physical custody of a newly adopted child under six years of age.

The company will not grant parental leave if the effect would be to enable the employee and the other parent of the child, if also employed, parental leave totaling more than the time set forth above or to grant any parental leave for any period of time in which the child's other parent is also taking parental leave from employment.

Employees seeking parental leave may also utilize any accrued vacation, sick leave or compensatory leave subject to the other terms and conditions of this policy manual.

Note: State and federal laws may differ regarding which employers are required to provide leave, which employees are eligible for the leave, the duration of the leave, family members to which the right to leave attaches, and an employee's right to reinstatement. Because of the complexity of the laws in this area, consult with your company counsel before using this policy.

Pregnant Employees

Policy   4090.1

In addition to the family leave policy, pregnant employees may request, if reasonably necessary, a temporary transfer to a less strenuous or hazardous position for the duration of the pregnancy. Company may require a medical opinion regarding the need for transfer.

Pregnant employees may also take a leave of absence on account of pregnancy for a reasonable period of time if the leave is reasonably necessary, the employee requests the leave in writing, and the company can reasonably accommodate the request. Pregnant employees may also use any accrued vacation time or other compensatory time off.

Upon return, any pregnant employee shall be entitled to any seniority, vacation credits, or other benefits which have accrued as of the date of the leave and were not used in conjunction with the leave. No employee benefits accrue during the leave. Upon return, the company will endeavor to return the employee to her former job or its equivalent.

If company's circumstances have so changed that the employee cannot be reinstated to the former or an equivalent job, the employee shall be reinstated to any position which is available and suitable. However, the company is not required to discharge any employee in order to reinstate the employee to any other job other than her former job. If any issue arises as to the employee's physical capacity to return to work, the company may request a medical opinion.

Note: State and federal laws may differ regarding which employers are required to provide leave, which employees are eligible for the leave, the duration of the leave, family members to which the right to leave attaches, and an employee's right to reinstatement. Because of the complexity of the laws in this area, consult with your company counsel before using this policy.

Bereavement Leave   4100

Comment

It is standard policy to allow employees to take time off to attend funerals. Among the questions that arise are how much time should be allowed and whether the time off should be paid time.

If your company has a personal leave policy, you may want to provide for bereavement leave within that policy. Another alternative is to provide paid time off for two or three days, allowing the employee to take additional days as unpaid time off.

You may also let the employee choose between unpaid time off or personal leave, or both. In the development of your company policy, management should provide guidelines which are consistent and evenhanded. It is unusual for states to legislate in this area, but it would be wise to check for any applicable laws or regulations.

Alternative policies are presented in this section. Their provisions may be combined to achieve management's desires.

Bereavement Leave

Alternate Policy 1   4100.1

The company will provide time off for employees to attend the funerals of family members and friends. Your supervisor will approve whatever period of time is necessary and appropriate under the circumstances.

If the conditions warrant and the supervisor/manager agrees, paid leave will be granted, but the amount of paid leave time will not exceed three days at regular straight-time wages. Such leave is in addition to all other paid leave time.

Typically, paid leave is reserved for the death of immediate family members.

Bereavement Leave

Alternate Policy 2   4100.2

The company will pay for time off in the event of death of the following immediate family members:

Spouse	Grandparent	Father-in-law
Parent	Brother	Sister
Child or Stepchild	Grandchild	Mother-in-law

The employee and supervisor/manager will determine the amount of time the employee will be absent from work. The maximum paid leave is (ADD NUMBER) days, in addition to all other paid leave.

Leave for attendance at the funeral of a non-immediate family member or person with an especially close relationship may be granted with or without pay. Determination will be made by the employee's supervisor after consultation with upper management.

Jury Duty   4110

Comment

It is generally required by law that you allow employees to take time off for jury duty, without discrimination. You will find variation in state statutes and company policies on whether this time away from work is paid or unpaid.

Some companies pay for all of the time, others pay for only a portion. Some companies don't pay for any time. Some companies also extend this benefit to serving as a witness when a subpoena is issued for testimony in a criminal or civil case, or before a grand jury, but not usually for the employee's own case. Even if time off is fully or partially paid, employees should not be required to sign over to the company their jury duty stipend or expense checks received for serving on the jury.

In many states, statutes penalize an employer for failure to reinstate, promote, or otherwise restore an employee who loses employee status or benefits because of service as a juror or witness.

Alternative Policy 2 contains a time limitation which limits the employer's obligation to pay. In light of certain lengthy and notorious trials, employers would be wise to include such a limitation.

Jury Duty

Alternate Policy 1   4110.1

Time off for mandatory jury duty or court appearances required as a result of a valid subpoena or court order is excused and paid at full salary, provided that proof of duty is verified by the employee's supervisor.

There will be no adjustment in the employee's salary for receipt of jury duty pay, witness fees, or expenses. The employee is expected to report for work when it does not conflict with court obligations.

It is the employee's responsibility to keep his or her supervisor/manager periodically informed about the amount of time required for jury duty or court appearances.

Jury Duty

Alternate Policy 2   4110.2

(COMPANY) will grant employees time off for mandatory jury duty or court appearances as a witness when the employee must serve or is required to appear as a result of a court order or subpoena. A copy of the court order or subpoena must be supplied to the employee's supervisor/manager when requesting time off.

The employee is entitled to full pay for each day of jury duty or service as a witness up to a maximum of (ten) days per year, in addition to any other paid leave. However, time off for court appearances as a party to any civil or criminal litigation shall not be compensated, and the employee must arrange for time off without pay or use accrued vacation or personal leave for such appearances.

Voting   4120

Comment

Some states require that you give your employees a specific amount of time (e.g., two hours) with pay to vote.

Your company may also be required by law or regulation to post the availability of paid time off for employees to vote. Usually the law or regulation specifies that the employee must give a defined amount of notice to the company.

State and local laws or regulations should be consulted, and your policy should be tailored to conform to the applicable law.

Voting

Policy   4120.1

(COMPANY) encourages all employees to vote. Employees are encouraged to use flextime hours for this purpose or to take advantage of polling hours prior to the beginning or following the end of your workday.

Note: This is applicable, if your company has a flextime policy.

If this cannot be arranged, your supervisor/manager will approve time off to vote either at the beginning or end of your workday, provided that you give at least one day's notice to your supervisor/manager.

Pension, Profit-Sharing, and Retirement Plans   4130

Comment

Pension plans and other deferred income benefit plans are generally thought to be the most costly and complicated portions of a company benefits program. The plan must provide adequate and non-discriminatory benefits, meet the approval of a number of federal agencies, such as the IRS and U.S. Department of Labor, and comply with a variety of federal and state laws, such as The Employee Retirement Income Security Act of 1974 (ERISA).[1]

These programs are attractive for two main reasons.

1. Employees like to have a nest egg which will provide them with some degree of assistance in continuing the same lifestyle upon retirement that they enjoyed while working.

2. Tax laws and regulations allow the employer to gain immediate deductions for contributions to these plans while the employees can defer tax obligations on this income until income tax rates are presumably more favorable in their later years.

Before your company develops a pension or profit-sharing plan, it is important to seek help from a qualified attorney, possibly a pension consulting firm, and your accountant or CPA firm.

Certain plans will be tailor-made for your company. Under other plans, known as prototype plans, you use a form plan prepared by an institutional lender or insurance company. The former are more flexible and expensive. Prototype plans are less flexible and less expensive. The characteristics of any such plans and the legal requirements, especially the reporting requirements, are complex. With that in mind, some generalizations can be made as long as you approach this subject with caution. The laws and regulations governing this area are not only complex, but they are also changed frequently.

The Internal Revenue Code (I.R.C.) and ERISA recognize two principal types of "qualified" plans: defined contribution and defined benefit plans. A defined contribution plan pays a participant solely from the amounts contributed into the plan, plus any income or gains from the investment of those sums and less any expenses or losses. No specific dollar amount is guaranteed for any participant.

A defined benefit plan is any plan which is not a defined contribution plan. Defined benefit plans pay a scheduled or guaranteed sum to a participant. It is up to the employer to invest adequate sums to provide that guaranteed benefit. Because of these differences, defined contribution plans tend to be more common. Although two principal types of qualified plans are recognized, many combinations and variations are available. Check with your legal or professional adviser.

A "qualified" plan is one that meets a variety of requirements set by the I.R.C. Generally, these requirements ensure the plan is non-discriminatory (that is, it does not discriminate in favor of company officers, directors, or highly paid employees), adequately covers a minimum number or percentage of the employees, and guarantees non-forfeiture of the contributions after certain periods of time — a concept known as "vesting." Also, the plan must be permanent in the sense that the employer must make recurring and substantial contributions to the plan. However, an employer need not contribute something every year.

Simplified Employee Pension (SEP) plans have been around for a few years. They are equivalent to defined contribution plans that use an individual retirement account (IRA) as a funding medium to which an employer (including a sole proprietor or partnership) makes contributions. See I.R.C., Section 408(k).

In order to establish an SEP, an employer executes a written document which includes the company's participation requirements and a definite allocation formula for the employer contributions. The total contribution may vary annually at the employer's discretion. An IRA account must be opened for every individual employee who becomes a plan participant.

An example of this type of plan is commonly known as a 401(k) plan. These plans must meet all normal tax qualification rules. In recent years, Congress has indicated an intent to increase the flexibility of these plans to encourage retirement planning.

The following checklist can be of some assistance to employers who are thinking about adopting a pension, retirement, or profit-sharing plan. In covering each step, remember that your accountant and other professionals will need to assist you.

Initial Considerations

- Investigate the tax advantages of a qualified plan.
- Remember that certain requirements will have to be met, such as:
  - Minimum participation standards;
  - Minimum vesting requirements;
  - "Top-heavy" plans obeying other special provisions; and

□ Discrimination not permitted, especially in favor of highly compensated employees.

- Estimate what difference a plan will make to your profit.
- Investigate and estimate the set-up costs, including legal and tax help.
- Should plan be integrated with Social Security?

Plan Type

Using most common plan formats

- Defined benefit pension plan or defined contribution pension plan
- Profit-sharing plan
- Simplified Employee Pension (SEP) plan
- Employee stock ownership plan (ESOP), which invests primarily in the employer's stock
- 401(k) cash or deferred arrangements under which employees direct an employer to pay a certain amount directly to the employee in cash or to a qualified profit-sharing plan trust arrangement.

Plan Design

Issues to discuss with your legal adviser

- Will employee contributions to the plan be allowed?
- Eligibility requirements:
- Who can be legally excluded from coverage under the plan?
- Who and how many must be included?
- How and when do employee interests vest and become non-forfeitable?
- "Top heavy" provisions must be included in every qualified plan. Top heavy plans tend to discriminate in favor of key employees, and the top heavy provisions reduce this discriminatory effect by accelerating the vesting timetable for non-key employees and requiring either a minimum annual retirement benefit in the case of a defined benefit plan or a contribution at least equal to 3% of a non-key employee's annual compensation in the case of a defined contribution plan.
- If these provisions become effective, the added expense of compliance may deter employers from adopting a qualified plan.
- When are distributions under the plan required to be made for:
  □ Living employees
    - Who retire?
    - Who terminate?

     □ Deceased employees?

     □ Disabled employees?

- Are early withdrawals allowed?

- Are there limits for contributions to plans? Do these limits apply to employees as well as employers?

- What will be the maximum allowable tax deductions for employees?

- Will plan loans to participants be allowed, and if so, under what circumstances?

- How will distributions be taxed to employees?

- How do I obtain a determination letter from the IRS stating my plan is "qualified"?

- Remember that a lot of statistics, compensation data, and employee classification information will have to be compiled and submitted initially and at the conclusion of each plan year

- Are "rollover" contributions from one plan to another tax-free?

Footnotes

4020 — Vacation

1. Cal. Lab. Code, § 227.3.

4050 — Leave of Absence and Military Leave

1. Uniformed Services Employment and Reemployment Rights Act of 1994
2. Cal. Govt. Code § 12945(c).
3. Cal. Govt. Code § 12945(b)(2)-disability leave for a reasonable period of time, not to exceed four months is required.

4130 — Pension, Profit-Sharing, and Retirement Plans

1. Pub. Law 93-406.

Chapter 5

Employee Expenses

Introduction

In many ways, the policies in this chapter are a continuation of the communication established in Chapter 4. This chapter will help you define the monetary role your company will assume in order to support the following:

- To efficiently carry out business assignments, an employee may sometimes be required to make personal expenditures on behalf of the company;

- Your employees' educational and professional growth through organizational memberships, attendance at conferences or seminars, and enrolling in higher education courses;

- Relocation assistance for new or transferred employees.

In developing this section of your policy manual, you will want to achieve a balance between what your company can afford and what other companies — primarily your competition — are providing for their employees.

As you look at the competition, consider the non-monetary as well as the monetary benefits of the policies in this section. Does your company provide:

- A challenging work environment where people like to work;

- Activities or facilities to release job stress;

- The opportunity for association and interaction with highly-skilled and talented co-workers; and

- Opportunities for employee development and education?

In today's society where employees are asking for a higher quality work environment, these factors often rate above any monetary benefits or salary. It is not only important to address these four factors in your policies, but it is also important to stress in employee orientation meetings that they are benefits which your company provides.

The circumstances which many employee expense policies should resolve vary from situation to situation. They should be written with greater flexibility than other policies. For example, when negotiating with an out-of-state prospective employee, to what limits will your company go in paying relocation expenses?

Due to this emphasis on flexibility, as these policies are first initiated and interpreted, the management staff will have to become sensitive to the limits or allowances which upper management believes are desirable. You should consider training or guidance for managers who will be using or interpreting these policies. The training will enable them to be more consistent when applying the limits or allowances in appropriate situations.

Although flexibility is an important aspect of these policies, consider the following two points as well. They provide important management and budget consistency. Without a policy, these employee expenses and benefits could easily absorb available and necessary operational and marketing funds.

Employee-Incurred Expenses and Reimbursement 5010

Comment

Most businesses will want to consider the development of a policy to reimburse employees for out-of-pocket expenses which are necessary for the performance of company business.

The availability of an in-house purchasing department, the establishment of charge accounts with local businesses, or a procedure for submitting requests to the supervisor/manager on a set day each week for necessary supplies or materials may answer the need for a reimbursement policy for a company with less than 20 employees. As the number of employees increases, it becomes more important to place greater control on these expenditures. However, it may still be necessary for employees to use their own money for small, extraordinary purchases and when on travel status.

At a minimum, here are some actions you will want to take:

- Design a form to be used in requesting advance approval of company-related expenditures;
- Establish procedures and controls for the supervisor/manager to follow in approving such requests;
- Design an expense report form for use in all cases of employee reimbursement; and
- Establish a procedure for submitting and approving expense reports and reimbursing the employee.

Employers who have state and federal government contracts or subcontracts subject to specific cost accounting guidelines, such as Cost Accounting Standards, should probably be more detailed in their definitions of reimbursable expenses. It is to your advantage to use language taken directly from such guidelines in defining a proper, reasonable, and allowable expense. A reference in the policy to governmental standards for reimbursable expenses is also helpful in those cases where a question arises concerning whether or not a particular expense is allowable. You may still want to reimburse the employee for a reasonable and necessary expense and assume the risk that it might not be recoverable.

Federal income tax laws govern how entertainment expenses will be allowed as deductions. Without going into detail (your CPA or tax counsel should advise you), generally only 80% of your business entertainment expenses will be deductible. These expenses are allowed only if they can be shown to be directly related to or associated with the active conduct of a trade or business. Therefore, it is now important to break out these expenses on an expense report for later segregation and reporting. Also, you may need to pay attention to your entertainment expenses at clubs or associations which discriminate against races or by sex. Recent regulations and statutes may deny deductibility of such entertainment. Ask your tax expert.

Consider implementing a rule within this policy, and probably within other employee reimbursement policies, that the expense report or reimbursement form be submitted to the appropriate approval authority, such as the accounting department, within a certain period of time. Some companies require the employee to submit a form within one or two weeks or five to ten business days after the expenditure.

This kind of rule encourages the employee to submit a time report when dates and times are more easily recalled. It also ensures that expenses will be properly allocated to the company's fiscal quarter or year without having to adjust closing entries. A stale report is often an inaccurate report, and inaccuracies can cause disapprovals and misunderstandings which lead to poor morale. Obviously, enforcement of the rule must be tempered with some flexibility for an unusual situation, such as when an employee loses his or her briefcase and must reconstruct the itinerary and obtain duplicate receipts.

Some companies do take a very firm stand on timely reports. For instance, all reports which are 30 or 60 days late will be disapproved. Likewise, the company has a responsibility to reimburse the employee promptly. Again, this is an issue affecting morale and your policy should reflect this duty to return to the employee the money that is rightfully his or hers without delay.

Employee-Incurred Expenses and Reimbursement

Alternate Policy 1   5010.1

To ensure that all proper business-related expenses incurred by employees are reimbursed, the following procedure has been established:

1. All expenditures are to be approved in advance by the employee's manager unless circumstances prevent advance approval.

2. All business-related expenditures must be accompanied by a receipt or evidence of expenditure in order to receive reimbursement.

3. All items purchased or charged by the employee are to be itemized on the approved company expense report. All portions of the report must be filled out or marked "N/A" (not applicable), and the necessity and purpose of the expenditure must be explained in sufficient detail.

4. Expense reports must be signed and dated by the employee and initialed by the manager showing approval. Reports are due in the accounting department within 30 days of the expenditure. Reimbursement will be made by the fifth working day of the month following submittal of the expense report.

5. Managers are authorized to approve expenditures up to a limit of (ADD DOLLAR AMOUNT) for non-travel-related items, including local mileage reimbursement and one day trips for conferences, meetings, and the like. Any amounts over this limit must be approved by (VICE PRESIDENT). All travel-related expense reports, except for local mileage reimbursement or one-day trips, must be approved by the supervisor/manager.

Employee-Incurred Expenses and Reimbursement

Alternate Policy 2   5010.2

(COMPANY) will pay all actual and reasonable business-related expenses incurred by employees in the performance of their job responsibilities. All such expenses incurred by an employee must be approved by his or her manager before payment will be made by the accounting department.

Expense reports are to be submitted and supported by evidence of proof of purchase, e.g., receipts. Expense reports are due in the (ACCOUNTING DEPARTMENT) the last working day of each month.

Mileage Reimbursement   5020

Comment

When an employee is asked to use his or her personal vehicle in conducting company business, the employer should reimburse the employee for such trips. The use of personal vehicles to run company business errands, such as to the post office or office supply store, may start out as a casual request. However, the employee may later be asked to contribute many dollars out of his or her pocket considering today's gasoline prices and other auto-related expenses.

To avoid any questions or misunderstandings, you should establish a policy to specify the conditions under which such reimbursement will be made. Of course, you could adopt a policy which discourages use of personal vehicles for company-related trips. Some companies allow or require employees to use the company-owned vehicle for such trips.

The policy should establish:

- The rate of reimbursement;
- The definition of what constitutes company travel;
- A rule on whether or not reporting to work prior to company travel is required;
- The method to be used to calculate miles traveled;
- The company's policy relating to insurance; and
- The procedure to follow to request mileage reimbursement.

As a general rule, employers will be liable to third parties injured as a result of an accident caused by an employee on company-related business. This is probably true even if the employee uses his or her personal vehicle without being required to do so by the employer, as long as the employer knew or should have known of the employee's use of a personal vehicle. The employer's liability to the employee for his or her personal injuries in such a situation is governed by state workers' compensation law.

What is not clear, state to state, is whether the employer is liable to the employee for damage to the employee's vehicle. This issue depends on the facts, and especially, whether the employer required the personal vehicle to be used and the level of the employee's negligence in driving. Therefore, the employer should consider the value of employees using their personal vehicles against the potential liability involved. An attorney should be consulted for answers to specific questions regarding liability in such situations. Also, the employer who adopts a policy permitting personal vehicle use should consult the company liability insurer regarding coverage of employees and their vehicles.

It is also wise to state in your policy that use of a personal vehicle is for the employee's convenience, or words to that effect. However, this is no guarantee that your liability for your employee's negligence will be prevented. Never require use of personal vehicles, or else the liability becomes more certain. An employer should also take steps to determine, or require a written statement, that the employee has a valid driver's license and maintains satisfactory liability insurance prior to using a personal vehicle for company business purposes. Keep in mind that many personal insurance policies do not provide coverage for accidents that occur while making business use of an automobile.

If no mileage reimbursement is to be provided, employees may elect to compute and deduct actual auto expenses or deduct mileage at a rate of $0.30 (30 cents) per mile. This is subject, of course, to the rules and regulations of the Internal Revenue Code.

If the standard mileage rate is used, no separate deduction is available to employees for depreciation, maintenance and repairs, tires, gasoline (including gasoline taxes), oil, insurance, and registration fees.

Mileage Reimbursement

Alternate Policy 1   5020.1

For the convenience of the employee, when he or she desires to use his or her personal vehicle for company business, all employees of (COMPANY) shall be reimbursed for company-related business travel at the rate of (ADD DOLLAR AMOUNT) per mile. Use of a personal vehicle is never required by the company and is discretionary on the part of the employee.

Travel expenses between your home and your assigned work location are not reimbursable. If an employee is required to travel from home directly to a third location on company business and then to work, the company will reimburse the employee for the difference between the mileage the employee normally drives to work and the total miles driven for business purposes.

Requests for reimbursement of business-related travel will be submitted to your supervisor/manager for approval on a standard company expense report. Reimbursement requests will include the following:

1. Date of travel
2. Beginning and ending odometer readings for each trip
3. Travel destination
4. Number of miles traveled on company business
5. The reason for company travel

The expense report must be signed and dated by the employee and initialed by his or her supervisor/manager. The reports must be submitted to the accounting department and will be processed according to the policy, *Employee-Incurred Expenses and Reimbursement — Section 5010.*

The employee, in using his or her vehicle for company purposes, assumes liability for his or her vehicle. All employees who desire to use their personal vehicles for company business must sign statements verifying that they have a current driver's license and vehicle liability insurance in at least the minimum amounts required by state law.

Mileage Reimbursement

Alternate Policy 2   5020.2

Employees of (COMPANY) who use their personal vehicle for company purposes will be provided an automobile allowance of (ADD DOLLAR AMOUNT) per month. This allowance is intended to compensate the employee for all costs related to the operation of his or her personal vehicle on company business. The employee assumes liability for his or her personal vehicle in work-related travel. Use of a personal vehicle is always for the employee's benefit and will never be required by the company. Employees must sign a statement confirming that they have a valid driver's license and sufficient vehicle liability insurance.

Travel expenses between home and your work location are not reimbursable. Most company-related travel will originate from our company location. However, in those cases where it is advantageous, considering time and distance, to leave directly from your place of residence, the request for reimbursement should be based upon total miles traveled for the company less normal daily mileage to and/or from your work location.

Mileage reimbursement will be approved by your supervisor/manager by submitting an expense report detailing the purpose of such travel, date of travel, and mileage traveled. All such expense reports must be submitted for approval as soon as possible but no later than (ADD DATE).

Requests for reimbursement are due in the accounting department on the last working day of each month. The employee's reimbursement will be available on the third working day of the month following receipt by the accounting department.

Travel Reimbursement   5030

Comment

Travel is typically an important part of the cost of doing business because personal contact and communication are necessary to the success of many companies. The cost of travel and business conferences has become an increasingly substantial part of overhead especially for sales and service companies.

Employees should be required to make an advance travel plan by:

- Contacting clients prior to the visit;
- Coordinating visits to several proximate locations whenever possible;
- Making definite itineraries; and
- Confirming appointments in advance.

A clear definition of the purpose of each business trip is essential. Travel reimbursement policies generally define the purpose of company travel and the business ethics to govern reimbursement. This policy should provide as much flexibility as possible so that an employee is not caught in any location without the flexibility to adjust his or her schedule to meet a particular situation.

Most companies request a signed statement of travel-related expenses prior to reimbursing the employee. A sample travel reimbursement form follows the alternate policies on travel reimbursement. As a convenience to your employees, you may wish to print the form on an envelope providing them an easy way to collect and account for all expenses during their busy travel schedule.

It is wise to review the company travel policy with each employee at the time of issuing the advance reimbursement form.

Travel Reimbursement

Alternate Policy 1   5030.1

This policy establishes the general guidelines and procedures to be followed when business travel is required.

1. Travel-related expenses are to be detailed on the company travel reimbursement form.

2. Employees who prefer to use their personal vehicles for their convenience on company business, including trips to the airport, will be reimbursed at the standard company mileage rate, provided that the time and distance involved is reasonable under the circumstances.

3. All parking expenses and highway tolls incurred as a result of business travel will be reimbursed.

4. All air travel must be approved in advance by the employee's supervisor/manager unless unavoidable. All travel will be by coach class whenever possible. First class may be used when coach class accommodations are not available or when traveling with a customer who is traveling first class. The duplicate airline ticket receipt should be attached to the company reimbursement form.

5. The company insures employees who fly when traveling on company business with a travel accident rider to our regular group insurance policy. Purchase of additional air travel insurance is not a reimbursable expense.

Note: Delete this preceding statement if your company does not provide such travel insurance, but consider whether or not such insurance purchased by the employee should be reimbursable anyway.

6. Employees should request advance approval for use of a rental car at their destination. If a rental car is used, additional insurance should not be purchased because of our existing insurance coverage. A copy of the rental car agreement form must accompany the travel reimbursement form.

7. Employees should select moderately-priced lodging convenient to their destination to minimize time and expense. A detailed receipt from the hotel or motel must accompany the reimbursement form unless such is unavailable, in which case, a credit card receipt is acceptable.

8. Employees must submit receipts for meals with the reimbursement form. Reasonable tips, when paid by the employee and noted on the receipt, will be reimbursed.

9. Travel reimbursement requests are due in the accounting department on the last working day of each month.

Travel Reimbursement

Alternate Policy 2   5030.2
_____

All company travel, conference, and meeting expenses must clearly serve the objectives of the company and should not conflict with the ethical standards of our company. In preparing for company travel, prior approval must be obtained from your supervisor/manager by submitting a travel approval request memo detailing the itinerary, estimated cost, and business purpose of travel. Upon receiving approval from your supervisor/manager, contact the (ACCOUNTING DEPARTMENT) to obtain a travel number. This number must be used to claim reimbursement. If air travel is required, request the (ACCOUNTING DEPARTMENT) to make the reservations. All personnel will travel economy class unless extenuating circumstances require first class travel.

Lodging expenses are to be reimbursed at actual cost. Unless special circumstances dictate otherwise, mid-price lodging facilities shall be selected. Room accommodations will be honored only for one person per room, per night. Expenses for a non-employee are not reimbursable. Exceptions include meals for a customer or business associate when discussing business or for other legitimate business-related meetings and conferences. Should a non-employee companion accompany you on a business trip, the "single" rate for lodging should be noted on your copy of the bill and expense report.

Reimbursement for food and other incidental travel expenses are referred to as per diem expenses. Per diem is defined on the basis of the hours spent in travel, generally measured from point of departure to point of return. The full per diem allowance is (ADD DOLLAR AMOUNT) per day. Full per diem is granted for travel requiring an employee to be away from home for more than 15 hours. Half per diem is granted for trips involving 6 to 15 hours, and no per diem is allowed for trips less than 6 hours.

Note: *You may decide to reimburse employees for their actual meal and incidental expenses. Some companies give an employee the option to claim more than a modest per diem if they submit receipts showing expenses over the per diem.*

Travel advances are intended to allow employees the convenience of using the company's money for business purposes while traveling. However, only reasonable travel advances will be granted and only on (ADD NUMBER) days' prior request. Typically, the travel advance will

Travel Reimbursement

Alternate Policy 2 (continued)   5030.2

be equal to the per diem times the expected number of travel days unless the employee can justify a greater need. The advance must be accounted for on the travel reimbursement form by deducting it from the employee's claimed expenses.

All requests for reimbursement of company travel are due in the (ACCOUNTING DEPARTMENT) by the last working day of the month. Payment will be made to the employee by the fifth working day of the following month.

If the travel advance exceeds the claimed expenses, employees shall attach a check to the expense report made payable to the company for the difference.

Weekly Expense Envelope — Side 1

Week of _____ **19** _____

Expense Items		Sunday	Monday	Tuesday	Wednesday	Thursday	Friday	Saturday	Sunday	Totals
Breakfast	1									
Lunch	2									
Dinner	3									
Hotel	4									
Entertainment	5									
Local Transportation	6									
Phone	7									
Tips	8									
Transportation Plane — Auto	9									
Auto Rental	10									
Gasoline/Oil	11									
Misc. Car Expense	12									
Parking Fees	13									
Toll Charges	14									
Sundry	15									
Misc. Expenses	16									
Mileage Rate at	17									
Totals	18									
Speedometer End										
Start										
Miles Driven										
City										

Small Change Recap — Enter in proper column above

Date	Cab and Bus Etc.			Phone Calls		Tips and Parking Fees	
Sun.							
Mon.							
Tues.							
Wed.							
Thurs.							
Fri.							
Sat.							

Total Expenses _____

Less Advance or Personal Expense _____

Balance Due _____

Name _____ Department _____

Address _____

City _____

For Office Use			
Approved By	Date Paid	Check or Voucher #	Amount Paid

Weekly Expense Envelope — Side 2

Explanation of Entertainment and Special Expense

Save your receipts.

Hotel and motel receipts must be enclosed.

Keep receipts for: Any expenditure of $25 or more for entertainment, tips or gifts

Transportation such as railroad, auto rental, bus, airplane, etc.

| Date | Entertainment Details — Enter amounts in proper column | | | | |
	Company	Person	Where	Reason	Amount

Notes:

Use of Rental Car on Company Business   5040

Comment

Companies requiring their employees to rent automobiles to conduct company business should establish a policy to outline the company's reimbursement responsibilities.

One of the most frequent concerns of business travelers is their need for additional insurance coverage. A company may want to add a rider to its current liability policy to cover employee use of rental cars.

The company should also consider establishing an account with car rental agencies and assigning someone within the company the responsibility of making all company reservations. Then, if there are questions at any time concerning billings or special problems, the company will have an established point of contact for an immediate response.

Use of Company Vehicles

Certain employees are provided with vehicles for use are part of their employment with the company. Employees using company vehicles are required to observe the following:

- Personal use of company vehicles is prohibited.
- Employees are required to keep the interior and exterior of the car clean.
- It is the employee's responsibility to make certain that the vehicle is properly cared for. While not required to perform the work, the employee should check the oil, watch dates for preventive maintenance work, and make certain that the vehicle is scheduled for maintenance and repair by authorized service departments.
- No one other than the authorized employee shall be permitted to operate the vehicle.
- Use of company vehicles while under the influence of or after partaking of alcohol, drugs, etc. is prohibited.
- While operating the vehicle, the employee must wear a seat belt at all times and obey all rules of the road.
- Employees are responsible for any parking tickets and other citations which result from an employee's personal negligence or disregard of motor vehicle laws or regulations. In the event of an accident involving an automobile, the employee is required to obtain the following information:
  - The license numbers and registration information of all vehicles involved.
  - The names, addresses, and company affiliation of all occupants of all vehicles involved.
  - The names and addresses of any witnesses to the accident not directly involved in the accident.
  - A detailed narrative description of the accident.
  - The name and badge numbers of any investigating police officers.
  - The name, address, and insurance policy number of any insurance carrier covering any of the drivers or other vehicles involved in the accident.

In the event of an accident, provide the information described above to your supervisor. Cooperate with investigating police officials, but limit further discussions regarding the accident to your supervisor.

Use of Rental Car on Company Business

Alternate Policy 1   5040.1

The following guidelines are to be adhered to by our employees who, while performing company business, are required to rent a car:

1. Standard car rental will be an intermediate class automobile.

2. Car rental reservations will be arranged by the (ACCOUNTING DEPARTMENT). The traveling employee is responsible for picking up a car rental request form prior to departure, and upon return, submitting a copy of the car rental agreement with his or her expense report. The car rental request form will identify the date that the car reservation was made, the person making the reservation, the car rental company, the pick-up point, and a reservation number.

3. (COMPANY) is self-insured, so it is not necessary to incur an additional charge for collision or damage deductible waiver or any other optional insurance (e.g., higher liability limits) offered by the rental company. Therefore, charges for such optional insurance will not be reimbursed by the company.

4. If special conditions exist and other than the intermediate size car is necessary, document the reason on your expense report.

Use of Rental Car on Company Business

Alternate Policy 2   5040.2

Employees required to travel because of their job responsibilities may rent a car upon receiving the approval of their supervisor/manager.

An economy or compact size car will be the employee's first choice in obtaining a rental car. (COMPANY) is self-insured for damage to rental cars used on company business. Any additional insurance charges offered as an option by the rental company are not reimbursable.

A copy of the rental car agreement must accompany the employee's monthly travel expense report.

Conferences and Meetings 5050

Comment

Your company may want to establish a policy to encourage employees' participation in job-related professional conferences and meetings. Not only will the employee benefit, but the company will benefit as well through professional exchange of its employees.

Companies with tight budgets may want to limit the number of approvals of such requests or restrict approvals to local meetings. You should also consider whether an equivalent program is available closer to home or whether the program could be brought in-house and shared with a greater number of employees.

Conferences and Meetings

Alternate Policy 1   5050.1

Employees may request time off or company financial support or both to attend conferences or meetings sponsored by institutions or professional organizations. The subject matter to be presented must relate directly to the employee's position or provide beneficial information to be shared in the employee's department.

The employee's supervisor/manager and the (VICE PRESIDENT) must approve the employee's participation in the conference or meeting.

The company will pay for the following expenses if attendance is approved: tuition or registration fees, travel costs, lodging, and meal expenses not covered by registration.

Time off for attendance and travel during normal working hours will be paid at the normal rate of pay.

Conferences and Meetings

Alternate Policy 2   5050.2

Our company encourages employees to increase their job-related skills and knowledge through participation in professional conferences and meetings. Employees must submit a request to their immediate supervisor/manager for approval to attend such conferences or meetings. The request must identify the subject matter of the presentation, how it is job-related, and an estimate of the expenses.

If the request is approved, the company will reimburse the employee for 75% of his or her conference-related expenses: travel, registration fees, workbooks, and lodging and meals not included in the registration fees.

The time off for employee's attendance and travel will be paid at the employee's normal rate of pay.

Professional Memberships   5060

Comment

Your company may find it advantageous to pay for all or a part of membership fees for exempt employees who join job-related professional organizations.

Such sponsorship not only promotes the professional growth and development of your employee but also gives visibility to your company in professional circles. The advantages of a professional membership, such as publications and seminars, can ultimately benefit company productivity and know-how.

Your company may choose to select a number of professional organizations which an employee is entitled to join at company expense, or your policy may specify a dollar amount up to which an employee can receive as membership reimbursement every year.

Alternatively, your policy may ask employees to submit requests for company support of organizational memberships which will be approved on a case-by-case basis.

Professional Memberships

Alternate Policy 1   5060.1

(COMPANY) encourages its employees' job-related professional growth and development. In expression of this support, the company will reimburse each exempt employee up to $100 per calendar year for expenses incurred in joining professional organizations. Professional organizations are defined as (LIST APPLICABLE ORGANIZATIONS) and similar professional organizations which have job-related educational programs and publications.

Reimbursement will be made upon receipt of an expense report accompanied by proof of membership payment.

Professional Memberships

Alternate Policy 2   5060.2

Employees are encouraged to participate in and continue their professional development while employed by our company. The company will sponsor one membership in a job-related professional organization per exempt employee per year.

Employees are encouraged to invite other interested employees to appropriate organizational functions and to distribute publications and other organizational literature of general interest within the company.

Approval of a company sponsored membership in an appropriate professional organization will be the responsibility of the employee's department supervisor/manager.

Relocation of Current or New Employees   5070

Comment

You will need to establish a policy to cover the expenses incurred in relocating an employee and his or her family. Such a policy is an incentive to encourage present employees to relocate to other company locations or to attract out-of-area prospective employees to join your company.

The issues faced by a company attempting to negotiate the relocation expenses of a current employee or to entice a new employee to join the company are becoming more complex. Certain limits to relocation expenses must be set, and categories of expenses must be defined (e.g., house-hunting trip, lodging for the employee's family, number of automobiles allowed in one move). For example, to what extent is the company willing to assist the employee's spouse to find employment in the community? Will the company pay the relocation expenses of a friend who lives with the employee? Does the company have networking contacts for the introduction of the spouse or friend into a defined professional field or a company?

Housing and living costs are also a major consideration in the already complicated picture of relocation. Will the company buy the employee's house if the real estate market is slow, or guarantee a real estate loan in the new location? Such issues further involve the cost of appraisals, surveys, brokers' commissions, and other matters related to the purchase and sale of residential real estate.

Your company will want to consider establishing the length of time an employee must have worked for or must remain with the company before or after relocation in order to have expenses reimbursed. Other considerations include:

- The distance an employee can be expected to commute before relocation is required;
- Allowable relocation expenses;
- Number of reimbursable trips to seek out a residence prior to the actual move;
- Allowable subsistence for the pre-move trip, en route during the move, and upon arrival while waiting for housing; and
- Allowable costs related to transporting household goods, automobiles, and other personal effects.

It is wise to construct a policy that provides for certain minimum expenses the company will assume for all qualified employees or prospective employees.

Above the minimum (typical) expenses, the policy becomes a guideline for negotiating the upper limit and additional categories of reimbursable expense in certain appropriate circumstances. In other words, the policy guarantees the employee a fair level of reimbursement, assuming that defined expenses are actually and reasonably incurred.

The policy is not restrictive from the standpoint of an upper limit of dollars or in the categories of reimbursable expenses. For instance, if your company must hire a senior scientist who lives in Australia because the ten others in the world with his or her qualifications are unavailable, commitments to some novel relocation expenditures may need to be made. In this way, the company avoids having to redraft or violate its own policy.

Companies with government contracts should tailor their policy to the applicable cost regulations and Cost Accounting Standards. It may still be necessary, however, for a company to incur unallowable costs in order to hire or transfer a key employee. To that extent, your policy should not be restrictive.

Relocation of Current or New Employees

Alternate Policy 1   5070.1

When any new or current exempt employee is required to work full time, at company request, at a location beyond a reasonable commuting distance from his or her present residence, reasonable and necessary moving expenses will be paid by (COMPANY). A reasonable commuting distance is considered to be 50 miles or less one way. Work shall be deemed full time if it is for a continuous period in excess of (ADD TIME).

Employees who voluntarily terminate within twelve months from the date of relocation will be required to refund all expenses paid under this policy to the company. A statement to this effect will be included in the Relocation Request Form.

The following moving expense assistance items are provided for the following:

1. Shipment of household goods of up to (ADD NUMBER OF POUNDS);

2. Packing and unpacking of household goods;

3. Appropriate employee and dependent transportation from the former residence to the new location, including all reasonable and necessary means of travel, plus the reasonable cost of meals and lodging en route as required;

4. Storage charges for household goods in transit for a maximum of 30 days when approved in advance;

5. Automobile allowance of $0.30 (30 cents) per mile for up to two vehicles actually driven to a new location;

6. Premiums for insurance covering the shipment of goods;

7. Temporary living expenses of the employee for reasonable accommodations and meals for up to 30 days' duration when the employee transfers in advance of his or her family;

8. Reasonable employee expense for travel home, typically once every three months after transfer and before the family moves to the permanent location;

9. Normal and reasonable residence-finding expenses for a spouse for up to seven days while seeking a new residence, with a maximum of two trips;

10. Temporary living expenses for reasonable accommodations and meals for a maximum of one week after the employee transfers his or her family to the new location and before moving into a new residence.

Relocation of Current or New Employees

Alternate Policy 1 (continued)   5070.1

The company will also pay for the following:

1. Home Selling Cost — normal real estate commission, legal fees, and all normal seller's closing costs.

2. Home Purchasing Costs —

    a. Fees for mortgage loan service (POINTS) not to exceed the greater of three points or (ADD DOLLAR AMOUNT), unless prior written approval is obtained;

    b. Title insurance and/or title search and legal fees; and

    c. Recording, appraisal, survey, and transfer fees.

The company will not pay for the following:

1. Legal fees to clear substantial title defects;

2. Repairs to the property sold or purchased; and

3. Moving of perishables or large, bulky items such as trailers, recreational vehicles, horses, boats, extensive hobby equipment, and items for which an unusual amount of expense is incurred for insurance, safety, or protection, such as an extensive art collection. However, an exception will be made for a house trailer which will be the employee's permanent residence for at least six months.

A Relocation Request Form must be filled out and submitted to the (ACCOUNTING DEPARTMENT) as soon as possible following approval of relocation by the (VICE PRESIDENT). The request will include an estimate of the relocation expenses. The employee, his or her supervisor/manager and the (ACCOUNTING DEPARTMENT) will jointly review the reimbursement request prior to final approval.

Reimbursement will be made to the extent of all approved expenses subject to submittal of statements of charges or receipts of payment. Exceptions to the above policy may be approved by the (VICE PRESIDENT) or his or her designee.

Relocation of Current or New Employees

Alternate Policy 2   5070.2

(COMPANY) will pay for all reasonable and necessary moving expenses for any new or current exempt employee required by the company to transfer his or her full time work location. The new work location must be beyond a reasonable commuting distance from his or her present residence. A reasonable commuting distance is defined as 50 miles or less, one way. An employee who receives company relocation expenses is expected to remain with the company for at least one year.

The following summarize our company's requirements and conditions in the relocation of new or current employees:

1. The employee and his or her supervisor/manager will identify all major costs that the employee will incur as a result of the move. An estimated total dollar relocation figure will be arrived at and a relocation request will be prepared.

2. The employee, his or her supervisor/manager, and a representative from the accounting department will review the relocation plan and prepare the company reimbursement statement. The statement will be submitted to the (VICE PRESIDENT) for final approval.

3. Upon receipt of final approval, the (ACCOUNTING DEPARTMENT) will request estimates from two reputable and licensed carriers and select the carrier to move the employee's household goods. A copy of the carrier's estimate will be given to the employee.

4. The (ACCOUNTING DEPARTMENT) will review the estimate in relation to the approved reimbursement statement and process the expenditure. Any discrepancies must be accounted for and approved before processing for payment. A similar procedure will be followed for any changes to the reimbursement statement. The company will comply with IRS regulations and provide the employee with the necessary information on the taxable status of the relocation.

5. Transportation for personal and family relocation may be by private vehicle or by public transportation.

   a. Private automobile — Employee will be reimbursed at the current company approved mileage rate. Mileage allowance will be based on the most direct route between point of residence and new work location. Reimbursement will be limited to one family vehicle.

   b. Public transportation — If the employee chooses air travel, only coach or tourist class is authorized. If not available, the employee's supervisor/manager may authorize first class.

Relocation of Current or New Employees

Alternate Policy 2 (continued)   5070.2

6. Authorized travel in addition to actual move — One, three-day, pre-move trip to the new work location for house-hunting by the employee and spouse or friend may be approved by employee's manager in advance.

7. Miscellaneous expenses — The employee will be reimbursed $300 for miscellaneous (non-receipted) relocation expenses.

8. Subsistence — Reasonable food and lodging expenses of employee and his or her family are authorized. All requested reimbursements must be supported by a receipt.

9. Household goods — All costs of packing, unpacking, insuring, and shipping household goods are authorized in accordance with the approved carrier's estimate. The employee assumes full responsibility for any claims against the carrier arising from the move.

10. Shipment of a vehicle — Approval must be requested in advance with initial relocation plan.

11. Reimbursement — Following relocation, the employee assumes responsibility for providing all necessary documentation for relocation expenditures to expedite payment of all costs.

Should an employee voluntarily terminate his or her employment with (COMPANY) within one year of relocation, the employee will refund to the company a pro rata share of the total relocation expenses paid based on the difference between the number of days that the employee worked after relocation and 365.

An agreement to this effect shall be signed by the employee and attached to the company reimbursement statement before final approval. The agreement will also authorize the company to deduct the pro rata share of relocation expenses from the employee's final paycheck. If any amount remains owing to the company, the employee shall pay this amount to the company before termination is completed or make other arrangements for payment (a promissory note).

Temporary Assignment Allowance   5080

Comment

When employees are asked to assume a temporary assignment, the company must be willing to compensate the employee for the additional expenses incurred in such an assignment. Just as you have done in the previous policy, *Relocation of Current or New Employees*, identify and list the types of expenses which your company will pay when an employee accepts a temporary assignment.

A temporary assignment is one which is performed in a location some distance away from the employee's normal work location and is considered beyond reasonable commuting distance, for example, more than 50 miles one way. The length of a temporary assignment is also longer than one that is typically covered under the travel reimbursement policy. However, it is temporary, so that it would not be economically justifiable to relocate the employee who will return to his or her normal work location (usually more than one month and usually less than one year).

The purpose of this policy is to encourage employees to accept such assignments which, of necessity, take them away from family and friends, but at the same time, save the cost of typical travel or relocation allowances.

As in relocation situations, your policy should allow for flexibility depending on the employee's circumstances and the work location. For example, lodging costing $60 a day for three months is not cost effective. However, a small apartment, rented on a week-to-week or month-to-month basis for $500 per month, may be.

Temporary Assignment Allowance

Alternate Policy 1   5080.1

(COMPANY) will provide specified reimbursement for travel, reasonable accommodations, and other miscellaneous expenses to employees who are requested to take a business assignment which is beyond reasonable commuting distance and more than three but less than twelve months in duration.

Approval of temporary assignment allowances must be requested in advance and require the approval of the employee's supervisor/manager and the vice president. An expense allowance budget, prepared jointly by employee and supervisor/manager, will accompany the request.

Reimbursable expenses include the following when circumstances require them:

1. Coach class air travel for the employee;

2. Shipment of up to (ADD NUMBER OF POUNDS) of personal or household goods;

3. Home maintenance costs (grass cutting, snow shoveling, security service);

4. Housing expense at the new location, including full rent and utilities;

5. Leased car;

6. One, three-day trip to locate a temporary residence;

7. One round-trip, coach class, air fare every (ADD NUMBER OF WEEKS) to visit immediate family at the employee's permanent residence or for a spouse or friend to visit the employee. If the employee chooses to travel using his or her personal vehicle, mileage will be reimbursed at the company's current rate.

8. Personal vehicle mileage will also be reimbursed for all trips between the employee's temporary residence and temporary work assignment in lieu of leased car.

All reimbursable or charged expenses should be submitted monthly on a company expense report to the (ACCOUNTING DEPARTMENT) for processing and payment. Reimbursement will be made for all items listed in the approved expense allowance budget.

The employee may submit other reimbursement requests to his or her manager for review and approval. Approval of the (VICE PRESIDENT) is required for all non-budgeted requests in excess of $100. The employee may also request an advance of expenses of up to one month's budgeted expenses prior to travel.

Temporary Assignment Allowance

Alternate Policy 2   5080.2

This policy defines the expense allowance applicable when company employees are asked to accept a temporary assignment. A temporary assignment is defined as one for which the employee would have to travel on a continuous basis (e.g., daily) more than 50 miles one way from his or her present residence for a period of more than 30 days and less than one year.

The employee and his or her supervisor/manager will develop a temporary assignment budget, projecting allowable employee expenses. The budget will be approved by the (VICE PRESIDENT). The following expenses will be reimbursed by the company:

1. Meal Allowance — The company will provide a daily meal allowance of (ADD DOLLAR AMOUNT).

2. Vehicle —

   a. Personal. The company will reimburse mileage by personal vehicle to the temporary work location at the established company mileage rate. After arrival, no mileage reimbursement will be allowed until the final return trip.

   b. Rental. A rented or leased car may be provided by the company. The employee will be expected to reimburse the company for any personal use of the leased or rented car.

3. Air travel — The employee will be reimbursed for round-trip, coach class air fare to the assigned temporary work location. The employee will be granted one round-trip, coach class, air fare to and from the employee's permanent residence for every one month of continuous temporary assignment (may be used by the employee or one family member visiting employee). This assumes that the employee has not driven his or her personal vehicle to the temporary location.

4. Temporary residence — The company will reimburse for up to 30 days' lodging in a hotel or motel. For temporary assignments known to exceed 30 days, the employee will be expected to seek a furnished apartment or negotiate reasonable, long-term rates at a hotel/motel.

5. Temporary assignment expenses — Additional, reasonable temporary assignment expenses will be approved by the employee's supervisor/manager on basis of actual and necessary expenses related to the particular assignment. Expenses to be considered include, but are not limited to, telephone calls, business conferences, supplies, laundry, and postage.

Expense reports are to be submitted to the (ACCOUNTING DEPARTMENT) at the end of each work week. Receipts are required for lodging expenditures, car rental, air travel (submit the duplicate ticket receipt), and additional expenses approved per Paragraph 5 above. Reimbursement will be made within 5 working days of receipt of the report.

Educational Assistance   5090

Comment

An employee who takes steps to increase his or her personal education and skills development will often become more effective and productive on the job. An employer who has the resources to provide partial or total assistance to employees to enhance their job-related skills and education will often reap multiple rewards, including increased employee morale and productivity.

In developing such a policy, determine:

- The type of educational programs for which reimbursement will be provided;
- The eligibility requirements to be used;
- The percentage of company reimbursement;
- The grade requirements to be maintained, if any;
- The method and procedure for reimbursement; and
- The management staff who must approve the employee's request.

Educational Assistance

Alternate Policy 1   5090.1

To encourage the personal development of our employees, (COMPANY) provides (ADD AMOUNT) of tuition cost and laboratory fees to regular full time employees with at least one full year of continuous service who successfully complete approved courses.

The employee and his or her supervisor/manager must agree that the achievement of the employee's career goals will require that the employee participate in courses or training not provided by the company. The employee must submit a request for tuition reimbursement to his or her supervisor/manager at least five days before the course begins.

The supervisor/manager who recommends approval of courses for tuition reimbursement will forward the request to the (PERSONNEL DEPARTMENT) for final approval. The employee will be informed of the department's approval. Tuition aid may be approved for any course or training at an accredited college, university, or other institution of higher learning. Correspondence courses normally won't qualify for tuition aid. Supervisors/managers are authorized to adjust the employee's work schedule when the course is given only during company time. The employee is expected to make up any time off with pay.

Employees are required to submit copies of grade reports or other evidence of satisfactory completion to the (PERSONNEL DEPARTMENT) as proof of successful completion within 30 days after completing the course. Upon receipt of evidence of payment of tuition and proof of successful completion of the course or training, the (PERSONNEL DEPARTMENT) will forward the approved request and documentation to the (ACCOUNTING DEPARTMENT) for payment. The employee will receive (ADD AMOUNT) reimbursement.

Employees failing to successfully complete courses or training will not be eligible for reimbursement. If an employee voluntarily terminates his or her employment within one year following reimbursement for educational assistance, the employee will refund a pro rata share of the total educational assistance expenses paid based on the difference between the number of days that the employee worked after reimbursement and 365. An agreement to this effect shall be signed by the employee and attached to the company reimbursement statement before final approval. The agreement will also authorize the company to deduct the pro rata share of educational assistance expenses from the employee's final paycheck. If any amount remains owing to the company, the employee shall pay this amount to the company before termination is completed or make other arrangements for payment, such as a promissory note.

Educational Assistance

Alternate Policy 2   5090.2

Educational assistance is available to all full time employees beginning on the date of hire. The decision to provide this monetary assistance is based upon your supervisor's/manager's recommendation.

Courses must be attended on the designated premises of the sponsoring institution. An exception to this policy are courses offered by television. Courses qualifying for financial assistance are those directly related to the employee's present assignment or directly related to the employee's job family (knowledge that will be used within a reasonable length of time).

Educational assistance approval must be received in advance. The employee and his or her supervisor/manager will jointly prepare an educational assistance request. The request will include the course description; dates of enrollment; time off, if necessary; and the costs of tuition, registration fees, required textbooks, and laboratory fees. Final approval is made by the (VICE PRESIDENT) who will forward the request to the (ACCOUNTING DEPARTMENT).

Within 30 days of completion of the course, the employee must submit documents to the (ACCOUNTING DEPARTMENT) indicating that the course was satisfactorily completed, the grade received, if any, and original receipts for all approved expenses. For all graded courses, a minimum grade of "C" or its equivalent is required for reimbursement. No reimbursement will be made for incomplete coursework.

If a course is available on either company time or personal time, the employee is expected to use his or her personal time. Use or non-use of company time for class attendance is one of the determining factors in computing reimbursement. The percentage of normal reimbursement for approved expenses will be according to the following: 100% — Non-use of company time; 75% — combination of company time and employee personal time; 50% — total use of company time. Normally, the use of company time will be unpaid time off. An employee on formal probation is not eligible for educational assistance.

Should an employee voluntarily terminate his or her employment within one year following reimbursement for educational assistance, the employee will refund a pro rata share of the total educational assistance expenses paid based on the difference between the number of days that the employee worked after reimbursement and 365. An agreement to this effect

Educational Assistance

Alternate Policy 2 (continued)   5090.2

shall be signed by the employee and attached to the company reimbursement statement before final approval. The agreement will also authorize the company to deduct the pro rata share of educational assistance expenses from the employee's final paycheck.

If any amount remains owing to the company, the employee shall pay this amount to the company before termination is completed or make other arrangements for payment, such as a promissory note.

Required Management Approval   5100

Comment

In developing your company policies in the areas of travel, educational assistance, attendance at conferences or seminars, and other expense-related matters, it is impossible to predict all of the possible extenuating circumstances which may justify exceptions to a given policy.

Most companies resolve this problem by spelling out general guidelines in their policies and providing for evaluation of exceptional circumstances on a case-by-case basis at some management level. The management staff, schooled in the company philosophy, can usually determine if the employee's request for an exception is:

- Consistent with general guidelines or purposes expressed in the policy;
- In the business interest of the company;
- Reasonable to both the company and the employee; and
- In keeping with exceptions granted in other similar situations. The importance of keeping an historical record of exceptions and interpretations is stressed in *How to Use this Book*.

In the majority of employee reimbursement situations, it is important to have the employee request approval prior to any expenditure of monies. There will be times when extenuating circumstances may require a traveling employee to incur costs beyond those originally discussed and/or approved (e.g., being forced to accept a first class flight when he or she missed the original reservation, or accepting a more expensive rental car when reservations were misplaced).

In those situations, give the employee some judgmental leeway and an opportunity to justify his or her decision either on the expense report itself or in an attached statement.

Required Management Approval

Alternate Policy 1   5100.1

All travel expense requests, mileage or subsistence expense reports, purchase requisitions, educational assistance reimbursements, and other business-related expense reports must be approved by the employee's supervisor/manager before the request will be processed for payment by the (ACCOUNTING DEPARTMENT). Where a projected expense allowance budget was prepared for relocation of employees or temporary assignment, the request should be submitted to the (ACCOUNTING DEPARTMENT) following its approval by the (VICE PRESIDENT).

(COMPANY) managers may only approve expenditures which are business-related, reasonable, and consistent with the letter and intent of company policies. Occasionally, a policy will not cover a specific expenditure. Similarly, the facts and circumstances relating to a particular item or expense may justify an exception to the letter of a policy. In these events, a supervisor/manager should consult with the (ACCOUNTING DEPARTMENT) for guidance. Among the factors to be considered in resolving such issues are:

1. The intent or purpose of the policy;

2. The particular facts or circumstances surrounding the expense;

3. The necessity for the expense;

4. The amount involved; and

5. Previous similar situations. Employees who incur expenses, or charge expenses to the company, without prior approval do so at their own risk. Employees are invited to seek prior approval from management in questionable situations.

Required Management Approval

Alternate Policy 2   5100.2

All employee travel, educational assistance, mileage, subsistence, and relocation expenses must have a supervisor's/manager's approval. Employees are required to request approval in advance of expenditures whenever possible to ensure no delay in company reimbursement. All expense reports are due in the (ACCOUNTING DEPARTMENT) on the final working day of each month. Prior to being honored by the (ACCOUNTING DEPARTMENT), these reports must have the employee's signature and date and must be approved by the employee's supervisor/manager.

Child Care   5110

Comment

The last decade saw a tremendous increase in the number of families with two wage earners and single parent wage earners. With this increase has come a growing demand by employees for affordable child care and/or child care assistance from employers. Already, federal and state tax credits exist to offset some child care costs. Legislation has been introduced to provide additional methods of child care assistance as well. Many larger companies have gone even further by providing child care facilities located on or near company facilities.

The child care policy set forth here provides financial assistance through reimbursements of allowable child care expenses. The policy establishes eligibility requirements, the type of care for which reimbursements are provided, and the amount of reimbursement. As with many employment issues, proposed legislation may impact your policy.

Code Section 129 of the Internal Revenue Code allows an employer to deduct amounts paid by it under a dependent care assistance program.

The policy that follows is designed to comply with the Internal Revenue Code provisions subject to tailoring by your legal counsel to satisfy technical requirements. It also avoids loss of deductibility as a result of discrimination in favor of highly-compensated employees and the payment of more than 25% of the plan's benefits to persons owning more than 5% of the company.

Small companies may not have the resources to offer child care after school. However, they may provide limited options. When a business is located near a school or a bus stop, children may be allowed to come into the business under strictly controlled conditions to wait for their parent to get off work. The policy, *Children in the Workplace*, describes such a situation.

Child Care

Policy 5110.1

(COMPANY) recognizes that affordable and available child care is of great importance to families. To assist its employees, we are willing to reimburse certain child care expenses subject to the eligibility requirements and limitations set forth below.

To be eligible, an employee must be full time with at least (ADD NUMBER) days of continuous service. In addition, both the employee and his or her spouse must be employed full time or the employee's spouse must be enrolled full time in an accredited educational or training program or the employee must be the sole source of support for the child.

Under no circumstances will reimbursements be made to employees where the combined family gross income from all sources, including, without limitation, wages and salary, dividends, interest, cash awards or support or alimony payments, exceeds (ADD DOLLAR AMOUNT).

The following child care expenses are eligible for reimbursement: regular child care, including before and after school child care, at all times during employee's working hours; fees and charges of day care centers, after school programs, family day care or in-home sitters; and the normal fees of summer camp sessions. No reimbursements are available for child care expenses incurred during non-working hours, including vacations and holidays; transportation, teaching materials, uniforms or equipment; or costs associated with the education of any child enrolled at the first grade level or higher. It is the company's policy to reimburse expenses related to child care. These expenses do not include the costs of field trips, recreational, cultural or similar activities which may be offered at additional cost as part of the child care program.

The amount of reimbursement will be determined in accordance with the following schedule. The amount to be reimbursed will be equal to the rate assigned or 50% of eligible child care expenses actually incurred by the employee, whichever is less. Where an employee incurs eligible child care expenses for more than one child, reimbursement amounts shall in no event exceed, in the aggregate, an amount equal to twice the amount determined in the preceding sentence.

Child Care

Policy (continued)   5110.1

Type of Child Care	Care Rate Assigned
Full-time child care for school aged children Summers only	(ADD DOLLAR AMOUNT)
Part-time child care before or after school	(ADD DOLLAR AMOUNT)

Under no circumstances will amounts reimbursed exceed amounts actually paid by the employee to the child care provider. Amounts to be reimbursed shall be further reduced by amounts received by employee or employee's spouse under any other child care assistance program offered to employee or employee's spouse.

To obtain reimbursement, employees must provide written documentation of payment of eligible child care expenses paid in that month to (VICE PRESIDENT) on or before the last business day of each calendar month. Reimbursements, if any, shall be made on or before the 15th day of the following month.

Children in the Workplace

Policy   5110.2

(COMPANY) recognizes that due to child care limitations and emergencies, there are circumstances when children of employees should be allowed on the premises during business hours. Children, as with any other visitor, can present safety risks to the company. To minimize these risks, we ask that our employees agree to the following when their children are on the premises:

1. Obtain prior approval from their department manager.

2. Ensure that their children enter and exit through the main entrance to the building.

3. Ensure that their children sign in and out with the (COMPANY) receptionist.

4. Ensure that their children do not enter restricted highly trafficked areas without prior approval of the department manager in case of an emergency.

5. Ensure that their children remain in the breakroom area, except when they are in the restrooms. The children need to refrain from making excess noise, running around and wondering in the lobby and office areas. It is suggested that parents have their children bring something to read or provide some other quiet activity while they are waiting.

6. Ensure that their children do not use the company telephone.

7. Ensure that the breakroom area is clean when the children leave.

It is important that employees who take advantage of having their children visit the premises during work hours agree and follow these rules. By doing so, (COMPANY) will be able to continue this privilege for our working parents.

Chapter 6

Miscellaneous Policies

Introduction

This chapter includes a group of policies which are either relatively new to the workplace or are not applicable to every company or business.

The topics of employee privacy and ownership of patents and inventions have caused controversy in the workplace. As a consequence, there may be pending or recently passed legislation on these topics. For this reason, you may choose to adopt the policies in the preceding chapters and monitor federal and state legislative decisions before acting on these policies. This would give you additional research time, an opportunity to determine the best way to tailor these policies, and time to determine the procedure for implementing these policies in your workplace.

Your company may eliminate this chapter entirely from your policy manual and move the various policies to other chapters. For instance, the policy on employee privacy could justifiably be moved to the section on *Hiring Practices*. In either case, if there are applicable federal or state laws, you will be subject to those laws and regulations, regardless of whether or not you adopt a particular policy.

Some companies have found it beneficial to have department or company meetings to introduce the policies included in this chapter which will be added to their current company policy manual. The terms and conditions of these proposed policies and their implementation can be discussed in an environment that will eliminate many uncertainties and assist the company in further tailoring or restructuring these policies.

Announcement of New Positions   6010

Comment

As you plan for future human resource needs, consider how you will recruit for these positions. Some of the best candidates for your open positions may already be working for you. Your expressed willingness to allow present employees to improve their skills by advancing to other jobs may boost overall morale as well as productivity.

If you decide to post open positions, one consideration is whether or not to give employees advance notice of the open position before you recruit from the outside. However, giving your current employees a preference for certain jobs may be found to be discriminatory under certain circumstances. For example, it would be discriminatory if you offer preferences to current employees, who happen to all be white males, while qualified minority or female candidates apply from the outside and are rejected.

You may still give current employees advance notice of open positions, or ones due to open, as long as this does not create discriminatory results. It is also wise to require the employee–applicant to have some minimum amount of time in his or her current position to allow the employee to become experienced in the current job and to have his or her performance formally evaluated at least once.

Announcement of New Positions

Alternate Policy 1   6010.1

The availability of all job openings will be announced for five working days within the organization prior to outside recruitment for any position. The job requisition giving job title, class, department, job functions, and qualifications will be posted on all company bulletin boards.

All applicants must have at least (ADD LENGTH OF TIME) experience in their current position prior to applying for another company position. Employees may have only one application in process within the company at any one time.

Announcement of New Positions

Alternate Policy 2   6010.2

Our company believes that the best candidates to fill our job openings may well be some of our present employees. In so keeping, prior to any outside recruitment, we will announce all new positions within the company for five working days. All open positions will be announced on the company bulletin board.

All present employees are encouraged to review the requirements for each position and apply for those positions in which they are interested. Your application will be given the same consideration as outlined in the company recruitment policy *(Section 2020)*.

Confidentiality of Company Information   6020

Comment

The pace of today's technological advances and the competition to obtain and profit from them have caused many companies to establish confidentiality policies to protect trade secrets and proprietary information. Many techniques can be used to protect your confidential company information. Whatever techniques you employ should be defined in a policy or series of policies.

A confidentiality policy serves four main purposes:

- To create a structure of precautions that have been taken, or will be taken, to protect the company's proprietary information;
- To alert a new employee to the problem;
- To set limits for all employees on the disclosure of confidential company information; and
- To define procedures and state the consequences of failure to adhere to them.

Start with listing your confidential material, separating them into like categories, such as documents (financial data, customer lists, drawings, schematic diagrams), working models or prototypes, photographs, books, and computer media to name a few.

Next, evaluate your experience in protecting each category. What success have you had? What breaches of security have occurred? How did you solve the problems? How did the solution work? Now you are ready to determine the level of security needed. Here are several techniques you can use.

- Secure areas of the building — Only persons with a predetermined need to know and a pre-arranged clearance are allowed within the secured area. This area should have a guard or an alarm system or special access requirements such as combination or other special locks.

- Classified documentation system — Documents are assigned a classification depending on their sensitivity. Cover sheets defining the classification are typically used, and these cover sheets can be color-coded to the classification. Some companies stamp documents with a classification, such as "Company Confidential," "Proprietary to (COMPANY NAME)," or "Company Private." The importance of this is to notify anyone who handles these documents that they must be protected. Such notice is essential for an enforceable protection technique.

- Employee identification card — This controls traffic in and out of parts of the building. It is also a subtle technique which communicates to all that the building, or parts of it, are controlled.

- Computer access codes — This is a method for allowing only those with a need-to-know to have access to information on computer media, such as marketing information, sales forecasts, sensitive memos, and research and development information.

- Visitor registration — This is typically used in conjunction with an employee identification card technique. The visitor is issued a distinctive badge so that employees can determine who is not authorized in certain areas.

- Employee non-disclosure or secrecy agreement — All employees having access to protected information should be required to sign such an agreement. Ideally, the agreement defines what information is protected, states the measures that each employee having access is to employ, tells the employee what he or she cannot do with the information, and states the consequences of failure to adhere to the requirements.

- Electronic mail — Develop a clear policy respecting e-mail and company computers. The policy must indicate that the e-mail system is company property, that no personal or unauthorized use is permitted and that e-mail can be accessed from time to time by the employer.

- Telephone monitoring and electronic eavesdropping — Federal and state laws significantly restrict the ability of an employer to monitor telephone calls by electronic means. Check with your company counsel before instituting any electronic eavesdropping practices.

To enforce confidentiality requirements against employees and/or third parties who obtain protected information wrongfully, you must have a system which is reasonably communicated and enforced. However, absolute perfection is not required.

An enforcement technique to use when employees terminate is to have them read, sign, and date a written admonition regarding non-disclosure of confidential information. This can be done before the final paycheck is delivered to them. An exit interview is the logical time for this to be accomplished. It can also be signed at the time of employment and thoughts placed in the employer's personnel file.

Most states have legislation pertaining to trade secrets which should be consulted for further guidance. Also the Uniform Trade Secrets Act, issued by the National Conference of Commissioners on Uniform State Laws in 1979 and approved by the American Bar Association in 1980, may be helpful regarding definitions.

You may also wish to consider having employees with access to confidential information sign a non-competition agreement. If limited in time and geographic scope, a non-compete provision is generally enforceable. State laws vary greatly regarding non-competes, so check with your legal counsel before using one.

Confidentiality of Company Information

Alternate Policy 1   6020.1

It is the responsibility of all (COMPANY) employees to safeguard sensitive company information. The nature of our business and the economic well-being of our company is dependent upon protecting and maintaining proprietary company information. Continued employment with the company is contingent upon compliance with this policy. Each company supervisor/manager bears the responsibility for the orientation and training of his or her employees to ensure enforcement of company confidentiality. Sensitive company information is defined as trade secrets or confidential information relating to products, processes, know-how, customers, designs, drawings, formulas, test data, marketing data, accounting, pricing or salary information, business plans and strategies, negotiations and contracts, inventions, and discoveries.

All such information shall be appropriately marked or verbally identified to each employee. When such information is transferred from one employee to another, the transferor must do all of the following:

1. Determine that the transfer is necessary and in the interest of regular company business;

2. Determine that the transferee has a need to know the information and has the necessary clearance;

3. Ensure that all cover sheets or markings which identify the information as proprietary, or classified, are conspicuous;

4. Give the information directly to the transferee and verbally identify the proprietary or classified information as such. Do not give it to an uncleared employee, such as a secretary or office colleague, and do not leave it on the transferee's desk unattended.

Visitors to company premises must register at the receptionist's desk, be issued a visitor's card, and return the card at the conclusion of their visit.

Confidentiality of Company Information

Alternate Policy 2   6020.2

All employees are asked to sign the following statement at the time of employment:

"In consideration of my employment with (COMPANY), I will be exposed to information and materials which are confidential and proprietary and of vital importance to the economic well-being of (COMPANY). I will not at any time disclose or use, either during or subsequent to my employment, any information, knowledge, or data which I receive or develop during my employment which is considered proprietary by (COMPANY) or which relates to the trade secrets of (COMPANY). Such information, knowledge or data includes the following which is by example only: processes, know-how, designs, drawings, diagrams, formulas, test data, accounting or financial data, pricing or salary data, marketing data, business plans and strategies, negotiations and contracts, research, customer or vendor lists, inventions, and discoveries ('trade secrets').

I further agree that upon termination of my employment with (COMPANY), I shall promptly return any and all documents containing the above information, knowledge or data, or relating thereto, to (COMPANY). This agreement shall be binding upon my successors, heirs, assigns, and personal representatives and shall be for the benefit of the successors and assigns of (COMPANY). In the event that a dispute arises concerning this agreement and a lawsuit is filed, the prevailing party shall be entitled to reasonable attorney's fees and costs.

I acknowledge that the proprietary information and trade secrets are created at substantial cost and expense to (COMPANY) and that unauthorized use or disclosure would cause irreparable injury to (COMPANY). I hereby consent to the order of an immediate injunction, without bond, from any court of competent jurisdiction, enjoining and restraining me from violating or threatening to violate this provision.

I understand that my continued employment with (COMPANY) is contingent upon my compliance with this agreement."

_____   _____

Employee's Signature   Date

Confidentiality of Company Information — E-Mail

Alternate Policy 3   6020.3

Company computers and e-mail system are company property and should be used solely for company purposes.

Personal use of company computers or e-mail system is prohibited. (COMPANY) reserves the right to access the e-mail system from time to time without notice. Employees acknowledge that the e-mail system is not considered private and that by using the system, employees consent to the company's access to it.

To facilitate access, the use of passwords or other security devices by any employee is restricted by those passwords or security devices known and approved by an employee's supervisor/manager.

Note: Employers using an e-mail system should consider the addition of this policy to Alternate Policy 1 or 2.

Employee Orientation 6030

Comment

From the first day an employee joins your company and throughout his or her entire employment, it is mutually beneficial to establish effective communication. Many employers have found an employee orientation is one way to initiate communication. The importance of this initial orientation, whether it is formal or informal, cannot be overemphasized.

An effective orientation does not just happen within a company without a plan. To establish a plan which outlines the objectives of the company orientation program, consider the points listed below, among others, and tailor your policy to emphasize the objectives that you believe are important. Consider:

- A discussion of the spirit shared within the company;
- Some of the information included in *Chapter 1, Our Company*, which helps your employees become more familiar with the team they have joined;
- An explanation of employee responsibilities and requirements regarding starting and quitting times, breaks, meal times, sick days, vacation notices, and time sheets;
- A discussion of the company benefit program and participation eligibility dates; and
- An opportunity to ask questions and develop rapport with the management team.

The sample Orientation Checklist serves as a reminder to cover all important issues during the orientation. For the new employee, it serves as a reminder that each of the issues were discussed with a check-off date.

Employee Orientation

Alternate Policy 1   6030.1

All new employees will participate in an orientation meeting within one month of their hire date. The orientation is designed to acquaint the new employee with the company and its policies. Supervisors/managers will be responsible for ensuring the attendance of new employees at the company orientation sessions.

On the first day of employment, the employee's supervisor/manager is responsible for assisting the employee in completing all check-in and benefit enrollment procedures with the personnel and accounting departments. In addition, the supervisor/manager will ensure that the new employee receives an introduction within the company and is provided with in-depth information regarding his or her specific role and responsibilities within his or her department.

Employee Orientation

Alternate Policy 2   6030.2

All new employees will be provided with an orientation briefing which will be held within their first week of employment with the company. The employee orientation goals are:

1. To establish good employee-employer communication;

2. To reduce the anxieties of a new environment and new responsibilities;

3. To build teamwork spirit;

4. To inform the employee of the company's achievements;

5. To provide the employee with information about the company benefit package and to explain the participation eligibility dates for the various plans available;

6. To assist the employee in leaving the assigned job and the skills required for efficient job performance.

New Employee Orientation Checklist

Orientation

As a new employer, we would like to acquaint you with our policies and benefit programs in order that your employment with us will be as rewarding as possible. All employees, upon joining the staff at (COMPANY) will be asked to participate in an orientation. The orientation will be conducted by a representative from the Administrative and Information Department. The following checklist will serve as a guide to the orientation.

I. Issuance of Company Property

Item	Received
A. Company Policy Manual	
B. Equipment Manuals	
1.	
2.	
3.	
C. Building Keys	
D. SOS Alarm ID Card	
E. Other	
1.	
2.	

II. Review of Company/Life at (COMPANY)

Topic	Discussed
A. Classification	
B. Overview of Personnel Benefit Program	
C. Use of Time Sheet (& Time Clock if applicable)	
D. Overtime Policy	
E. Payday, Direct Deposit, and Pay Stub Info	
F. Use of Kitchen and Lunch Wagon Schedule	
G. Meal and Rest Period/Smoking Policy	
H. Food and Office Area or Work Station	
I. Calling Supervisor when Late or Absent	
J. Use of Telephone	
K. Parking	
L. Workers' Compensation	
M. Department Organization Structure at (COMPANY)	
N. Introductions	
O. Dress Code	

New Employee Orientation Checklist (continued)

III. Review of Company Policies

Topic	Discussed
A. Performance Review	
B. Insurance	
C. Vacation	
D. Paid Holidays and Floating Holidays	
E. Sick Leave	
F. Bereavement Leave	
G. Jury Duty	
H. 401 (k) Retirement Program	
I. Employment Gift	
J. Observance of Special Days	
K. Sales Persons on (COMPANY) Premises	
L. Grievance Procedure	
M. Special Lunches	

IV. Company Philosophy

Topic	Discussed
A. Relationship to Clients	
B. Quality Control and (COMPANY) Image	
C. Relationship to other Departments	
D. Use of (COMPANY) Facility	

V. History of (COMPANY)

Topic	Discussed
A. History	
B. Products	

My signature below indicates that I have received the items listed and the discussion topics specified above have been reviewed to my satisfaction.

_____   _____
            Signature   Date

Inventions and Patents   6040

Comment

Technological advancements raise the question: Who owns the various proprietary interests in the inventions and discoveries developed by the employee — the employer or the employee? There are several answers to this question.

Without a company policy or an employment agreement, federal or state law will govern. There is currently no federal statutory law on the subject of patent ownership rights between employee and employer. However, two pieces of legislation are pending in Congress which, if either become law, would probably preempt state laws on the subject. Briefly, one bill would give employees complete ownership rights if the patentable discovery was developed by the employee on his or her own time and without use of the employer's facilities, equipment, or data. Currently, many states have similar laws which have been applied by federal courts to cases before them.[1] The second bill would require employers to compensate employees, according to a defined set of factors, for all patentable discoveries developed on company time.

Until federal legislation preempts state laws, employers should determine what their state laws do or do not provide in regard to the ownership of patentable discoveries and copyrightable material. Regarding copyrightable material, the new federal Copyright Act specifies that a "work made for hire" belongs to the employer. There may be state laws governing ownership rights where the copyrightable material is not a "work made for hire," but is developed by an employee using the employer's facilities, equipment, or data.

Another reason for consulting your state law is because some state legislation may control or preempt any employment agreement or company policy to the contrary. Absent of any controlling state or federal law, your company policy or any employment agreement will govern the respective rights of the employer and employee. If you have neither, the employer's only recourse is the common law "shop right" doctrine, which basically grants the employer a non-exclusive, royalty-free and non-assignable license to use the patentable discovery, if the employee used the employer's time and materials.

Many companies already have policies which parallel the pending federal legislation discussed above. Others have policies which give all such rights or interests to the employer without any additional compensation to the employee except a pat on the back or a plaque.

Sometimes the employee retains a nontransferable license to use the patentable discovery or copyrightable material for his or her own purposes. Still other companies provide some compensation to the employee who develops a valuable discovery. The typical patentable discovery is usually the product of several employees' research, work, and time which makes apportionment of any reward difficult.

If you decide that your employees are entitled to some type of compensation for their discoveries, draft this policy carefully and apply it evenhandedly. You may wind up sharing millions of dollars with the employees involved in the development of a valuable patent. When the stakes are high, words are sometimes interpreted differently than one party intended, and then disputes arise.

Prior to any conflict or misunderstandings between employer and employee on the question of inventions and patents, establish a policy and discuss it with all employees. Develop an agreement for all employees to sign which sets forth the terms and conditions of your inventions and patents policy. Also, be aware that the laws of some states have mandatory language to be inserted in such an agreement.[2]

Inventions and Patents

Alternate Policy 1 6040.1

Employees are asked to read and sign the following agreement at the time of employment:

"As an employee of (COMPANY), I acknowledge that I am expected to make contributions of value to (COMPANY). Such contributions shall include, among other things, all processes, inventions, patents, discoveries, copyrights, and other intangible rights developed or conceived by me during my employment. Such contributions shall be the sole property of (COMPANY). I will be entitled to no other compensation for them other than my normal salary and benefits. I agree to disclose such contributions promptly to (COMPANY), to assign them to (COMPANY), and to assist (COMPANY) in obtaining patent or copyright protection. I understand that this agreement covers contributions conceived or made not only by me but with others as well, while I am employed at (COMPANY)."

_____   _____

Employee's Signature   Date

Inventions and Patents

Alternate Policy 2 6040.2

Employees are asked to read and sign the following agreement at the time of employment.

"In consideration of my employment with (COMPANY), I shall promptly disclose in writing all discoveries, inventions, and improvements conceived by me or with others during the course of my work at (COMPANY). (COMPANY) shall be free to use any such discoveries, inventions, or ideas without obligation of any sort to me as an employee. If patents or other intangible rights should result therefrom, I agree that all such rights shall be the sole property of (COMPANY). I will cooperate fully in signing documents to transfer and perfect full rights, title, and interest to and for (COMPANY). I understand that this agreement only applies to discoveries, inventions, and improvements conceived or developed during my working hours, or at any time while I was using (COMPANY) facilities, equipment, supplies, or trade secret information or data."

_____   _____

Employee's Signature   Date

Inventions and Patents

Alternate Policy 3   6040.3

All inventions conceived or developed by any employee of (COMPANY) during the term of his or her employment shall remain the property of the employee. However, as to all such inventions with respect to which the equipment, supplies, facilities, or trade secret information of the company was used, or that relate to the business of the company, or to actual or demonstrably anticipated company research and development, or that result from any work performed by the employee for the company, the company shall have a perpetual, royalty-free license to make, use, and sell products embodying such inventions or produced by means of such inventions. The license shall be exclusive as long as the employee continues to be employed by the company and for a period of (add length of time) following termination of employment for any reason, and shall be nonexclusive thereafter. When appropriate, this license shall be evidenced by written instruments that protect the parties' respective rights in such inventions. Each party agrees to execute such instruments on request of the other.

Note: If this policy is to be used, you may wish to couple it with a separate non-competition agreement barring the employee from providing services whether as employee, owner, consultant, or otherwise with any competitor or assigning any patent rights to a competitor for a specified period of time following termination and within a reasonable geographic area. Some states may require that non-competition agreements be entered into at the time of employment or promotion. You may choose to have all research and development oriented personnel execute such agreements.

Conflict of Interest   6050

Comment

In keeping with good business ethics, it is important to have a conflict of interest policy. The company should protect its interests by advising its employees of the ethical and moral integrity it expects from them. Some companies review a prospective employee's potentially conflicting business interests before employment. Others periodically review during employment. Conflict of interest can be defined broadly or narrowly. Here are some examples:

- An employee's involvement in an outside business interest which competes with the activities of employer;

- An employee's outside business which is a purchaser or supplier of goods or services to the employer;

- Outside business involvement which interferes with the employee's ability to devote full time and attention to his or her company responsibilities;

- The employee's outside business operates in such as manner as to reflect adversely on his or her present employer;

- The employee's relatives have business interests in companies which compete with, sell to, or buy from the employer; or

- The giving or receipt by an employee of gifts, money, or other items of value by customers, suppliers, or competitors.

Some states' laws forbid employers from restraining anyone, employees or former employees, from engaging in any lawful business activities. Other statutes provide that such restrictions in contract clauses are void.[1]

Because many courts view company policies as being contractual in nature, the latter type of statute probably applies to your policies. Statutory or public policy exceptions to these broad statutes are often available to employers. For instance, if an employee has an ownership interest in a competing business which is using confidential information or special knowledge obtained from the employer, this is not a lawful business activity. The employer can discharge the employee or possibly require the employee to give up any beneficial interest in the competing business as a condition of further employment. The same result would apply if the employee, while not using any information from his or her employment, interferes with the employer's prospective business advantage by steering potential customers to his or her own business.

Research your state law for statutes or court opinions which define conflict of interest and what the company can and can't do to protect itself. Read *Sections 6070* and *6080* for related policies.

Conflict of Interest

Alternate Policy 1   6050.1

No employee of (COMPANY) shall maintain an outside business or financial interest, or engage in any outside business or financial activity, whether as an officer, director, shareholder (other than the holder of less than five percent of a publicly-traded company), partner or otherwise, which conflicts with the interests of the company, or which interferes with his or her ability to fully perform job responsibilities.

For example, and not by limitation, if your job responsibilities include purchasing, or you are in a position to influence such purchases, you should have no proprietary or financial interest in any business that furnishes products, materials, or services to the company or in any related transaction. Nor may you benefit directly or indirectly from a third party who furnishes products, materials, or services to the company. Violation of this policy will result in immediate dismissal.

Conflict of Interest

Alternate Policy 2   6050.2

No employee of (COMPANY) shall engage in the same or a similar line of business or research as that carried on by the company. An employee shall not have a financial interest in a company which is a competitor of or supplier to the company.

Financial interests held by an employee or by his or her immediate family members in such companies are to be disclosed immediately to the company so that a determination can be made as to whether a conflict exists. Members of the employee's immediate family include spouse, children, and any other relative sharing the same home as the employee.

Grievance Procedure   6060

Comment

Companies strive to treat all of their employees fairly. Yet there will always be circumstances when employees believe that they have been treated unfairly or when rumors spread within a company about unfair treatment. Among companies, what is fair treatment of employees depends to some extent on the company's experience with past practices, industry-wide expectations, and the employees' perceptions.

A company's decision about instituting a grievance policy and procedure falls into this inquiry about fairness. An employer who has a heavy employee turnover rate and who emphasizes and preserves the employment at will doctrine may not want such a policy. Other employers may see a grievance procedure as another example of management's philosophy of ensuring productivity by giving the employee a right to be heard. In other words, management is not always right, and employees do have standing to object to certain practices or decisions which affect them.

When you adopt a company grievance procedure, you must follow it exactly as it is written. If you apply it differently from how it is understood, or apply it to the letter in one case and not in the other, you may be giving the affected employee an opportunity to prove discrimination or, in some cases, a breach of an employment agreement. In one case where a senior employee was denied use of the company's grievance procedure, the employee was able to establish a "wrongful discharge" and actionable lack of good faith and fair dealing.[1]

If you have adopted a policy similar to the corrective counseling policy in this book, your grievance procedure and your corrective counseling procedures should be consistent. At the very least, each policy should refer to the other where appropriate. Remember that grievances may be about policies or conditions, not just disciplinary matters.

Some disputes, especially where termination is a possible result if the employee's grievance is not successful, are important enough to consider an independent mediator or decision-maker. Some employers would consider this solution drastic and too much delegation of management authority. However, other employers may think that private outside mediation or arbitration is worth the price, especially where wrongful discharge litigation is rampant. Employers who bargain with unions have been doing this for years. The way to preserve your freedom here is to write the policy to make outside mediation or arbitration, or both, the option of the employer as a condition of allowing the employee to begin the grievance process in the first place.

Your written grievance form can include this as a stated, boldface condition on the top of the page. It is an expensive alternative, but you can preserve it for the really important disputes.

Alternate Policy 1 is a simplified approach to grievances, but it concludes with a high-level determination which demonstrates the policy's importance to management and the need to resolve the issues at lower levels before upper management gets involved. Alternative Policy 2 is a more structured policy best left for supervisor/management guideline books.

Alternate Policy 3 attempts to combine an informal dispute resolution mechanism with a more formal method of resolution, if informal methods do not succeed. A sample Grievance Form for both Alternate Policy 2 and Alternate Policy 3 follows each policy.

Grievance Procedure

Alternate Policy 1   6060.1

In coordination with the *Performance Improvement Policy*, an employee may express a verbal grievance to his or her immediate supervisor/manager. If the concern is not resolved to the employee's satisfaction within one week, the employee may put in writing the details of his or her grievance and submit the grievance to the immediate supervisor/manager.

The written statement will be reviewed by the (PRESIDENT), who will appoint a person to decide the matter. The employee and his or her supervisor/manager will request a hearing with the appointed person for resolution of the problem. The problem will be discussed in the presence of the employee and supervisor/manager. Final resolution of the grievance will be made by the appointed person and discussed with the employee and supervisor/manager.

The decision will be reduced to writing, a copy given to the employee and supervisor/manager, with the original kept by the personnel director. A copy will be filed in the employee's personnel file when appropriate.

Grievance Procedure

Alternate Policy 2   6060.2

A grievance is defined as any dispute or complaint arising between an employee and the company.

Grievance Procedure

Step 1   The employee should take up the problem with his or her supervisor/manager within a reasonable time. The employee will receive a written answer within five working days.

Step 2   If the grievance is not settled in Step 1, the grievance may, within five working days after the answer to Step 1, be presented to the department head or a designee. The grievance, at this time, shall be reduced to writing and signed by the grievant. As in Step 1, the employee shall receive a written answer within five working days.

Step 3   If the grievance is not settled in Step 2, the employee may present it to the personnel director or a designee. The employee will receive a written answer within five working days.

The employee may have another company employee represent him or her at any of the grievance procedure steps if he or she desires.

Specified time limits are exclusive of Saturdays, Sundays, and holidays. Should the grievance still remain unresolved after completion of Step 3, it may be referred by the company to an outside arbitrator for an impartial and binding decision. The employee does not have this option. Referral by the company to arbitration is binding on the employee and the company, and neither may pursue another remedy. The costs of arbitration will be borne equally by the parties. All other costs will be borne by the party incurring them.

The employee may be represented by counsel at his or her own choosing and at his or her own expense. The award of the arbitrator in all cases is final, conclusive, and binding upon the company and the employee. In lieu of arbitration, both the employee and the company may agree to resolve the dispute through an outside mediator.

Grievance Form

Employee Name: _____   Social Security #:_____

Department: _____   Date of Hire: _____

Job Title: _____   Date Submitted: _____

Complete details of grievance, including references to any law or policies: _____

_____

_____

_____

_____

Remedy Requested: _____

_____

_____

Employee's Signature   Date

Disposition-Step 1 Date Received: _____

Disposition: _____

_____

Accepted ____ Appealed ____

_____
Supervisor   Date Communicated

Disposition-Step 2 Date Received: _____

Disposition: _____

_____

Accepted ____ Appealed ____

_____
Department Head   Date Communicated

Disposition-Step 3 Date Received: _____

Disposition: _____

_____

Accepted ____ Appealed ____

_____
Personnel Director   Date Communicated

Grievance Procedure

Alternate Policy 3   6060.3

(COMPANY) recognizes the value of a grievance procedure that provides for the timely review of employee grievances in a fair yet workable manner. A grievance is considered to be any dispute between an employee and the company, which impacts on an employee's ability to perform his or her job.

Although purely personal matters between employees would not ordinarily give rise to a grievance subject to this grievance procedure, any matter which adversely affects an employee's ability to perform his or her job could be the subject of a grievance. Use good individual judgement and common sense as your guide.

The grievance procedure being utilized encourages the informal resolution of grievances at several stages. Informal resolution can be obtained through department supervisors/managers or a member of the grievance review team assigned to that particular grievance. More formal review can be obtained from the grievance review team whose names will be posted on the company bulletin board or a management review team consisting of (PRESIDENT) and (VICE PRESIDENT).

The attached grievance form will serve as the appropriate form for submitting a grievance. You may attach any additional information which you feel necessary to fully state your grievance.

The following guidelines shall be applicable to all phases of the grievance process.

1. All employees should endeavor to create a work environment that encourages an employee to discuss a grievance. The atmosphere created should be free from interference, coercion, restraint, and discrimination.

2. All employees shall cooperate fully with the grievance review team and the management team.

3. Grievances should not be discussed openly throughout the company. Interviews and investigations should be conducted in as private a setting as possible.

4. A grievance may be withdrawn at any time prior to the issuance of a written report by the grievance review team or management team.

5. Specified time limits are exclusive of Saturdays, Sundays, and holidays.

Grievance Procedure

Alternate Policy 3 (continued)   6060.3

Grievance Procedure

Step 1 To encourage informal resolution, an employee should bring his or her grievance to the attention of his or her supervisor/manager. No written grievance form would need to be completed. The supervisor/manager and employee would discuss the grievance and determine a plan to resolve it. The supervisor/manager and employee will then implement the plan. The grievance should be raised within 30 days following the events or circumstances giving rise to it, and the employee and his or her supervisor/manager shall endeavor to resolve it within 5 days thereafter.

Step 2 If Step 1 is not successful or if the grievance is against am employee's supervisor/manager, an employee shall submit written grievance to one of the grievance review team members whose names are posted on the company bulletin board. The grievance should be submitted within 35 days following the conduct which led to the grievance.

Step 3 The grievance review team will assign the grievance to one of its members for review. The assigned team member will also seek an informal resolution to the grievance, and may conduct such investigations as necessary, including discussions with the person submitting the grievance, the persons against whom the grievance is submitted and any other employees who have personal knowledge of any matters related to the grievance. If an informal resolution is achieved, the assigned team member shall prepare a brief written statement setting forth the resolution. The statement shall be signed by the person submitting the grievance and the person or persons against whom the grievance was directed. Copies shall be given to each of these persons. One copy shall be retained by the grievance review team. Efforts to resolve the grievance under Step 3 should be concluded within 10 days following the submission of the written grievance.

Step 4 If no informal resolution is reached, the assigned team member will, at the written request of the employee submitting the grievance, convene the grievance review team for the purpose of reviewing the grievance. The employee's request should be made within 5 days following the conclusion of Step 3 activities by giving the assigned team member a signed writing that states, "Please convene the grievance team." The grievance review team will review the grievance form filed and consider

Grievance Procedure

Alternate Policy 3 (continued)   6060.3

any information obtained by the assigned team member. The grievance review team can conduct additional investigations if it chooses, but it is not obligated to do so. The grievance review team shall prepare a brief written report setting forth its recommendation for grievance resolution within 10 days following the employee's request. The recommendation shall be distributed to the party filing the grievance and the party against whom the grievance was directed. A copy of the report shall be retained by the grievance review team.

In the event that the grievance is against a member of the grievance review team, the grievance should be submitted initially to either of the remaining two grievance members. The two remaining members will select a third person to serve on the grievance review team for the purpose of that grievance.

Step 5   Either the employee filing the grievance or the employee against whom the grievance has been filed may appeal the recommendation of the grievance review team to the management team consisting of the (PRESIDENT), (VICE PRESIDENT), and (PERSONNEL DIRECTOR). To initiate this process, the employee must provide written notice of his or her intention to pursue a Step 5 appeal, and submit the written notice to the assigned team member of the grievance review team within 5 days following the conclusion of the issuance of the Step 4 process. The written notice need only contain the statement, "I intend to pursue a Step 5 appeal." If the grievance was originally filed against a member or members of the management team, the appeal shall be reviewed by the remaining member or members of the management team. The management team shall review the original grievance and discuss the grievance with the employee submitting the grievance, the person against whom the grievance was directed, and the assigned team member. The management team may conduct such other investigation as it may choose. The management team will issue its recommendation within 10 days following the notice of appeal.

Grievance Form

Name of Employee:_____Department: _____Date of this Report: _____

State your grievance in detail, including the date of act(s) or omissions causing grievance:

_____

_____

Identify other employees with personal knowledge of your grievance:_____

_____

Briefly state your efforts to resolve this grievance: _____

_____

Describe the remedy or solution you would like: _____

_____

_____

Employee's Signature: _____ Date: _____

Step 3 Date Received: _____ Actions Taken: _____

_____

Disposition: _____

Accepted _____ Appealed _____

_____   _____
Assigned Team Member   Date Communicated

Step 4 Date Received: _____ Actions Taken: _____

_____

Disposition: _____

Accepted _____ Appealed _____

_____   _____
Grievance Review Team   Date Communicated

Step 5 Date Received: _____ Actions Taken: _____

_____

Disposition: _____

Accepted _____ Appealed _____

_____   _____
Management Team   Date Communicated

Gratuities to Government Employees or Officials   6070

Comment

Federal and state laws and regulations specifically state that government employees and officials may not accept gratuities from the private sector and prohibit company representatives from making or offering to make gratuities available.

Therefore, the company's responsibility is to ensure that all employees are informed of and maintain adherence to this policy.

Gratuities to Government Employees or Officials

Alternate Policy 1   6070.1

Any form of a business gift to federal, state, or municipal employees is strictly forbidden by (COMPANY). Management is charged with the responsibility of informing all employees of this policy and maintaining adherence to it.

Violation of this policy will be treated as a major violation and, depending on the circumstances, may be grounds for immediate termination or other appropriate action.

Gratuities to Government Employees or Officials

Alternate Policy 2   6070.2

In adherence to government regulations, no employee may offer a gratuity to any government employee or official on behalf of, or in pursuance of, (COMPANY) business. Gratuities are defined as meals, drinks, gifts, expenses, cash, or any other item of value, including personal service.

An offer to provide, or the actual provision of, any form of gratuity to a government employee or official will constitute grounds for immediate termination.

Gratuities to Customer or Supplier Representatives   6080

Comment

It might appear easy to establish and enforce a policy that your company will not give or accept gifts or gratuities within a customer or supplier business relationship. However, consider what action a company should take when a gift arrives that, if returned, might offend the giver? Also, what action does the company take when employees attend seminars, conventions, or group meetings that include meals or entertainment paid for by a customer?

From time to time, company employees may be invited to participate in trips or outings arranged to create or maintain good will, such as hunting, fishing, cultural activities, or sporting events. Participation in such activities could be in the best interests of the company and would contribute to a good working relationship with the customer who extended the invitation. Management has to consider situations such as these individually. If it is mutually agreed that an employee's participation will serve a useful and ethical purpose, possibly the invitation should be accepted.

In answer to the question of what to do with gifts that would offend the giver if returned, some companies have adopted a policy of donating all such gifts to a charitable organization. Consideration of the following five questions will help you write a policy regarding gratuities:

- Does acceptance of the gratuity violate any law?
- Was the gratuity in exchange for preferential treatment?
- Is the value of the gratuity so insignificant it could not be construed as a bribe or payoff? Even if insignificant, does it create an appearance of impropriety?
- Would public disclosure of the facts surrounding the gratuity embarrass the company or its employees in any way?
- Does your company have a drug-free workplace policy?

A "Yes" response to any of these questions could indicate a potential legal or practical problem pertaining to the gratuity. Policies concerning gratuities can become quite complex. Management must provide a means to review situations that do not fall into the above prohibited categories. Alternate Policy 3 addresses the issue of alcoholic beverages as gifts. In an effort to avoid offending suppliers, companies can develop a supplier letter requesting cooperation with the policy. See sample letter on page 301.

Gratuities to Customer or Supplier Representatives

Alternate Policy 1   6080.1

This policy establishes the ethical conduct to be maintained by employees in relationships with customers and suppliers.

As an employee, you may not receive, give, pay, promise, or offer to our customers anything of value whether cash or any other property for the purpose of securing or appearing to secure preferential treatment. This also includes any form of gratuity to or from employees of our customers or members of their families.

Violation of this policy in any form will require immediate disciplinary action.

Gratuities to Customer or Supplier Representatives

Alternate Policy 2   6080.2

Employees of (COMPANY) may not offer to give, or accept a gift, cash or other item of value — including personal service — from an existing or prospective customer, supplier, or a representative of either in pursuance of business or in conjunction with negotiating business on behalf of this company.

Expenses for meals as part of a seminar, convention, or business meeting are not within the definition of gratuities for purposes of this policy. Invitations extended by a customer or supplier to participate in any program or activity, such as a party or football game, should be referred to your supervisor/manager for approval on a case-by-case basis.

Any violation of this policy will constitute grounds for immediate termination.

Gratuities to Customer or Supplier Representatives

Alternate Policy 3   6080.3

(COMPANY) employees (including management) shall not solicit, accept, or offer entertainment, gifts, or gratuities which have the appearance or effect of influencing the judgment of the recipient in the performance of their duties.

Business decisions must be made impartially and on the basis of such factors as price, quality, service, financial responsibility and the maintenance of reliable sources of supply. Employees must ensure that any business courtesy offered or received does not influence or appear to influence, business decisions.

In compliance with our *Drug-Free Workplace Policy*, alcoholic beverages are not allowed on property owned by (COMPANY). Suppliers are reminded not to bring alcohol onto company property, even if the alcoholic beverage is covered by a promotional box or wrapping.

Gratuities to Customer

Sample Letter

Dear Valued Supplier:

As the holiday season approaches, we, at (COMPANY) wish to express our appreciation for the support and valuable products and services provided by our suppliers this past year.

We are proud of our association and believe ethical behavior has been our hallmark and must continue to guide all of our business activities. We would like to reconfirm our *Gift and Gratuity Policy* as the holidays approach.

(AN EXACT STATEMENT OF THE COMPANY POLICY)

Please make every effort to comply with these policies so that our relationship may continue unhindered. Thank you for your help in this matter.

Sincerely,

(COMPANY NAME)

President

Political Activities   6090

Comment

This policy describes the requirements and limits that should be maintained when encouraging individual employees to voluntarily participate in civic and political activities and when granting time off to engage in such activities. It may also limit or prohibit political activities within the company premises.

There are a number of federal and state laws which regulate or limit your company from using its money, property, equipment, supplies, or facilities to aid in partisan political activity. Such restrictions are more common if your company has a government contract.

Also, what someone may do as an individual may not be allowed for corporations. Your company should pursue the necessary research to determine if you are restricted in these areas and tailor this policy accordingly.

Political Activities

Policy 6090.1

In recognition of its responsibilities as a business citizen, (COMPANY) encourages its employees to accept the personal responsibility of good citizenship, including participation in civic and political activities, in accordance with their interests and abilities.

(COMPANY) accepts without reservation the basic democratic principle that all employees are free to make their own individual decisions in civic and political matters. Therefore, no employee's status with the company will be affected, in any way, whatsoever, because of participation or non-participation in lawful civic and political activities.

Participation in civic and political activities is considered to be a personal matter and, as such, is generally to be carried on outside of normal working hours. No political activities or solicitations will be carried on within company premises.

Political activities are defined for purposes of this policy as activities in support of any partisan political issue or activities in support of, or in concert with, any individual candidate for political office, or a political party, which seek to influence the election of candidates to federal, state, or local offices. The definition includes employees who are or may be candidates for political office.

The company reserves the right to deny time off for political activity where the activities, in the opinion of the company, would unduly interfere with the employee's fulfillment of any obligations to the company. When an employee's full time is required for political activity, however, a leave of absence without pay may be granted (refer to *Section 4050*).

Employee Privacy   6100

Comment

As companies become more keenly aware of their need for company confidentiality, they should also recognize the importance of their employee's rights to privacy. This recognition has been accelerated by the increasing numbers of employees who are speaking out against or taking action to limit a company's release of information contained in their employment records. Companies are learning the hard way, through costly court cases, that careless disclosure of information about their employees can be counterproductive. This is especially true where a prospective employer contacts the employee's previous employer for personnel information. Disclosure of other than factual information about dates of employment, positions held, and salary data may lead to a lawsuit for defamation or invasion of privacy. See the *Comment* to *Section 2060*.

A sample of an Authorization to Provide Information Form is provided for you on page 307. Before the personnel department investigates references, you may wish to use this sample when you know the top three potential applicants for any position. The sample Consent to Release Information Form on page 308 can be used upon the termination of employment by a current employee. Before using these forms, check with your legal adviser. Certain areas relevant to the hiring process but not included on these forms, such as credit or criminal record checks, may or may not be permitted by your state. Use caution in the collection and use of information concerning current or prospective employees.

Some states also have laws requiring an employer to allow an employee to inspect his or her personnel or other employment records.[1] The statutes may allow the employer to limit this access in certain reasonable ways, such as during normal business hours, on employee's own time, by written request or appointment, allowing a company official to be present, or limiting the frequency of access. Check your state laws for similar requirements.

Federal and state laws (and some government contracts) require you to retain employment records for certain periods of time. The federal requirements are set forth in the *Guide To Record Retention Requirements* which is available from the Superintendent of Documents, U.S. Government Printing Office, Washington, D.C., 20402. As you develop your policy, be concerned about:

- Controlling the internal and external release of employee information; and

- Establishing a procedure which permits your employees to examine or copy, request corrections to, or dispute any information contained in their employment records or personnel file.

Employee Privacy

Alternate Policy 1   6100.1

(COMPANY) recognizes our employees' rights to privacy. In achieving this goal, the company adopts these basic principles:

1. The collection of employee information will be limited to that which is needed by the company for business and legal purposes.

2. The confidentiality of all personal information in our records will be protected.

3. All in-house employees involved in recordkeeping will be required to adhere to these policies and practices. Violations of this policy will result in disciplinary action.

4 Internal access to employee records will be limited to those employees having an authorized, business-related need-to-know. Access may also be given to third parties, including government agencies, pursuant to court order or subpoena.

5. The company will refuse to release personal information to outside sources without the employee's written approval, unless legally required to do so.

6. Employees are permitted to see the personal information maintained about them in the company records. They may correct inaccurate factual information or submit written comments in disagreement with any material contained in their company records.

Employee Privacy

Alternate Policy 2   6100.2

(COMPANY) believes that nothing should be placed in an employee's personnel file unless there is a clear business reason for doing so. Our employee privacy philosophy is further reflected in the following statements:

1. Personnel files will include only job-related information pertinent to your employment.

2. Employees may see information in their personnel files. If an employee disagrees with the information, he or she may submit written comments which will be attached to the information.

3. When asked to do so by an employee, the company will explain its need for certain personal information.

4. Personnel files are open only to company personnel on a business-related, need-to-know basis unless the company is legally required to release them by court order or subpoena.

5. Employees must give their written permission before there will be external disclosure of their personal information, with the exception of the following information:

    a. Verification of dates of employment, positions held, and salary when requested by the employee's prospective employer;

    b. Personal information which the company is legally required to reveal by court order or subpoena. In the latter case, the employee will be informed prior to the disclosure if reasonably possible.

Authorization to Provide Information

Note: The following form is used to obtain information about a prospective employee.

I, authorize (COMPANY) to conduct a complete background investigation in order to assess my eligibility for a position requiring a high level of reliability and trustworthiness. I authorize all persons who may have information relevant to this investigation including, without limitation, prior employers, doctors, landlords, creditors and others to disclose it (including photocopies where requested) to (COMPANY) or their agents. I hereby release and hold harmless from liability all persons on account of such disclosure. I understand that the investigation may include verification of past employment, review of personnel records maintained by any prior employer, education, and opinions of references.

This authorization shall be valid for a period of time not to exceed one year following the date indicated below or until employment is terminated, whichever occurs first. The release and hold harmless contained herein shall remain in full force and effect with respect to all disclosures provided within this time period.

I authorize that a photocopy of my signature below may be used to obtain information regarding the investigation.

_____   _____

Employee's Signature   Date

_____

Social Security Number

Consent to Release Information

I, authorize (COMPANY) to release information to prospective employers of mine who identify themselves to you as such. This authorization is unconditional and permits disclosure of the complete content of my personnel file.

I acknowledge that I have had the opportunity to review my personnel file and receive copies of information contained in it. I hereby release and agree to hold harmless (COMPANY), its directors, officers, shareholders, employees, successors and assigns from any and all claims, cost, liability or expense, of any kind or nature whatsoever, including, without limitation, reasonable attorney fees, arising out of or resulting from the release of information respecting the undersigned by (COMPANY).

This authorization shall permit the release and disclosure of information for a period of 90 days following the date indicated below. The release and hold harmless shall remain in full force and effect with respect to all disclosures made within this time period.

_____   _____

Employee's Signature   Date

_____

Social Security #

Telephone   6110

Comment

The abuse of the telephone is often noted as one of the most aggravating and hidden expenses within a company. However, it is difficult for a company to effectively address the issue without a telephone policy which defines the limits that the company places on an employee's personal telephone use during company time.

In the development of a policy, it is important to realize that there are situations when employees must make personal phone calls from work. In equal defense, the policy should restrict usage to a reasonable limit.

Telephone

Alternate Policy 1   6110.1

A large percentage of the company's business is transacted by telephone. The telephone equipment is provided for the purpose of providing service to our customers. Therefore, it is necessary to limit your personal calls to an absolute minimum number.

Personal calls should only be made in case of absolute necessity or emergency. If non-emergency personal calls must be made, please arrange to make them during your break or lunch period. No long distance personal calls may be made on company phones.

Telephone

Alternate Policy 2   6110.2

The company requests your cooperation in limiting outgoing or incoming personal calls to an absolute minimum. Please instruct your friends and family not to call at work except in emergencies.

Telephone lines must be kept clear for company business. A pay telephone is provided for employee use and is located in the lunch room.

Telephone

Alternate Policy 3   6110.3

Personal calls of short duration, i.e., two to three minutes, may be received and made at your desk or work station. No long distance calls will be tolerated unless prior permission to make such a call is received from a supervisor/manager, and the necessity is apparent, e.g., an emergency. Personal telephone call privileges are subject to change or termination at any time. For instance, and not to be limiting, if the company telephone lines become overloaded with calls or an employee is found spending more than just limited time on personal calls, this privilege will be revoked either generally or specifically as to the offending employee.

Dress Code 6120

Comment

How an employee dresses for work impacts your business in several ways. First, employees who have contact with customers or suppliers create a public image of the company. Second, and more importantly, dress must be suitable for the demands and hazards of the job. Good individual judgment is the guideline. An employee should have the latitude to reflect individuality but in a manner which does not have a negative impact on your company's image or compromise company safety.

A more casual dress trend appears to be gaining support in corporate and small business America. Strong communication reigns when such a policy is initiated. Be sure to communicate the appropriate dress through videos or group discussions so employees don't show up in beach clothes.

Results from casual dress codes often show improved communication. Without the clothes that signal the status barrier, communication has opened up within the company. Other companies have seen it as an "empowerment statement" — the company was no longer doing business as usual.

In some instances, the issue may be nearly eliminated if uniforms are required. In this case, the policy should only require that the uniforms be properly fitted, cleaned, and maintained.

Dress Code

Policy   6120.1

Employee dress should be neat in appearance and in a manner consistent with a professional atmosphere. The impression made on customers, visitors, and other employees and the need to promote company and employee safety should be kept in mind.

Good individual judgment is the best guideline.

Kitchen – Break Room   6130

Comment

Many companies provide kitchen facilities or break rooms or both for the benefit of employees. Because these facilities are used by employees throughout the day, a policy must be drafted to promote the clean-up of the area. This policy must also be drafted in a manner consistent with any smoking policy that is instituted.

Companies are also providing exercise rooms, locker rooms, and shower rooms for the convenience of their employees. The following policy pertaining to the Kitchen — Break Room could be easily modified to accommodate these types of facilities as well.

Kitchen — Break Room

Policy 6130.1

(COMPANY) provides a kitchen–break room for the benefit of its employees. Employees shall be responsible for the general clean-up of the area, including the washing of personal dishes and utensils.

All trash should be disposed of in the trash container. Any empty aluminum cans or glass bottles shall be disposed of in the trash container marked "Aluminum Cans Only" or "Glass Bottles Only," whichever is applicable.

Employee Recognition 6140

Comment

Employees deserve to be recognized for their efforts. Whether an employee has provided the company with years of service, been recognized in some public forum for outstanding community service, or individual excellence in some area, such efforts should be recognized.

Individual honors and achievements attained in individual pursuits during non-work hours often cast a favorable public image on the company. Recognition can be made through the award of a service pin or plaque, an announcement in a company-wide newsletter, or by posting a notice concerning the effort on a company bulletin board.

Recognition can be more elaborate, such as an awards banquet or similar gathering. If an employee knows that he or she has an opportunity to be recognized by fellow workers, he or she will work hard to be recognized. The costs to recognize service and outstanding efforts can be nominal, but the benefits may be immeasurable.

Employee Recognition

Policy   6140.1

(COMPANY) believes that the good efforts of its employees are to be encouraged and rewarded. To that end, the company will recognize the faithful service of its employees by providing recognition of service plaques to all five-year employees and the opportunity to select a gift from a selection of gifts chosen by the company for employees with at least ten years of continuous service and at five-year intervals from and after the tenth anniversary.

The company also encourages the involvement of its employees in cultural, social, service, and recreational activities during their non-work hours. (COMPANY) will be happy to recognize individual honors and achievements in these areas as well by reporting such items in the company newsletter or posting results on the company bulletin board.

Promptly notify your supervisor/manager of any such honors or achievements.

Customers   6150

Comment

Without customers, we have nothing. Unfailing commitment to customer service is a requirement for any successful business. Enough said.

Customers

Policy   6150.1

It is company policy to provide its customers with the best possible service in a courteous and thoughtful manner at all times. The customer comes first and should be treated in the same manner that you would want to be treated.

Visitors   6160

Comment

Non-customer visitors to company facilities can breach company security, create safety concerns, and distract employees.

Visitors should be discouraged to avoid these adverse consequences. To minimize the risks, visitors should secure prior permission or be permitted only at designated times in designated areas.

Law enforcement and government officials, including health or fire inspectors, with proper authority, court order, or subpoena should be directed to the appropriate corporate officer or manager to minimize disruption.

Visitors

Policy   6160.1

Non-customer visitors present safety and security risks to the company. To minimize these risks, visitors are not allowed on company property without prior written approval of (VICE PRESIDENT) or in the case of emergency.

Visitors may drop off employees at the beginning of a work shift or pick up employees at the end as long as the drop-off/pick-up occurs within designated areas. Law enforcement or government officials, including health or fire inspectors, shall be directed immediately to (VICE PRESIDENT), who shall determine proper governmental authority, review court orders or subpoenas, and assist the law enforcement or government officials in a manner which provides full cooperation with minimal disruption to company operations.

Recreational Activities–Sponsorships   6170

Comment

To enhance a positive image among employees and the public in general, companies often host social gatherings for its employees, such as picnics or dinners, sponsor one or more athletic teams for its employees, or provide other social and recreational opportunities during non-working hours on or off company facilities.

Liability issues which impact the decision of whether or not to host these recreational or social gatherings are discussed in *Substance Abuse — Section 2060.*

Simply stated, whenever the company may be linked to an activity, the potential for inclusion as a defendant in any litigation exists. To minimize liability, any recreational activities must be voluntary and the company should minimize its direct control over such activities.

General guidelines respecting the voluntary nature of participation, the duration of the activity, and the requirement that participating employees act in a courteous and responsible manner should be utilized. Prohibitions on the use of alcohol should also be considered.

Companies are frequently asked to sponsor athletic teams or cultural events that may or may not involve employees. Examples include youth baseball or soccer teams, community theatre, or community sports events such as fun runs or bicycle rides. Whether or not a company chooses to engage in these activities depends in part on:

- Whether such activities will promote a favorable public image;
- Whether the activities fit within the company's marketing plan;
- The cost of the activity; and
- The risk of liability. Does the organizing entity carry liability insurance which provides coverage for participants as well as spectators, and will your company be included as an additional insured?

Two alternative policies are presented in this section. The first represents a decision by the company not to provide recreational or social activities or sponsorship.

The second policy indicates the company's willingness to engage in such activities on a case-by-case basis.

Recreational Activities–Sponsorships

Alternate Policy 1   6170.1

(COMPANY) encourages its employees to engage in social, recreational, community service, and cultural activities during non-working hours. Recognizing that the decision to engage in such activities is a purely personal one and further recognizing the need of employees to enjoy quality time with family and friends, the company has determined not to provide financial assistance or facilities for the promotion of these activities.

Such activities are indeed commendable but are to be undertaken solely on an individual basis by employees.

Recreational Activities–Sponsorships

Alternate Policy 2   6170.2

(COMPANY) recognizes that recreational, social, community service, and cultural activities during non-working hours are beneficial to the company, its employees, their families, and our community. Employees are encouraged to participate in such activities but are under no obligation to do so. Company financial assistance for equipment, supplies, fees, and similar expenses may be made on a case-by-case basis. Requests for such assistance shall be made to (VICE PRESIDENT) and such requests shall describe the activity in detail, including specific information respecting the use of the assistance provided. Employees are solely responsible for their safety and well being while traveling to or from or participating in the activity.

The company will also consider reasonable requests for financial assistance or sponsorships of youth recreational teams or community organizations on a case-by-case basis. Any such requests shall provide the same detailed information as required in the preceding paragraph and shall be directed to (VICE PRESIDENT). Under no circumstances does the company assume any liability or responsibility for personal injuries or property damage which might occur during or arise out of the activity for which financial assistance or sponsorship is provided. Any employee participation in such activity shall be voluntary.

Outside Employment   6180

Comment

Many employees moonlight with a second or third job. For employers, moonlighting employees raise questions concerning employee loyalty and potential conflict of interest.

Employees working more than one job may be more fatigued or under more stress raising legitimate safety concerns. Similarly, employees may be tempted to use company facilities or resources or company time to perform tasks or services on behalf of the second employer.

In these situations, employers generally select from one of two options: a complete ban on moonlighting or a limited ban subject to the approval of supervisory personnel. Two alternate policies are presented in this section that illustrate these approaches. If moonlighting is acceptable, Alternate Policy 2 can be easily modified to permit it. Moreover, the absence of a policy on outside employment probably permits such employment by implication.

Outside Employment

Alternate Policy 1   6180.1

Full time employees are expected to be working solely for (COMPANY).

To further employee safety and well-being, no exceptions to this policy will be permitted.

Outside Employment

Alternate Policy 2   6180.2

Employees are expected to be working solely for (COMPANY). Any outside employment should be promptly disclosed to (VICE PRESIDENT). In certain circumstances, outside employment will be approved, but the company retains the right to review and evaluate each situation on an individual basis.

Note: Because outside employment is related to conflict of interest issues, you may wish to include this policy in Section 6050, Conflict of Interest.

Employer Security   6190

Comment

The policies discussed in this section relate to an employer's right to secure its facilities through the use of identification badges, strict controls on access to company property, or by the search and/or seizure of privately-owned or company-owned property within company premises. Related security issues, such as confidentiality, conflicts of interest, and outside employment, are described in *Sections 6020 — Confidentiality of Company Information; 6050 — Conflict of Interest; and 6180 — Outside Employment.*

As a general rule, employers may freely restrict access to their facilities to those who display proper identification or other indicia of proper authority. Questions relating to searches and/or seizure of property are more difficult to answer. Policies permitting searches should be made after careful consultation with the company's legal counsel.

The federal and state constitutions limit the right of public sector employers to search their employees. For public sector employers, one must balance the employee's reasonable expectation of privacy versus the employer's rights to a safe and secure workplace and need to supervise its employees.

Private sector employers are generally not constrained by constitutional restrictions. Nonetheless, employees generally are afforded certain privacy rights, even with respect to company furnished lockers or desks, that may not be invaded in the absence of a strong company policy eliminating any expectation of privacy. Where such a policy exists, private sector employers would seem to have the right to search lockers, desks, lunch or tool boxes and similar items brought onto or taken from company facilities. Employees should provide written consent to search and/or seizure at the time of hire, and a detailed report of all searches and seizures should be made at the time of search and at the time of disposition of property seized. Reports should be maintained in the employee's personnel file.

In a related issue, many employers are concerned about the increase of on-the-job violence. As part of any employer's security program, employers must utilize careful pre-employment screening to avoid hiring unstable or violence prone individuals. In addition, supervisors and managers ought to be trained to recognize signs of trouble and to be sensitive to employee concerns. Finally, employers should have emergency procedures in place and a written policy identifying what steps are to be taken in the event of an emergency related to on-the-job violence.

Employers are also urged to check with legal counsel concerning the applicability of other federal or state statutes which may restrict the imposition of additional security measures, such as telephone taps, telephone monitoring, or polygraph tests.

The policy which follows is designed to be utilized — after consultation with company legal counsel — by private sector employers with no significant government contracts or controls.

Employer Security

Policy   6190.1

To promote a safe and healthful workplace environment for all and to protect the company property, confidential, and proprietary information, (COMPANY) shall require that all employees display at all times during working hours an identification badge which shall contain an employee's photograph, name, department, and signature.

The company expressly reserves the right to search from time to time without prior warning or notice all persons and/or property of any kind or nature found upon, brought onto, or taken from company property including, without limitation to, lockers, desks, tool boxes, lunch boxes, duffel bags, briefcases, and similar items. The company shall confiscate any and all materials or items found during a search which the company reasonably and in good faith believes to violate any law or regulation, endanger company or employee safety and welfare, or otherwise violates company policy.

Confiscated items will be surrendered to government authorities where appropriate, returned to proper owners, if necessary, or returned to the searched employee within (ADD TIME PERIOD) business days following the search.

Security or supervisory personnel conducting a search shall prepare a detailed report setting forth the time, date, and place of search; the name, address, telephone number, and job description of person(s) whose person or property has been searched; inventory of items, if any, found and confiscated; and the disposition of items confiscated.

Note: Consult with legal counsel prior to adopting any policy regarding employer security.

Emergency Closings   6200

Comment

Periodically, due to inclement weather, national crisis, or other emergency, a business will close for all or part of a normally-scheduled workday.

A company's policy in this regard acknowledges the possibility of such an occurrence, sets forth a mechanism for communicating this information to employees, and indicates whether or not such an occurrence will be assessed against an employee's sick leave or vacation leave.

A similar policy could be tailored for businesses which shut down periodically during the year to provide for maintenance or retooling.

Emergency Closings

Policy   6200.1

Except for regularly-scheduled holidays, (COMPANY) will be open for business on Mondays through Fridays during normal business hours. The company recognizes that circumstances beyond its control, such as inclement weather, national crisis, or other emergency, do occur. On such occasions, the company may close for all or part of a regularly-scheduled work day.

In such event, the company will endeavor to notify all supervisory personnel for the purpose of contacting employees. Employees may also contact their supervisor/manager or company offices. Any closing longer than one full work shift shall be assessed against employee's sick leave or vacation time, whichever may be applicable and, if none, the closing shall be regarded as unpaid personal leave.

Note: Employers not wishing to assess emergency closings against employee sick leave or vacation time should delete the last sentence.

Parking   6210

Comment

Parking often presents unanticipated problems. Unregulated parking can result in long walks for customers, suppliers, or other visitors to the business. By reserving spaces for visitors, this problem can be minimized.

Similarly, where a company's work force works multiple shifts, close-in parking should be reserved for employees working late night shifts to minimize security problems.

If you share a building with other tenants, work with the landlord or other tenants to develop a parking policy that will be workable for all of the tenants.

Parking

Alternate Policy 1   6210.1

Recognizing the need of our customers, suppliers, and visitors to have easy access to (COMPANY) facilities, employees may park their automobiles in spaces reserved for employee parking.

Under no circumstances should any employee park in areas reserved for business parking or in any manner which might block access to company facilities by any delivery vehicle or truck. The company assumes no responsibility or liability for employee automobiles. Lock your cars and take your keys.

Parking

Alternate Policy 2   6210.2

Employee parking is available on a first-come, first-served basis in designated areas of the (COMPANY) parking lot. No employee parking is permitted at any time in spaces reserved for visitors.

Only cars displaying a parking sticker may park in employee parking lots. Cars not displaying the sticker may be ticketed or towed at the owner's expense. Parking stickers are available from the personnel department.

Employees are urged to carpool to minimize congestion, assure an adequate number of parking spaces for all employees, and conserve energy. Under no circumstances will the company be responsible or liable in any way for property damage to employee-owned cars while parked on company parking lots. Lock your cars and take your keys.

Mail, E-mail, and Shipping   6220

Comment

Mail constitutes an important part of every business. With regular increases in postage, mail represents an growing percentage of operating budgets as well. Due to the volume of incoming and outgoing mail, many businesses have set up mail rooms or shipping departments utilizing employees who work entirely in those areas. In smaller companies, clerical employees are assigned mail duty. In either case, the handling and processing of mail takes time and costs money.

For these reasons, many companies have adopted mail policies to prohibit the personal use of the company mail system. The prohibition contained in the accompanying policy is absolute. No personal mail is permitted, even pre-stamped mail. Some employers may choose to permit the deposit of pre-stamped mail as a convenience to employees.

Provision is made to assist employees in shipping personal items at certain times during the year. This policy is relevant only where a business regularly ships goods, and it requires that employees reimburse the cost of shipping.

E-mail

The growing popularity of e-mail in the workplace has added a broadened responsibility to the employer. Be aware of your potential responsibility in e-mail messages that create a hostile work environment or demonstrate discriminatory practices. This policy should state your right to monitor e-mail messages for evidence of discriminatory material.

Mail and Shipping

Policy   6220.1

(COMPANY) is dependent upon an efficient and economical system of receiving and sending mail. Postage and shipping costs represent a significant part of the company operating budget. In addition, the handling and processing of mail requires the time and effort of employees. To facilitate the efficient and economical receipt and dispatch of mail, no personal use of the company's mail system shall be permitted including, without limitation, the use of company stationery or envelopes, postage or postage meters for personal purposes, or the deposit of pre-stamped personal mail with company mail.

From time to time, employees shall be permitted to utilize the company's shipping department to arrange for the shipment of personal goods. Any personal use is subject, of course, to the availability of shipping department personnel and to the priority of business related shipments. Any costs associated with personal shipments shall be charged back to the employee and shall be promptly reimbursed by the employee to the company.

Note: The above last paragraph should only be used where applicable. Otherwise, it should be deleted.

E-mail

No personal use of the company's computerized electronic mail system is permitted. Computer files including e-mail files are company property and subject to inspection or copying by the company. (COMPANY) employees are to honestly disclose who they are when they send e-mail. Attempting to subvert this policy is a serious offense. E-mail will be regularly monitored by employers and managers of the company.

Footnotes

6040 — Inventions and Patents

1. Cal. Lab. Code § § 2870-2872.
2. Cal. Lab. Code § § 2870-2872.

6050 — Conflict of Interest

1. Cal. Bus. & Prof. Code § 16600.

6060 — Grievance Procedure

1. Cleary v. American Airlines, Inc. 111 Cal. App.3d 443, 168 Cal. Rptr. 722 (1980).

6100 — Employee Privacy

1. Cal. Lab. Code § 1198.5.

Index

Successful Business Library

A Complete Franchise Solution.

From The Oasis Press®

Understand the nuances of running a franchise or turning your existing business into a successful franchise model. Each of these books offer unparalleled expertise in helping you make the most of operating a franchise in today's marketplace...

The Franchise Redbook
Easy-to-Use Facts and Figures
Roger C. Rule

An accurate and user-friendly reference that will help determine your best franchise opportunity. While there are several other reference books available, The Franchise Redbook is up-to-date, comprehensive, and by far the easiest to use for determining your franchise options. The organized listings make it easy to weigh the pros and cons of the franchises within your area of interest. Ideal for selecting a franchise, doing market and comparative analysis, preparing a marketing or business plan, preparing contact lists, or doing any other research on franchises.

Paperback $34.95   750 Pages   ISBN 1-55571-484-6

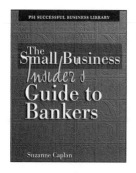

No Money Down Financing for Franchising

Roger C. Rule

An essential resource for securing finances and building the foundation to a winning franchise. Broken down into three logical progressions, this book explores every resource available for franchise financing, including many methods that require no money down and explains the vital points that will prepare you in obtaining these goals.

Paperback $19.95   240 Pages   ISBN 1-55571-462-5

The Small Business Insider's Guide to Bankers

Suzanne Caplan & Thomas M. Nunnally

This book will show you how the banking industry operates, and how to speak its language. It tells you how and why you should take a leading role in developing and nurturing a lasting partnership with your bank.

Paperback: $18.95   163 Pages   ISBN: 1-55571-400-5

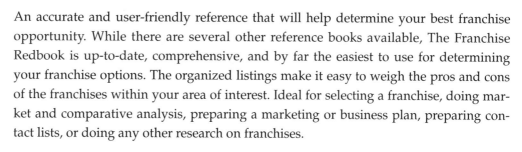

The Oasis Press®
Successful Business Library
Tools to help you save time and money.

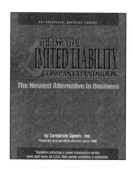

The Essential Limited Liability Company Handbook

Tells you everything you need to know about setting up a limited liability company or converting an existing business. Presents difficult financial and legal concepts in simple language and answers the questions most asked by entrepreneurs and small business owners when considering an LLC formation. Provides you with a certificate of formation and a sample operating agreement.

Paperback: $21.95   Pages: 276   ISBN: 1-55571-361-0

Which Business?

A compendium of real business opportunities, not just "hot" new ventures that often have limited earning potential. Which Business? will help you define your skills and interests by exploring your dreams and how you think about business. Learn from profiles of 24 business areas, reviewing how each got its start and problems and successes that they have experienced.

Paperback: $18.95   Pages: 376   ISBN: 1-55571-390-4

Friendship Marketing

If you have every wondered how to combine business success and personal significance, author Gerald Baron has numerous practical suggestions. After years of working with executives and entrepreneurs, he's found that business success and personal meaning can share common ground. Using dozens of examples, he shows how building relationships is the key to business development and personal fulfillment.

Paperback: $18.95   Pages: 187   ISBN: 1-55571-399-8

Delivering Legendary Customer Service

"Goes far beyond the basics . . . provides the detailed specifics necessary to effectively manage relationships with customers, management and your team."

- Bill Rose, Managing Director SOFTBANK, and
Founder, Software Support Professionals Association

Paperback: $14.95   Pages: 232   ISBN: 1-55571-520-6

OASIS
PRESS®
BOOKS

ALL MAJOR CREDIT CARDS ACCEPTED

CALL TO PLACE AN ORDER
– or –
TO RECEIVE A FREE CATALOG
1-800-228-2275

International Orders (541) 245-6502   Fax Orders (541) 245-6505
Web site http://www.psi-research.com   Email sales@psi-research.com

PSI Research   P.O. Box 3727   Central Point, Oregon   97502
U.S.A.

businessplan.com (2nd ed.)
L. Manning Ross

Now you can ready your business for the age of digital commerce. businessplan.com is a step-by-step guide for creating your Web-woven plan. It gives you the tools to integrate your real and virtual offices for increased profits and efficiency.

Paperback: $19.95   Pages: 200   ISBN: 1-55571-531-1

Improving Staff Productivity
By following the easy-to-implement techniques, you can expect to potentially generate significant time and money savings and improve your overall operations and custom service.

Paperback: $16.95   Pages: 113   ISBN: 1-55571-456-0

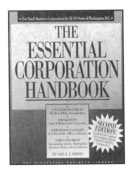

The Essential Corporation Handbook
The *Essential Corporation Handbook* takes the mysteries out of corporate formalities, and shows owners what they must do and what they may do with their corporations. By knowing the rules to follow, you can avoid time-consuming, expensive mistakes, and you can keep your energy focused where you want it – on running your business.

Paperback: $21.95   Pages: 245   ISBN: 1-55571-342-4

Before You Go Into Business, Read This!
Ensures you that the simple things are kept simple, and that the complex things are made simple. It is designed to give the average entrepreneur basic definitions of terms and conditions within all industries and the general concepts of running a business. A must for any new business owner!

Paperback: $17.95   Pages: 280   ISBN: 1-55571-481-1

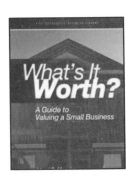

What's It Worth?
Determine what your business or investment is really worth. Whether you're buying or selling a business or franchise, this unique guide will quickly show you how to get the best deal. This book is ideal for anyone wanting to purchase a new business, to establish a fair selling price for a going business, or simply to have a better understanding of a professional appraiser's process.

Paperback: $22.95   Pages: 320   ISBN: 1-55571-504-4

how to order

Mail: Send this completed order form and a check, money order or credit card information to: **PSI Research/The Oasis Press®, P.O. Box 3727, Central Point, Oregon 97502-0032**

Fax: Available 24 hours a day, 7 days a week at **1-541-245-6505**

Email: info@psi-research.com (Please include a phone number, should we need to contact you.)

Web: Purchase any of our products online at our Website at **http://www.psi-research.com/oasis/**

Inquiries and International Orders: Please call **1-541-245-6502**

Indicate the quantity and price of the titles you would like:

title	binder isbn	paper isbn	binder	paperback	qty.	total
Advertising Without An Agency		1-55571-429-3		☐ 19.95		
Before You Go Into Business Read This		1-55571-481-1		☐ 17.95		
Bottom Line Basics	1-55571-329-7 (B)	1-55571-330-0 (P)	☐ 39.95	☐ 19.95		
BusinessBasics		1-55571-430-7		☐ 16.95		
The Business Environmental Handbook	1-55571-304-1 (B)	1-55571-163-4 (P)	☐ 39.95	☐ 19.95		
Business Owner's Guide to Accounting and Bookkeeping		1-55571-381-5		☐ 19.95		
businessplan.com		1-55571-455-2		☐ 19.95		
Buyer's Guide to Business Insurance	1-55571-310-6 (B)	1-55571-162-6 (P)	☐ 39.95	☐ 19.95		
California Corporation Formation Package		1-55571-464-1 (P)		☐ 29.95		
Collection Techniques for a Small Business	1-55571-312-2 (B)	1-55571-171-5 (P)	☐ 39.95	☐ 19.95		
College Entrepreneur Handbook		1-55571-503-6		☐ 16.95		
A Company Policy & Personnel Workbook	1-55571-364-5 (B)	1-55571-486-2 (P)	☐ 49.95	☐ 29.95		
Company Relocation Handbook	1-55571-091-3 (B)	1-55571-092-1 (P)	☐ 39.95	☐ 19.95		
CompControl	1-55571-356-4 (B)	1-55571-355-6 (P)	☐ 39.95	☐ 19.95		
Complete Book of Business Forms		1-55571-107-3		☐ 19.95		
Connecting Online		1-55571-403-X		☐ 21.95		
Customer Engineering	1-55571-360-2 (B)	1-55571-359-9 (P)	☐ 39.95	☐ 19.95		
Delivering Legendary Customer Service		1-55571-520-6 (P)		☐ 14.95		
Develop and Market Your Creative Ideas		1-55571-383-1		☐ 15.95		
Developing International Markets		1-55571-433-1		☐ 19.95		
Doing Business in Russia		1-55571-375-0		☐ 19.95		
Draw the Line		1-55571-370-X		☐ 17.95		
The Essential Corporation Handbook		1-55571-342-4		☐ 21.95		
Essential Limited Liability Company Handbook	1-55571-362-9 (B)	1-55571-361-0 (P)	☐ 39.95	☐ 21.95		
Export Now	1-55571-192-8 (B)	1-55571-167-7 (P)	☐ 39.95	☐ 24.95		
Financial Decisionmaking		1-55571-435-8		☐ 19.95		
Financial Management Techniques	1-55571-116-2 (B)	1-55571-124-3 (P)	☐ 39.95	☐ 19.95		
Financing Your Small Business		1-55571-160-X		☐ 19.95		
Franchise Bible	1-55571-366-1 (B)	1-55571-526-5 (P)	☐ 39.95	☐ 27.95		
The Franchise Redbook		1-55571-484-6		☐ 34.95		
Friendship Marketing		1-55571-399-8		☐ 18.95		
Funding High-Tech Ventures		1-55571-405-6		☐ 21.95		
Home Business Made Easy		1-55571-428-5		☐ 19.95		
Improving Staff Productivity		1-55571-456-0		☐ 16.95		
Information Breakthrough		1-55571-413-7		☐ 22.95		
Insider's Guide to Small Business Loans		1-55571-488-9		☐ 19.95		
Keeping Score: An Inside Look at Sports Marketing		1-55571-377-7		☐ 18.95		
Kick Ass Success		1-55571-518-4		☐ 18.95		
Know Your Market	1-55571-341-6 (B)	1-55571-333-5 (P)	☐ 39.95	☐ 19.95		
Leader's Guide: 15 Essential Skills		1-55571-434-X		☐ 19.95		
Legal Expense Defense	1-55571-349-1 (B)	1-55571-348-3 (P)	☐ 39.95	☐ 19.95		
A Legal Road Map for Consultants		1-55571-460-9		☐ 18.95		
Location, Location, Location		1-55571-376-9		☐ 19.95		
Mail Order Legal Guide	1-55571-193-6 (B)	1-55571-190-1 (P)	☐ 45.00	☐ 29.95		
Managing People: A Practical Guide		1-55571-380-7		☐ 21.95		
Marketing for the New Millennium		1-55571-432-3		☐ 19.95		
Marketing Mastery	1-55571-358-0 (B)	1-55571-357-2 (P)	☐ 39.95	☐ 19.95		
Money Connection	1-55571-352-1 (B)	1-55571-351-3 (P)	☐ 39.95	☐ 24.95		
Moonlighting: Earning a Second Income at Home		1-55571-406-4		☐ 15.95		
Navigating the Marketplace: Growth Strategies for Small Business		1-55571-458-7		☐ 21.95		
No Money Down Financing for Franchising		1-55571-462-5		☐ 19.95		
Not Another Meeting!		1-55571-480-3		☐ 17.95		
People-Centered Profit Strategies		1-55571-517-6		☐ 18.95		

| | | | | **Sub-total for this side:** | | |

title		isbn	binder	paperback	qty.	total
People Investment	1-55571-187-1 (B)	1-55571-161-8 (P)	☐ 39.95	☐ 19.95		
Power Marketing for Small Business		1-55571-524-9 (P)		☐ 19.95		
Proposal Development	1-55571-067-0 (B)	1-55571-431-5 (P)	☐ 39.95	☐ 21.95		
Prospecting for Gold		1-55571-483-8		☐ 14.95		
Public Relations Marketing		1-55571-459-5		☐ 19.95		
Raising Capital	1-55571-306-8 (B)	1-55571-305-X (P)	☐ 39.95	☐ 19.95		
Renaissance 2000		1-55571-412-9		☐ 22.95		
Retail in Detail		1-55571-371-8		☐ 15.95		
The Rule Book of Business Plans for Startups		1-55571-519-2		☐ 18.95		
Secrets of High Ticket Selling		1-55571-436-6		☐ 19.95		
Secrets to Buying and Selling a Business		1-55571-489-7		☐ 24.95		
Secure Your Future		1-55571-335-1		☐ 19.95		
Selling Services		1-55571-461-7		☐ 14.95		
SmartStart Your (State) Business		varies per state		☐ 19.95		
Indicate which state you prefer:						
Small Business Insider's Guide to Bankers		1-55571-400-5		☐ 18.95		
Start Your Business		1-55571-485-4		☐ 10.95		
Strategic Insights		1-55571-505-2		☐ 19.95		
Strategic Management for Small and Growing Firms		1-55571-465-X		☐ 24.95		
Successful Network Marketing		1-55571-350-5		☐ 15.95		
Surviving Success		1-55571-446-3		☐ 19.95		
TargetSmart!		1-55571-384-X		☐ 19.95		
Top Tax Saving Ideas for Today's Small Business		1-55571-463-3		☐ 16.95		
Truth About Teams		1-55571-482-X		☐ 18.95		
Twenty-One Sales in a Sale		1-55571-448-X		☐ 19.95		
WebWise	1-55571-501-X (B)	1-55571-479-X (P)	☐ 29.95	☐ 19.95		
What's It Worth?		1-55571-504-4		☐ 22.95		
Which Business?		1-55571-390-4		☐ 18.95		
Write Your Own Business Contracts	1-55571-196-0 (B)	1-55571-487-0 (P)	☐ 39.95	☐ 24.95		

Success Series	isbn		paperback	qty.	total
50 Ways to Get Promoted	1-55571-506-0		☐ 10.95		
You Can't Go Wrong By Doing It Right	1-55571-490-0		☐ 14.95		

Oasis Software	format	binder		qty.	total
Company Policy Text Files CD-ROM	CD-ROM ☐		☐ 49.95		
Company Policy Text Files Book & CD-ROM Package	CD-ROM ☐	☐ 89.95 (B)	☐ 69.95 (P)		
Winning Business Plans in Color CD-ROM	CD-ROM ☐		☐ 59.95		

Subtotal from other side	
Subtotal from this side	
▶ Shipping	
TOTAL	

Ordered by: *Please give street address*

NAME   TITLE

COMPANY

STREET ADDRESS

CITY   STATE   ZIP

DAYTIME PHONE   EMAIL

Ship to: *If different than above*

NAME   TITLE

COMPANY

STREET ADDRESS

CITY   STATE   ZIP

DAYTIME PHONE

Shipping:

YOUR ORDER IS: ADD:

0-25	5.00
25.01-50	6.00
50.01-100	7.00
100.01-175	9.00
175.01-250	13.00
250.01-500	18.00
500.01+	4% of total

PLEASE CALL FOR RUSH SERVICE OPTIONS.
INTERNATIONAL ORDERS, PLEASE CALL FOR A QUOTE ON CURRENT SHIPPING RATES.

Payment Method:
☐ CHECK   ☐ MONEY ORDER
☐ AMERICAN EXPRESS   ☐ DISCOVER
☐ MASTERCARD   ☐ VISA

CREDIT CARD NUMBER

EXPIRATION (MM/YY)   NAME ON CARD (PLEASE PRINT)

SIGNATURE OF CARDHOLDER (REQUIRED)

Fax this order form to: (541) 245-6505 or mail it to: P.O. Box 3727, Central Point, Oregon 97502
For more information about our products or to order online, visit http://www.psi-research.com

04172000